REASSURANCE FOR THE SEEKER

Three Spiritual Luminaries of Twentieth-Century Cairo

Book 1

REASSURANCE FOR THE SEEKER

A Biography and Translation of Ṣāliḥ al-Jaʿfarī's *al-Fawāʾid al-Jaʿfariyya*, a Commentary on Forty Prophetic Traditions

Book 2

A LIFE IN PRAISE OF GOD

An Annotated Translation of ʿAbd al-Ḥalīm Maḥmūd's Autobiography, *Hadhi ḥayātī l-ḥamdu li-Llāh*

Book 3

IN THE PROPHET'S FOOTSTEPS

The Life and Teachings of a Sufi *Ḥadīth* Master

Muḥammad al-Ḥāfiẓ al-Tijānī

REASSURANCE FOR THE SEEKER

A Biography and Translation of Ṣāliḥ al-Jaʿfarī's
al-Fawāʾid al-Jaʿfariyya, a Commentary on Forty
Prophetic Traditions

Samer Dajani

2013

First published in 2013 by
Fons Vitae
49 Mockingbird Valley Drive
Louisville, KY 40207
http://www.fonsvitae.com
Email: fonsvitaeky@aol.com

Library of Congress Control Number: 2012953106
ISBN 9781-887752-985

Printed in Canada

Editing: Valerie Joy Turner
Typesetting: Neville Blakemore, Jr. and Muhammad I. Hozien
Book design: www.scholarlytype.com

Contents

Illustrations

Publisher's Note

Arabic terms and names have been transliterated according to the *International Journal of Middle East Studies* (*IJMES*). A variety of honorific glyphs have been used in the text, as follows.

سبحانه وتعالى	'Praise be to Him most high'—used after the mention of God.
عليه السلام	'Peace be upon him'—used after the mention of a prophet.
عليهم السلام	'Peace be upon them'—used after the mention of more than one prophet.
صلى الله عليه وسلم	'May the peace and blessings of God be upon him'—used after the mention of the Prophet Muḥammad.
رضي الله عنه	'May God be pleased with him'—used after the mention of a male Companion of the Prophet Muḥammad, or any righteous person or scholar.
رضي الله عنها	'May God be pleased with her'—used after the mention of a female Companion.
رضي الله عنهما	'May God be pleased with them'—used after the mention of two Companions.
رضي الله عنهم	'May God be pleased with them'—used after the mention of several Companions.
رحمه الله	'May God have mercy on him'—used after the mention of a person who passed away.

بسم الله الرحمن الرحيم

Foreword

With a piercing look, a warm smile, and palpable signs of grandeur, one could easily spot Shaykh Ṣāliḥ al-Jaʿfarī from the crowd surrounding him. He was an erudite scholar, an eloquent orator, and a valuable addition to the long list of luminary scholars of al-Azhar who not only succeeded in safeguarding the Islamic discourse by remaining truly faithful to the long-standing scholarly legacy and religious heritage, but more importantly by reviving it. They did this by addressing challenges that Muslims faced in their daily lives, and finding new juristic solutions through the use of independent legal reasoning (*ijtihād*).

One of the salient features of Shaykh Ṣāliḥ which indeed made him stand apart from other accomplished scholars of his time was his unique intellectual discernment and sharp intellect, along with his unmatched affinity to the religious sciences. He realized that Islamic civilization was built on knowledge. The early Muslims established intellectual disciplines that served the core of their civilization: the Holy Book. They adhered to this core, served it, followed it, and made it a standard for acceptance, rejection, and evaluation. Muslims developed new intellectual disciplines, in addition to transmitting knowledge from communities that preceded them, and this aided them in understanding reality, comprehending the world as it is, and grasping metaphysical truth. They compiled this knowledge and passed it on to their contemporaries and those who came after them.

Shaykh Ṣāliḥ's vigorous efforts to master the Islamic sciences were crowned with his appointment as the Imam of al-Azhar Mosque. He was a staunch opponent of the loud cacophony of secular voices that clamored to denounce the traditional Islamic sciences as irrelevant and backward. He asserted that an essential distinction needs to be made between the scientific methodologies and the juristic and linguistic tools that the classical Islamic scholars used in their endeavor to resolve issues of contention in their own time, and the findings of the independent legal reasoning they pursued and the legal rulings they reached, which certainly served their age but may not very well serve ours. He believed that a true scholar could be measured by his ability to reach a fine equilibrium between staying true to long accumulated, valuable religious scholarship and legal traditional works without turning a blind eye to contemporary issues which need fresh legal treatment. Shaykh Ṣāliḥ indeed had this ability.

Shaykh Ṣāliḥ was also known for his unwavering zeal for giving public lectures and conducting religious lessons in al-Azhar Mosque. His lectures drew huge Cairene crowds and people greatly admired his firm grasp of religious knowledge, which matched his unique moral characteristics. He was also known for his prominent position as a spiritual guide. He used to conduct circles of remembrance in one of the halls of al-Azhar Mosque every Thursday.

For thirty-three years, Shaykh Ṣāliḥ did not leave al-Azhar Mosque; a small chamber was set up for him inside one of its teaching halls. This enclosed chamber was for his seclusion and became his home for the rest of his life. He never walked out of al-Azhar Mosque except to go to pilgrimage in Mecca and to visit the Prophet's grave in Medina and the graves of the descendants of the Prophet in Cairo.

I had the privilege of being one of the students of Shaykh Ṣāliḥ—no one could miss the glowing radiance on his face and his veritable love for the Prophet Muḥammad ﷺ. His own servant, Sayyid, who tended to his affairs at al-Azhar Mosque, tells us that Shaykh Ṣāliḥ used to circle the grand hall of al-Azhar Mosque at night after everyone had left, holding his long beads, praising God. He recalls that once, while circling the hall, he turned to him saying, "hold on to the love of the Prophet Muḥammad, Sayyid, hold tight to it." I gathered that the noble Shaykh did not only mean to advise his servant Sayyid but rather wanted to advise all of us on the imperative of keeping the Prophet Muḥammad at heart. He composed long beautiful poems praising the Prophet Muḥammad and his eminent status, and these circulated widely among Egyptians.

This brief introduction about Shaykh Ṣāliḥ does not do justice to his noble legacy; my aim is to shed some light on his prominent personality and his religious scholarship, to trigger the appetite of both researchers and scholars to delve deeply into his works and for ordinary readers to find religious knowledge and spiritual guidance.

This translated work of Shaykh Ṣāliḥ is timely, as it represents a voice of true traditional knowledge based on solid religious scholarship and unique spiritual realization. I pray that this work will be the start of a series of translations of Shaykh Ṣāliḥ's books to provide English speakers a closer look at the works of this prominent Muslim scholar who enriched the Islamic scholarly legacy and acted as a beacon of spiritual guidance for generations to come.

Shaykh Ali Gomaa
Grand Mufti of Egypt

Translator's Introduction

This book offers the first English-language biography of Shaykh Ṣāliḥ al-Jaʿfarī, accompanied by a translation of one of his most important works: a collection of forty *aḥādīth*, or reports about the statements and actions of the Prophet Muḥammad.[1] Shaykh Ṣāliḥ al-Jaʿfarī was one of the great scholars of al-Azhar in the twentieth century and the imam and orator of its mosque for almost thirty years.

Al-Azhar has been the Muslim world's premier institution of religious learning and its most authoritative voice for centuries. After World War II, Arab nationalism reached its peak and Egypt became allies with the USSR. Communist ideology was on the rise, especially among the Middle Eastern elite, and many of its tenets posed a serious threat to Islam. However, perhaps more dangerous in the view of al-Azhar's scholars were intellectual movements from within Islam that began to question many traditionally held beliefs of Sunni Islam, such as the continuous presence of the miraculous even after the passing of the Prophet Muḥammad.

Some of those movements went on to criticize the long-held association of Sunni Islam, especially in al-Azhar, with the four surviving schools of jurisprudence (Ḥanafī, Mālikī, Shāfiʿī, and Ḥanbalī), and the two main schools of theology (Ashʿarī and Māturīdī). Sufism, with its emphasis on matters of the spirit and the hereafter, was also criticized by the Western-inspired voices of modernization that came out of both liberal and conservative Muslim reform movements. Al-Jaʿfarī's book represents an answer from the heart of the Sunni world's leading institution to the challenges that Islam faced, and still faces, in the Muslim and Arab world.

---

1. *Ḥadīth* for the singular and *aḥādīth* for the plural. The word *ḥadīth* can also be used for reports about the Prophet's Companions, like *ḥadīth* 26 in this collection.

The biography is based mostly on Arabic biographies that are in turn based largely on accounts gathered from his own works and lessons. I have tried to allow al-Jaʿfarī's voice to be heard as much as possible, especially when he speaks of his teachers at al-Azhar, because it gives us a glimpse of a generation of scholars about whom we know next to nothing.

Born in Sudan to a family of Egyptian origin, and then living most of his life in Cairo inside al-Azhar mosque itself, al-Jaʿfarī dedicated his life to spreading the teachings of his spiritual guide and role model, the Moroccan shaykh Aḥmad b. Idrīs. Ibn Idrīs spent the latter half of his life teaching in Mecca and Yemen, punctuated by occasional trips to Egypt. Also included in this book is a short work by Ibn Idrīs which is a commentary, composed toward the end of his life in Yemen, on the *Ḥadīth al-sunna al-Muḥammadiyya* (The *Ḥadīth* of the Muḥammadan Sunna). *Sunna* means the lofty and noble way, path, or practice of the Prophet. In this *ḥadīth*, the Prophet summarizes his way by describing some of his states and qualities, so that the seeker who wishes to follow in his path may be able to emulate him. Shaykh Ṣāliḥ al-Jaʿfarī found this commentary printed in a small treatise that was copied from a manuscript written by the hand of its author's descendant Muḥammad b. ʿAlī l-Yamanī l-Idrīsī. The latter was a scholar in his own right who collected the works of Ibn Idrīs and contributed to the Idrīsī tradition himself. He was also a religious and political leader and a revolutionary: he founded the Idrīsī state of ʿAsīr. Shaykh Ṣāliḥ al-Jaʿfarī edited and published the work as *Shahd mushāhadat al-arwāḥ al-taqiyya min baḥr ʿulūm jadd al-sāda al-idrīsiyya* [The honey that pious souls drink from the ocean of the sciences of Shaykh Aḥmad b. Idrīs].

We thus have two works of *ḥadīth* commentary that belong to the same tradition of scholarship and spirituality, one from the second quarter of the nineteenth century, and the other from the last half of the twentieth century. Because of the importance of Ibn Idrīs' teachings to the life and thought of Shaykh Ṣāliḥ al-Jaʿfarī, and because reference to Ibn Idrīs is found often in al-Jaʿfarī's book, I begin with a short biography of Ibn Idrīs before commencing with the biography of his intellectual and spiritual student. Ibn

Idrīs and the Idrīsī tradition have already received much attention from Western academia. R. S. O'Fahey wrote a biography entitled *Enigmatic Saint*,[2] and some of Ibn Idrīs' works have been translated into English in *The Exoteric Aḥmad b. Idrīs*[3] and *The Letters of Aḥmad b. Idrīs*.[4] A good study that places Ibn Idrīs' teachings in their broader context is *Saints and Sons*,[5] which recounts the spread and evolution of one of the main branches of the Idrīsī tradition in the Middle East and Southeast Asia. *Sufi and Scholar on the Desert Edge*[6] discusses Ibn Idrīs' most famous student, al-Sanūsī, and his efforts to spread the path of his teacher in the Hijaz and modern-day Libya. *The Idrīsī State in ʿAsīr*[7] studies the political state that was established by Ibn Idrīs' aforementioned descendant Muḥammad b. ʿAlī l-Yamanī. I have therefore chosen to focus on the teachings of Ibn Idrīs, with only the briefest introduction of his life, based on his own writings and the writings of his students. In doing so I attempt to avoid what has already been discussed at length and aim to shed light on aspects that have not been given due attention. In addition to the full translation of al-Jaʿfarī's book I provide explanatory notes.

Finally, I want to extend special thanks to Gray Henry of Fons Vitae Publications for showing great enthusiasm for this book, my editor Valerie Joy Turner for her meticulous and wonderful work, and Muhammad Hozien for his beautiful typesetting and design. I

---

2. R. S. O'Fahey, *Enigmatic Saint: Aḥmad b. Idrīs and the Idrīsī Tradition* (London: C. Hurst and Co., 1990).
3. Bernd Radtke, et al. *The Exoteric Aḥmad b. Idrīs: A Sufi's Critique of the Madhāhib and the Wahhābīs* (Leiden: Brill, 2000).
4. Ibn Idrīs, *The Letters of Aḥmad Ibn Idrīs*, edited and translated by Albrecht Hofheinz and Einar Thomassen (London: Hurst and Company, 1993).
5. Mark Sedgwick, *Saints and Sons: The Making and Remaking of the Rashīdi Aḥmadi Sufi Order, 1799–2000* (Leiden: Brill, 2005).
6. Knut S. Vikør, *Sufi and Scholar on the Desert Edge: Muḥammad b. ʿAlī al-Sanūsī and his Brotherhood* (London: Hurst and Company, 1995).
7. Anne K. Bang, *The Idrīsī State in ʿAsīr 1906–1934: Politics, Religion and Personal Prestige as Statebuilding Factors in Early Twentieth-century Arabia* (London: Hurst and Company, 1996).

owe thanks to Sara Swetzoff for her generous help in reviewing and editing the first draft of the manuscript, and to all those friends who helped review different parts for me, especially my wife Nishat Lal. Most importantly, I thank my parents for their constant love and support in all my endeavors.

Shaykh Ṣāliḥ al-Jaʿfarī: A Biography

Shaykh Ṣāliḥ al-Jaʿfarī's grandfather, Ṣāliḥ b. Rifāʿī, was an Egyptian scholar from the town of Salamiyya near Luxor in Upper Egypt. He came from the ʿAlawiyya subtribe of the larger Jaʿāfira tribe in the Luxor region, which traced its lineage to a prince from that area called Ḥamad. Prince Ḥamad's lineage, in turn, went back to Morocco, and from Morocco to the great descendant of the Prophet, Jaʿfar al-Ṣādiq (d. 148/ 765) in Medina. Al-Ṣādiq was a descendant of the Prophet's grandson al-Ḥusayn, and was renowned for his piety, knowledge, and wisdom. Ṣāliḥ b. Rifāʿī acquired religious learning in al-Azhar and moved to Dongola in Sudan for the sake of spreading knowledge. He set up a Qurʾān teaching school in the ancient Grand Mosque of Dongola, where residents memorized the Qurʾān at his hands. Shaykh ʿAbd al-ʿĀlī also taught in the same mosque, where he spread the teachings of his father, the great Moroccan scholar and Sufi shaykh, Aḥmad b. Idrīs. That was the beginning of the link between Ibn Idrīs and Ṣāliḥ al-Jaʿfarī. The latter would go on to spread Ibn Idrīs' teachings from the heart of al-Azhar Mosque, the Muslim world's greatest and most respected institution of religious education.

The Way of Ibn Idrīs

An Arab proverb states that the multitude of names indicates the honor of the named. One is certainly reminded of this when attempting to speak of Aḥmad b. Idrīs (d. 1837). His students knew him as "the teacher," or often referred to him by the title Abū l-ʿAbbās al-ʿArāʾishī, in reference to his birth near the Moroccan port city of Larache.[1] He is also known as "al-Fāsī," after the city of

1. It is not clear where the nickname "Abū l-ʿAbbās" came from, as he had no son by the name of ʿAbbās. Since it is associated with the name of his hometown, it is likely that he acquired this full title in Fez. It is possible that it was a title expressing his powerful presence and his roaring voice

Fez where he studied the religious sciences, and western academics often refer to him as "the enigmatic saint" and "the enigmatic imam" because of what little was known about him in relation to the impact that he left on the Muslim world.[2] But there is one other name by which he was known, a name that was said to have been given to him by the Prophet Muḥammad himself. This was the name that was used for him in the spiritual realm, the world of realities (*ḥaqāʾiq*), and that therefore expressed his true role in the world; that name is *al-Shifāʾ*: the healing.[3] This phenomena of a duality of names, one in the ephemeral physical world and one in the world of everlasting realities, is an old one in Islam, and is but another example of the binary of the outward and the inward, the material and the spiritual. Tradition states that when Adam was created, he was told that his title in the world would be "the father of humanity," but that his title in paradise would be Abū Muḥammad (the father of Muḥammad). When asked why he was given this title, he was told that Muḥammad was the pinnacle of creation: "Had it not been for him, I would not have created you, nor created any heavens or earths." In the same divine address he was also told about his greatest descendant, "his name in the Heavens is Aḥmad, and on Earth Muḥammad."[4] The name Muḥammad means "the praised one," and reflects the Prophet's position as the greatest of God's creations. But in the Qurʾān (on the statement of Jesus) the name given to him is Aḥmad: "the greatest in praising God." This name is believed to reflect the true reality of the Prophet, which was his role before the creation of the physical universe, and likewise the role

---

in the lessons he gave in Fez, as shown in the story of his meeting with his master al-Tāzī below. Al-ʿAbbās is one of the Arabic words for lion, referring specifically to the lion from which other lions flee.

2. On the influence of Ibn Idrīs, see Sedgwick, *Saints and Sons* and O'Fahey, *Enigmatic Saint*.
3. This is an appellation for Ibn Idrīs used regularly by his students. On the Prophet giving him this name, see al-Jaʿfarī, *al-Sīra al-nabawiyya al-Muḥammadiyya*, p. 82. On the use of this name in the spiritual realm, see the quote of al-Sanūsī in al-Jaʿfarī, *al-Muntaqā l-nafīs*, p. 41.
4. al-Qasṭalānī, *al-Mawāhib al-ladunniyya* (Beirut: al-Maktab al-Islāmī, 2004), vol. 1, pp. 69–70.

that he will play on the Day of Judgment. In this world he appeared as Muḥammad, but his beginning and end is Aḥmad. Of the former reality and role the Prophet said,

> I was a light in front of God ﷻ two thousand years before Adam was created. That light was glorifying God ﷻ, and the angels were glorifying God ﷻ by imitating it. When God ﷻ created Adam He deposited that light into his clay.[5]

Of the latter role, the Prophet said that he will be raised on the Day of Judgment holding the banner of praise in his hand, and that God will give him spiritual openings, inspiring in him ways of praising God that he had never known before, praises by the virtue of which all of creation will be saved from the terror of waiting for the Judgment to begin.[6] The two prophets, Adam and Muḥammad, are not the only early examples of such a duality of names. The pious caliph ʿUmar b. ʿAbd al-ʿAzīz, the eighth caliph of the Umayyad dynasty, who the Muslims call the fifth of the rightly-guided caliphs, saw the Prophet in a dream before he held that position, and he told him, "You will be given the leadership of my community, so keep blood from spilling, keep blood from spilling, for your name among the people is ʿUmar b. ʿAbd al-ʿAzīz, and your name with God is Jābir (the one who fixes what is broken)."[7] This name is meant to represent his role as the caliph who took over from a line of corrupt leaders and rehabilitated the situation of the Muslim community, a role for which he is celebrated in Islamic history.

In the memory of his students, then, Ibn Idrīs' true role in this world was to be a source of healing—perhaps because he combined

5. This *ḥadīth* is from the *ḥadīth* collection of Muḥammad b. Abī ʿUmar al-ʿAdanī (d. 243 AH), who was the teacher of the famous traditionists Muslim, al-Tirmidhī, and Ibn Māja. Al-Jaʿfarī, *Dars al-jumuʿa bi-l-Azhar*, vol. 8, p. 88, n. 2.

6. See the *aḥādīth* in *Ṣaḥīḥ Muslim*, vol. 1, pp. 104–105, and *Sunan al-Tirmidhī*, vol. 2, pp. 798–799.

7. Ibn Abī l-Dunyā, *al-Manāmāt*, pp. 93–94. A later example is the Sufi Abū Madyan, who, according to Ibn ʿArabī, "was known in the higher world under the name of Abu-l-Naja." Claude Addas, "Abū Madyan and Ibn ʿArabi," p. 172.

within himself the greatest levels of mastery of the outward knowledge of the law and the inward knowledge of the spiritual realities; perhaps it was his reformist approach, which aimed to bring new life and vitality to Islam, while also striving to unite the Muslims.[8] Perhaps it was his insistence on absolute purity of faith, whether in regard to creed, jurisprudence, or spirituality; a purity and authenticity that can only be achieved by direct attachment to God and His Prophet, and by reducing attachments to anything else.[9] Or perhaps it was the way that he responded to the most difficult questions posed to him by the great scholars of his age, answers that they frequently described as healing to their minds and hearts. Perhaps for one or all of these reasons, Ibn Idrīs is still known by his followers as "the healing."

Aḥmad b. Idrīs was born in Morocco in 1750 to a family of prophetic descent. He memorized the Qurʾān and several Islamic texts before going to Fez at the age of twenty to study at al-Qarawiyyīn, one of the Muslim world's leading centers of religious learning. As a result of reforms by the rulers of the time, education at al-Qarawiyyīn focused almost entirely on studying primary *ḥadīth* collections and their commentaries, instead of the short codified compendia of law that were popular from the thirteenth century, or other types of second and third-hand texts.[10] Ibn Idrīs excelled as a student and became a teacher in Fez in the 1780s and 1790s. At the same time he took as his spiritual guide a Mauritanian scholar named Muḥammad Limjaydrī b. Ḥabībullāh, who would visit Fez from time to time. Limjaydrī eventually took him to meet his own shaykh, ʿAbd al-Wahhāb al-Tāzī (d. 1792 or 1798), who lived in Fez and attended Ibn Idrīs' lessons. Al-Tāzī was impressed by Ibn Idrīs' great eloquence and his booming voice. When Ibn Idrīs came to him as a disciple, al-Tāzī remarked at the difference in the way he was speaking before him, saying, "What happened to that roaring voice, Aḥmad?"[11] Al-Tāzī was considered to be a master in two

8. O'Fahey, *Enigmatic Saint*, p. 76.

9. Sedgwick, *Saints and Sons*, pp. 14–16.

10. O'Fahey, *Enigmatic Saint*, pp. 33–34.

11. Thābit, *Min aqṭāb al-umma*, p. 114. I thought to include this story, not

ancient Sufi paths, the Shādhiliyya and the Naqshbandiyya, as well as in a third, new spiritual path, the Khaḍiriyya, which had begun with his own teacher, ʿAbd al-ʿAzīz al-Dabbāgh (d. 1720). Ibn Idrīs took all three of these paths from his master, and later on in his life also took the Khalwatiyya *ṭarīqa* in Egypt.[12] It is believed that both al-Dabbāgh and al-Tāzī reached such a spiritual state that they eventually took their paths directly from the Prophet Muḥammad, and al-Tāzī expressed his desire to bring Ibn Idrīs to the same level.[13] Ibn Idrīs spent four years with him until his death, and then took another man as his shaykh, Abū l-Qāsim al-Wazīr (d. 1799 or 1800). Al-Wazīr was a shaykh of the Nāṣiriyya branch of the Shādhiliyya, the most elite and honored branch of that *ṭarīqa* in Morocco, one which was only given to scholars.[14] Ibn Idrīs was appointed one of al-Wazīr's *khalīfas* (representatives or lieutenants), and described reaching spiritual maturity at his hands.[15]

After al-Wazīr's death, Ibn Idrīs recounted seeing the Prophet Muḥammad in a vision and receiving his own litanies: a formula of remembrance, a formula of sending blessings upon the Prophet, and a formula of asking for God's forgiveness. The Prophet told him that these three litanies contained within them the benefits of all other formulas of remembrance, blessings, and prayers of forgiveness, and even more. After this, the Prophet addressed him,

---

only because it is often repeated in Ibn Idrīs' biographies and gives us an insight into his demeanor as teacher and as disciple, but to correct a translation error by his biographer O'Fahey. O'Fahey mistook *hadra* (a roar) as *hadara* (a waste), which led him to translate the phrase as "Where is that worthless man, Aḥmad?" The comment in the biographies that follows, which explains, "by that he was referring to the roaring voice from his teaching," thus did not fit, leading O'Fahey to mistake "teaching" for "learning." He concluded that al-Tāzī meant that "Ibn Idrīs' 'book-learning' still left him worthless in the Sufi sense." (*Enigmatic Saint*, pp. 43–44).

12. O'Fahey, *Enigmatic Saint*, p. 53.
13. On visions of the Prophet in sleep and awake, see *ḥādīth* 11, 12, and 33 along with their commentaries.
14. O'Fahey, *Enigmatic Saint*, pp. 38–46. On the Nāṣiriyya being restricted to scholars, see al-Jaʿfarī, *al-Muntaqā l-nafīs*, p. 87.
15. Sedgwick, *Saints and Sons*, p. 10.

saying, "O Aḥmad, I have given you the keys of the heavens and the Earth; saying them once is equal to the greatness of everything that is in this world and the next, many times over."[16] After this, Ibn Idrīs spent several years occupying himself with the Qurʾān and its meanings, until he saw the Prophet in another vision, making him and the Qurʾān brothers, and saying to the Qurʾān, "Reveal to him what you contain of knowledge and secrets," or according to a different source, he was addressing Ibn Idrīs, saying, "I will reveal to you what it contains of knowledge and secrets."[17] These visions sum up the path and method of Ibn Idrīs, as we will explain in more detail below. In the year 1799, at the age of forty-nine, Ibn Idrīs arrived in Mecca, having passed by Cairo and Upper Egypt on the way, intending to spend the rest of his life in the two holy sanctuaries. He spent almost thirty years there, teaching mostly in Mecca, but also in Medina and Ta'if.[18] Then, in 1827, he decided to move to Yemen, where he spent the last ten years of his life. We will speak of his role and influence in those lands below.

The cornerstone of the spiritual path of Ibn Idrīs was closely following the Qurʾān and the Sunna.[19] "The way which he traveled, and to which he called others, was complete devotion to contemplating the meanings of the Book of God," said his great student the celebrated Yemeni Mufti ʿAbd al-Raḥmān b. Sulaymān al-Ahdal (d. 1835).[20] He also instructed his students to study several *ḥadīth* collections, especially those pertaining to jurisprudence, "for it is not permissible for anyone to embark upon anything without knowing God's ﷻ ruling on the matter and its proof."[21] In his determination to

16. al-Jaʿfarī, *Miftāḥ mafātiḥ*, pp. 15–16.
17. Thābit, *Min aqṭāb al-umma*, p. 114. The wording recalls the Prophet's pairing of his Companions into "brothers" when he migrated to Medina.
18. O'Fahey, *Enigmatic Saint*, pp. 57–60.
19. As stated by his student, the Yemeni judge al-Ḥasan b. ʿĀkish (al-Jaʿfarī, *al-Muntaqā l-nafis*, p. 21).
20. al-Jaʿfarī, *al-Muntaqā l-nafis*, p. 21.
21. Recommended were *Ṣaḥīḥ al-Bukhārī*, considered to be the most authentic collection of prophetic *ḥadīth*, and the *Muwaṭṭaʾ* of Mālik, usually held in even greater esteem by followers of the Mālikī school of jurisprudence. Also Ibn Ḥajar al-ʿAsqalānī's *Bulūgh al-marām*, a

follow the example of the Prophet, Ibn Idrīs was greatly concerned with reviving forgotten practices and teachings of the Prophet Muḥammad, no matter how small or trivial they might seem to others. This becomes clear from the lecture notes preserved by his students, and from his own works, including his *ḥadīth* collection called *Rūḥ al-sunna* [The spirit of the Sunna]. In this collection of 208 traditions, he not only wanted to bring together the prophetic teachings that embody the spirit of the prophetic message, but he also wished to provide several traditions about small matters of practice that had been neglected by many Muslims.[22] Ibn Idrīs would send his students as missionaries to Muslim lands to revive the example of the Prophet. He sent his student al-Mirghanī as a missionary to the lands of modern-day Eritrea, where his great success aroused the hostility of the local ruler, who attempted to poison him. He later sent him to different regions in Egypt, and then to the Sudan. We also know that he sent a party from Mecca to Upper Egypt "for the sake of establishing the Sunna there."[23]

It seems that one of Ibn Idrīs' most passionate concerns was to improve the situation of the Muslims and strengthen their faith by strengthening their connection to God, and that was achieved through the ritual prayer. In his lessons, his *ḥadīth* collection, the letters sent to or from him, his treatises, and even in his debate with the Wahhābī scholars in Yemen, correcting the way of prayer was always a prominent subject. Ibn Idrīs wrote several treatises on the proper way to pray, both in terms of the movements and recitations, and in terms of the spiritual quality of the prayer, and sent them to

---

collection of *ḥadīth* pertaining to jurisprudence, especially that of the Shāfiʿī school, and Ibn Abī Zayd's *Risāla* in Mālikī jurisprudence, which is recommended for containing "about 4,000 *aḥādīth*, 600 of them in the wording of the Prophet, and 3,600 in their meaning" (al-Jaʿfarī, *Aʿṭār azhār aghṣān*, p. 110).

22. Some examples include praying a voluntary prayer before (and not just after) the sunset prayer, lengthening the prayers, wearing footwear during the prayer instead of praying barefoot, sitting down in order to drink, and shortening one's garment so that it does not drag on the floor.

23. O'Fahey, *Enigmatic Saint*, pp. 72, 147–148.

his students in different lands. When he arrived in Yemen, he spent two years traveling up and down the coast—his frail health only allowing him one trip inland—concentrating his teachings on the proper way to pray.[24] His arrival in Yemen was also described by one study as contributing to a revival of Sufism there.[25] Ibn Idrīs' student al-Sanūsī wrote two large works on oft-debated matters in prayer, such as the movement of the arms during prayer, and other issues.[26] Likewise, his other student al-Mirghanī devoted four pages, in his otherwise very concise Qurʾānic commentary, to a description of the correct way of praying, an inclusion that might seem odd and out of place for those who did not understand the importance given to the perfection of prayer by the Idrīsī tradition.[27] The Yemeni judge, al-Ḥasan b. ʿĀkish, wrote,

> In his night worship he would finish the entire Qurʾān in one prayer of two units, and sometimes he would repeat a single verse in one cycle and cry until the morning. . . . I have never seen a scholar perfect and beautify the prayer with its prophetic etiquettes as faithfully and completely as him, and whoever prayed with him no longer enjoyed praying with anyone else.[28]

Likewise the Yemeni Mufti ʿAbd al-Raḥmān b. Sulaymān al-Ahdal wrote of him,

> All the people—the elect and the commoners—crowded around him and benefited from him greatly in the matters of their religion, because of the guidance of this noble master in his worship and in his dealings is the prophetic guidance. This is especially apparent in the prayer, for he, may God ﷻ increase our benefit from him, used to pray in the most perfect way that is described in the authentic *aḥādīth* of the 'teacher of the *sharīʿa*.'[29]

24. Ibid., pp. 82–85.
25. O'Fahey, "Enigmatic Imam," p. 207.
26. al-Sanūsī, *Bughyat al-maqāṣid* (*al-Masāʾil al-ʿashar*), pp. 149–271, and *Shifāʾ al-ṣadr* (pp. 5–75), in al-Sanūsī, al-*Majmūʿa al-mukhtāra*.
27. al-Mirghanī, *Tāj al-tafāsīr*, pp. 35–40. Al-Jaʿfarī devoted the 9th and 10th *aḥādīth* in his collection to the subject.
28. al-Jaʿfarī, *al-Muntaqā l-nafīs*, p. 36.
29. al-Jaʿfarī, *al-Muntaqā l-nafīs*, pp. 32–33.

Al-Ahdal's description of Ibn Idrīs' prayer as being in accordance with the most authentic narrations about the Prophet refers to the fact that Ibn Idrīs did not imitate in his prayer any of the four schools of jurisprudence, but followed what his knowledge and evidence led him to believe is the most correct way to pray. Ibn Idrīs rejected blind following of the schools of thought, especially for people of knowledge, and he believed himself to be an absolute independent *mujtahid*, meaning that he had reached the rank in which one did not need to follow any of the established schools of law, but could extract his own opinions from the Qurʾān and *ḥadīth*. In order to test this claim, some Meccan scholars decided to test his memorization of the vast corpus of *ḥadīth*, including not only the actual prophetic statements, but also the entire chain of narrators that transmitted each statement. They collected a list of traditions that had full chains back to the Prophet, and others that were not fully connected, and chose chains that were strong and others that were weak. They then mixed up the chains of transmission and questioned him. Ibn Idrīs corrected all the mistakes and returned every statement to its rightful chain. The scholars also collected for him a list of questions from every branch of knowledge, and he answered every question correctly. He thus proved himself a true master not only in the science of *ḥadīth* and its transmission, but also in every other Islamic science.[30]

Ibn Idrīs taught that knowledge of every thing, large or small, old or new, until the end of time, is found in the Qurʾān and the Sunna, and there is no need for the use of deductive analogy or speculation to come up with any answer. This is why the Prophet's cousin Ibn ʿAbbās said, "Were I to lose a camel shackle, I would find it again in the Book of God." However, the key to a real understanding of the Qurʾān and Sunna and the ability to discover in them the answer to every problem is to fear God (have *taqwā*).[31] The Qurʾān states, *And fear God and God will teach you* (2:282), and *If you fear God He will provide you with higher discrimination* (8:29).

30. O'Fahey, *Enigmatic Saint*, p. 77.

31. Refer to *ḥadīth* 39 and its commentary for a more detailed explanation of *taqwā*.

Taqwā, he taught, is acting in accordance with what one knows. He wrote,

> The Messenger of God, God's blessings and peace be upon him and his family, said, "Whoever acts in accordance with what he knows, God will bequeath to him knowledge of what he does not know." This is the meaning of the other *ḥadīth*, "Knowledge comes through being taught," i.e., by God, when a person has pious fear of Him and He then teaches him. On the other hand, if a person does not fear God, then He does not teach him but rather leads him into error; even with regard to what he has memorized, God hinders him from understanding it, and he resembles *a donkey carrying a load of books* (62:6).[32]

Al-ʿĀkish wrote,

> Among the things I took from him is the knowledge of jurisprudence according to the earliest generations such as the four imams and the other founders of the schools who extracted it from the prophetic *aḥādīth* and Qurʾānic verses. In that regard he ﷺ was the greatest wonder, the like of which has never been heard of in the East or West! He was never asked about a new issue without answering immediately—as if it was obvious—with a clear text from the Book or the Sunna, in a way that no one but him could have been guided to. Many would search to see whether anyone else had been guided to that or not, and no one has been found who even came close to this.[33]

Ibn Idrīs attracted a great following in Mecca. He taught a circle of some of the Muslim world's greatest scholars and Sufis—people who changed the face of the Muslim world and its history. Chief among them is Muḥammad b. ʿAlī l-Sanūsī (d. 1859) who was born in modern-day Algeria and was educated in al-Qarawiyyīn in Fez. After accompanying the great spiritual masters of the west, most notably Aḥmad al-Tijānī and al-ʿArabī l-Darqāwī, he felt that he had not yet found the master he was looking for and traveled east.

---

32. Bernd Radtke, et al., *The Exoteric Aḥmad b. Idrīs*, pp. 96–98, 104, with minor changes to the translations.
33. al-Jaʿfarī, *al-Muntaqā l-nafīs*, p. 38.

In Mecca, he saw the Prophet in a dream telling him that he would reach his spiritual illumination at the hands of Ibn Idrīs. When he found Ibn Idrīs disputing the idea of scholars being bound to one school of jurisprudence, he hesitated and felt some doubt, until he saw two further dreams of the Prophet commanding him to go to Ibn Idrīs.[34] Ibn Idrīs appointed al-Sanūsī as his deputy when he left for the Yemen, and ordered him to construct a *zāwiya*, or a center, for all of his students. Al-Sanūsī oversaw the construction of seven more *zāwiya*s in Mecca, Medina, Ta'if and other parts of the Hijaz, and more then fifty others in different parts of the Muslim world. Twenty-five of those *zāwiya*s were in the Cyrenaica in modern-day Libya where al-Sanūsī settled to spread his master's teachings, and the rest were mostly in neighboring areas such as Egypt, Tunisia, and Algeria.[35]

When Ibn Idrīs moved to Yemen he received a great reception from its scholars, which is believed to be due in part to the recommendation given to him by Yemen's greatest scholar at the time, Muḥammad al-Shawkānī, who was the chief judge of Sanaa from 1759 until his death in 1834.[36] Though he never met Ibn Idrīs, they had corresponded with each other by mail, and al-Shawkānī "lavished praise on him and advised people to obtain as much of his learning as possible. He asserted that this knowledge (i.e., of Ibn Idrīs) was new and not something anyone possessed before."[37] Ibn Idrīs finally settled in Ṣabyā, where he was buried, and which because of him, according to al-ᶜĀkish, became

> the Kaᶜba of all those seeking God ﷻ, and people thronged about him from every district and at every time and moment. . . . When he had settled down here, a large crowd joined him from the land of Jabart (Eritrea and northern Ethiopia) and the Sudan and from elsewhere. . . . And also present with him

34. O'Fahey, *Enigmatic Saint*, pp. 134–135.
35. Vikør, *Sufi and Scholar on the Desert Edge*, p. 184.
36. O'Fahey, "Enigmatic Imam," p. 207.
37. Bernd Radtke, et al., *The Exoteric Aḥmad b. Idrīs*, p. 187.

> was a group of religious scholars from the Tihāma, one of whom was myself.[38]

Ibn Idrīs was concerned with removing or reducing the hold of any attachments beside those of God and His Messenger on the believers. He thus did not want any rigid attachments to any school of jurisprudence or theology. He believed that the ultimate authority over Muslims had to be God and His Messenger, and that sometimes attachment to different schools of thought came in the way of the faithful following of God's words and the teachings of His Messenger and led to factionalism and division among Muslims. He said,

> Fanatical devotion to one's school, the formation of factions, accusing each other of heresy as if it were a matter of different religions—and this can easily be seen by anyone who understands the world and reads what people write—such things we disapprove of and forbid every Muslim to have anything to do with. That is because they are one community—the best community—and their Prophet ﷺ is one, and their Book is one, and the direction of their prayers is one. So why should we have this factionalism and fanaticism? We have always forbidden people to have anything to do with them, both in the district of Mecca and Medina and elsewhere.[39]

In terms of theology and creed, he believed that the only thing that Muslims needed to believe is what he called "The Creed of Imam al-Shāfiʿī," namely this:

> I believe in God and in what came from God, according to what was meant by God. I believe in the Messenger of God and in what came from the Messenger of God, according to what was meant by the Messenger of God. O God, I believe in what You know to be the truth with You, and I declare to You my disassociation from what You know to be false with You. So take it from me as a whole, and do not demand from me the details![40]

38. Ibid., pp. 178–179. The Tihāma is a coastal strip now divided between Saudi Arabia and Yemen.
39. O'Fahey, *Enigmatic Saint*, pp. 75–76, with slight changes.
40. Yaḥyā Muḥammad Ibrāhīm, *Madrasat Aḥmad b. Idrīs al-maghribī wa atharuhā fī l-Sūdān*, pp. 113–114.

He argued that the only sure way to understand the meaning of God's descriptions in the Qurʾān is through God's self-disclosure to the servant.

> The people of this persuasion (i.e., the philosophers and scholastic theologians) believe in God according to what they understand, while the people of God are people who believe in God inasmuch as He makes Himself known to them. And what a great difference there is between the two persuasions, because he who believes inasmuch as God makes Himself known to him places his intellect behind his belief, so that he believes whether his intellect accepts it or not. And he who has this kind of belief, God informs him of what he did not know before by means of inspiration, not through the intellect.[41]

Even in the field of Sufism and the spiritual path, Ibn Idrīs wanted his followers to be completely attached only to God and His Messenger, not even to himself as a teacher and guide.[42] He used to say, "Sufism is to empty the heart of anything but God."[43] He said,

> Every prophet is given one supplication that will be answered by God ﷻ,[44] and every friend of God ﷻ has one request with His Prophet ﷺ. When the time for it came, I asked Him to take charge of my companions himself, that He give them spiritual support and nourishment from His own person. He said, "Whoever associates himself with you, I will not entrust him to the guardianship of anyone else but me or their care. I will be his guardian and his guarantor."[45]

---

41. O'Fahey, *Enigmatic Saint*, p. 74, replacing "revelation" with "inspiration."
42. O'Fahey, *Enigmatic Saint*, p. 110.
43. al-Jaʿfarī, *al-Muntaqā l-nafīs*, p. 22.
44. "Every Prophet is given one supplication that will be answered by God" is a statement of the Prophet as narrated by al-Bukhārī (p. 1283) and Muslim in their respective *Ṣaḥīḥ*s.
45. The words used are *walī* (guardian) and *kafīl* (guarantor). The latter refers mostly to those who take charge of the upbringing of others, such as orphans, and those who ensure that they receive their rights. In this case it refers to the protection of the spiritual seeker from

Ibn Idrīs would mention this to his students whenever they asked anything of him, saying, "We have transferred you to he who is better than us, and he has accepted the transfer, so turn to him and present your question and need to him."[46] One might consider the spiritual *ṭarīqa* a link between the seeker and the Prophet through a chain of spiritual successors and inheritors who pass on the teachings, wisdom, and spiritual knowledge of the Prophet from generation to generation; Ibn Idrīs wanted his students, like himself, to receive everything directly from the Prophet without intermediaries. That is why Ibn Idrīs called his path the Muḥammadan path, al-Ṭarīqa al-Muḥammadiyya, because those who take this path have no shaykh but the Prophet himself, who takes care of their spiritual upbringing.[47] Al-Sanūsī said, "Our shaykh ﵁ used to call his way 'al-Muḥammadiyya,' after the Prophet ﷺ, and sometimes would call it 'al-Aḥmadiyya,' after himself."[48]

For Ibn Idrīs, the purpose of the path was to achieve a perfect following of the prophetic model. He said, "The greatest portion of our aim is in following the Prophet ﷺ, footstep after footstep."[49] For him, the greatest honor and gift that God could bestow upon a servant is not the miraculous type of gift (*karāma*).[50] Instead, the greatest *karāma* is *istiqāma*, which is to be righteous and upright in following the correct path, and to remain constant and unwavering on that path. He said,

> Remaining upright (*istiqāma*) is the ultimate *karāma*. And we are,

---

deviating, and their spiritual upbringing "as the father raises his child" (al-Jaʿfarī, *Fatḥ wa fayḍ*, p. 156).

46. al-Jaʿfarī, *Miftāḥ mafātiḥ*, p. 26.
47. al-Jaʿfarī, *Fatḥ wa fayḍ*, p. 68.
48. Ibid., p. 153.
49. ʿAbd al-Ghanī l-Jaʿfarī, *al-Kanz al-tharī*, p. 110.
50. *Karāmāt* (sing. *karāma*) "are tokens of honor or favor, and when used in the discussion of a religious man the word refers to those actions that God has allowed the man to perform as a token of his piety. They can thus range from acts of miraculous healing or other contraventions of the 'natural' order of things to simply showing great wisdom or some other virtue." (Voll, "Two Biographies of Aḥmad b. Idrīs al-Fasi," p. 638, n. 21). On this topic see the commentary on *ḥadīth* 11.

> praise be to God, following the straight path which was followed by our example, the Messenger of God. As for these (other types, i.e., miraculous) favors, they are like shadows that come and go. They are of no importance on the path to God, except for those whose status is imperfect. For the perfect, his good fortune lies in having the Qurʾān as his ethos as had the Messenger of God.[51]

In order to follow his path, one must first receive its litanies from an authorized shaykh, and then undertake the foundation of the path. The foundation consists of a ritual bath, and one ritual prayer, accompanied by certain supplications, followed by making an intention to follow the path of Ibn Idrīs. After this, the seeker must recite the main formula of remembrance of the Aḥmadiyya Muḥammadiyya path 70,000 times. This is the formula that Ibn Idrīs was given in his vision and which the Prophet told him combined within it the benefit of all other formulas. It consists of saying the standard confession of faith, "There is no god but God, Muḥammad is the Messenger of God," adding to it, "With every glance and every breath, as many times as all that is contained in the knowledge of God."[52] During or after finishing the spiritual foundation of the path, says Ibn Idrīs, "he will, without doubt, see in his sleep either a sign or a message, depending on the sincerity of the seeker." Then he must go back to the shaykh and receive his daily litanies. "And through God is success. Praise be to God, Lord of the Worlds: God is the Succor, and there is no other than He."[53]

---

51. O'Fahey, *Enigmatic Saint,* p. 13, with slight changes to the translation.
52. Meaning, multiplied by the number of all things that God created and will create, and whose number He knows. God's knowledge is pre-eternal and does not change (*Fatḥ wa fayḍ*, pp. 150–151). During the lifetime of Shaykh Ṣāliḥ al-Jaʿfarī, his students were required to repeat it 70,000 times for their foundation. After his death, and with the emergence of his own litanies to replace those of Ibn Idrīs, the number required for the foundation was reduced to 10,000.
53. O'Fahey, *Enigmatic Saint*, pp. 208–209, with slight changes to the translation.

Spiritual Successors

When Shaykh Aḥmad b. Idrīs left Mecca for Yemen, he appointed Shaykh Muḥammad b. ʿAlī l-Sanūsī as his deputy in Mecca. When Ibn Idrīs passed away, his youngest son ʿAbd al-ʿĀlī (d. 1859) was only seven years old. Eleven years after that, ʿAbd al-ʿĀlī left Yemen for Mecca and became a student of al-Sanūsī. Al-Sanūsī was the most illustrious of Ibn Idrīs' great students, and as early as his fifteenth day of discipleship, his teacher told him that he had now become just like him. As al-Sanūsī's grandson narrates,

> On the fifteenth day of (al-Sanūsī's) taking from (Ibn Idrīs), the latter said to him, "You are us and we are you (*anta naḥnu wa-naḥnu anta*)." (Al-Sanūsī) replied, "Master! What has the moist earth in common with the heavenly constellations; what has the dim star, Suhā, in common with the midday sun?" (Ibn Idrīs) answered, "This is a favor of God, who dispenses as He wishes."[54]

ʿAbd al-ʿĀlī remained with his teacher al-Sanūsī for twelve years, until his death in 1859. They spent their first five years in Mecca, and the rest in the Cyrenaica in modern-day Libya, where they spread the wisdom of "the teacher" Ibn Idrīs and built around sixty *zāwiyas*. This Libyan branch of the Aḥmadiyya Muḥammadiyya path later became known as the Sanūsī movement, or Sanūsī *ṭarīqa*. ʿAbd al-ʿĀlī became the greatest of al-Sanūsī's students and was entrusted by him to teach during al-Sanūsī's own lifetime; al-Sanūsī even said to his student what the latter's father had said to him, "You are us and we are you." This meant that Ibn Idrīs passed to his youngest son a complete spiritual inheritance via al-Sanūsī. It seems that ʿAbd al-ʿĀlī was very concerned with following his father's teachings, to the extent that he said, "We did not neglect to take a single footstep that our father took; we took each one ourselves."[55] By that he probably meant that he was a perfect follower of his father, as well as a perfect inheritor of his father's spiritual states. This is not to imply, however, that either al-Sanūsī or ʿAbd al-ʿĀlī ever thought they rivaled their teacher Ibn Idrīs, and his unique

54. Ibid., p. 134, with corrections to the translation.
55. al-Jaʿfarī, *Miftāḥ mafātiḥ*, p. 42.

rank remains preserved until today among his followers. Al-Sanūsī's famed grandson, Shaykh Aḥmad al-Sharīf al-Sanūsī, said,

> As for our Shaykh Abū l-ʿAbbās al-ʿAraʾishī [Ibn Idrīs], he had in that (i.e., in taking directly from the Prophet) such a well-established rank that no one could attain his spiritual relationship (*aḥwālihī*) with the Prophet.[56]

One year after the death of al-Sanūsī, ʿAbd al-ʿĀlī left for Egypt, where he lived for twelve years; he arrived with his eldest son Muḥammad al-Sharīf (d. 1937) in Dongola in the year 1877. The Turco-Egyptian governor of the province invited them to stay and ʿAbd al-ʿĀlī taught there but died a year later, on 24 November 1878. He was buried in the main mosque of Dongola.[57] The burial there of ʿAbd al-ʿĀlī indicates his importance to the residents. After just one year, he had gained enormous respect in the town. A story narrated by his son Muḥammad al-Sharīf provides a glimpse of this: Muḥammad was once walking behind his father in Dongola while people were crowding around him, showing him great veneration and respect. Muḥammad al-Sharīf said that he began to think to himself, "Would I, when I reach my father's age, receive the same kind of respect and veneration that my father has received?" At this point, he said, his father turned to him and said, "And even more than this, O Muḥammad!" And it was as his father had said.[58]

In this last year of his life, Shaykh ʿAbd al-ʿĀlī gave lessons day and night.[59] Shaykh Ṣāliḥ al-Jaʿfarī's grandfather Ṣāliḥ b. Rifāʿī used to attend those lessons and take his son Muḥammad with him.[60] They would also go together to visit Shaykh ʿAbd al-ʿĀlī in his home, where they said they would always find him sitting with books all around him, putting one down and picking up another.[61] After ʿAbd al-ʿĀlī's death, Muḥammad al-Sharīf succeeded him in spreading the

---

56. O'Fahey, *Enigmatic Saint*, p. 142.
57. Ibid., p. 127.
58. Thābit, *Min aqṭāb al-umma*, p. 123.
59. al-Jaʿfarī, *al-Muntaqā l-nafīs*, p. 164.
60. ʿAbd al-Ghanī l-Jaʿfarī, *al-Kanz al-tharī*, p. 30.
61. al-Jaʿfarī, *al-Muntaqā l-nafīs*, p. 164.

path of Shaykh Aḥmad b. Idrīs in Egypt and the northern Sudan; for forty-nine years he taught, thirteen of these years in Upper Egypt and the rest in Dongola.[62]

When Shaykh Ṣāliḥ al-Jaʿfarī was born in 1328/1910, his father Muḥammad was so happy that he told his father that he wanted to name his son after him. Shaykh Ṣāliḥ b. Rifāʿī, whose grandson described him as a man of great spiritual knowledge, answered, "If you name him after me, you will be giving him as a gift to God ﷻ, and you will not benefit from him in your work or your agriculture." The father replied, "Then I have given him up as a gift to God ﷻ."

When al-Jaʿfarī was a young child, his father wanted to teach him a trade, so he took him to work at his brother's shop. But the young Ṣāliḥ's heart was too attached to the Qurʾān: he would run away from his uncle and go to the old mosque of Dongola to sit in the circles of Qurʾān lessons. There he would learn at the hands of venerable shaykhs who had learnt the Qurʾān from his own grandfather. Thus the young Ṣāliḥ al-Jaʿfarī spent his childhood enamored of the Qurʾān, passing his days neither at his uncle's shop nor playing with other children, but always in the mosque of Dongola learning and memorizing the Qurʾān. Even when he slept, he says, he kept the Qurʾān at the side of the bed, so that if he woke up at any time of the night he would continue its recitation. At the age of fourteen, he finished the Qurʾān, and at that very young age he also got married.[63]

There in that same mosque which housed the tomb of Shaykh ʿAbd al-ʿĀlī, his son and successor Shaykh Muḥammad al-Sharīf taught. Al-Jaʿfarī's father would get angry with his son for leaving the shop, until one day, when al-Jaʿfarī was sixteen years of age, he went and spoke to Shaykh Muḥammad al-Sharīf about it. The shaykh replied to him, "Have you forgotten that you have given him up as a gift to God ﷻ? Send your son to al-Azhar."[64]

It seems that Shaykh Muḥammad al-Sharīf watched over the young Ṣāliḥ, and saw something special in him. Al-Jaʿfarī says that whenever

62. Those were the years of the rule of the Mahdi movement, from 1885 to 1898, during which he did not want to remain in Sudan.

63. ʿAbd al-Ghanī l-Jaʿfarī, *al-Kanz al-tharī*, pp. 22–23.

64. Ibid., pp. 21–22.

he used to meet Shaykh Muḥammad, the shaykh would greet him by saying, "Welcome, our shaykh!" This would embarrass the young Ṣāliḥ who wondered why he was always singled out with the phrase "our shaykh" even when he was in the presence of many venerable shaykhs. Even his shaykhs who taught him the Qurʾān once asked him the reason, when Shaykh Muḥammad greeted them all, he called the young man "our shaykh" and did not use that phrase for them. The young Ṣāliḥ said, "God ﷻ knows best."[65]

At the age of nineteen, al-Jaʿfarī decided to follow the spiritual path of Shaykh Aḥmad b. Idrīs, and became a student of Shaykh Muḥammad. He spent a year in his company, serving him, learning at his hands, and joining him in his circles of remembrance of God. Muḥammad al-Sharīf gave al-Jaʿfarī an *ijāza* in the path, meaning an authorization to pass that spiritual chain to others, but he does not say if he received the *ijāza* at that young age or at a later meeting.[66] In that year, al-Jaʿfarī began to develop a strong spiritual connection with Shaykh Aḥmad b. Idrīs and his son Shaykh ʿAbd al-ʿĀlī and would see them in his dreams. In one dream, he saw Shaykh Aḥmad b. Idrīs say to him, "God ﷻ is with you. Study the jurisprudence of the four schools of law." When he asked a shaykh to interpret this dream for him, the shaykh replied that it meant that he will go study in al-Azhar. This was followed by another vision that confirmed for him the need to go to al-Azhar. Al-Jaʿfarī relates,

> Before I came to al-Azhar, someone from town brought a volume of al-Nawawī's commentary on *Ṣaḥīḥ Muslim*, so I borrowed it from him and began to study it. So I saw (i.e., in a dream vision) my master ʿAbd al-ʿĀlī l-Idrīsī ؓ sitting on a chair, and with him his travel bags, and I heard someone saying, "The *sayyid* wants to travel to Egypt, to al-Azhar."[67] I went and greeted him and kissed his hand, and he said to me sharply, "Knowledge is taken from the chests of men, not from books!" And he repeated it. I woke up from my sleep and was inspired

65. Thābit, *Min aqṭāb al-umma*, pp. 88–89, 121.
66. ʿAbd al-Ghanī l-Jaʿfarī, *al-Kanz al-tharī*, pp. 111–113.
67. *Sayyid* literally means chief or liege-lord, and is a term of honor used for descendants of the Prophet Muḥammad.

> by my Lord to travel to al-Azhar. And when I reached it I found the *ḥadīth* scholar Shaykh Muḥammad Ibrāhīm al-Samālūṭī teaching al-Nawawī's commentary on *Ṣaḥīḥ Muslim*![68]

At twenty years of age, the young Ṣāliḥ al-Jaʿfarī left his parents, his wife, his son ʿAbd al-Ghanī, and his daughter Fatḥiyya, for what was then a very arduous trip by land and river to Cairo, a trip in which he spent many nights in mountains and valleys. Part of his greatest excitement for Cairo was due to the presence of the tombs of his ancestor al-Ḥusayn, the grandson of the Prophet, his sister Zaynab, his daughters Sukayna and Fāṭima, and many other famous figures from the family of the Prophet Muḥammad for which he had felt a great love since his childhood. He thus said in one of his most famous poems, *al-Burda al-Ḥasaniyya al-Ḥusayniyya*,

> I traveled from one country to another,
> until I came to them in their homes
>
> And slept on one mountain after another,
> asking my Lord to behold their beauty.[69]

Ṣāliḥ al-Jaʿfarī the Student

Al-Jaʿfarī arrived in Cairo at the age of twenty, around the year 1930. He was greatly troubled by the city's westernization and the dress of women there, which was far different from the very conservative dress of the women in Dongola, as well as by the free mixing of the sexes and the crowded streets. Saddened by what he found, he decided to go back home, and went to visit the tomb of al-Ḥusayn, hoping to find peace in the presence of his blessed soul. There he found Shaykh Muḥammad Ibrāhīm al-Samālūṭī (d. 1934)

68. al-Jaʿfarī, *Fatḥ wa fayḍ*, pp. 18–19. Al-Nawawī (d. 676/1278) authored the most famous commentary on the *ḥadīth* collection of *Ṣaḥīh Muslim*, which is considered one of the two most authentic collections of *ḥadīth*; the other being *Ṣaḥīḥ al-Bukhārī*. This commentary is quoted by al-Jaʿfarī in some of his *ḥadīth* commentaries, such as *ḥadīth* 22 and *ḥadīth* 26.
69. ʿAbd al-Ghanī l-Jaʿfarī, *al-Kanz al-tharī*, pp. 24–25.

of al-Azhar, who used to teach *ḥadīth* in the mosque of al-Ḥusayn, and whose lesson was the first he attended.[70] As if he had read his mind, the shaykh said to him,

> Do not think that the Friends of God ﷻ[71] only live in rooms of seclusion and escape from people to mountain caves. The true friend of God is he who lives among scorpions, and yet they are not able to sting him. Remain here and struggle against your self's desires, and struggle against those people!

At that point, al-Jaʿfarī said to himself, "This shaykh is a knower of God ﷻ, I will not leave him as long as I live." He therefore remained in Cairo and began his studies at al-Azhar.[72] Al-Jaʿfarī believed that the scholar had exhibited *kashf*:[73] the ability to see what normal people cannot see, and a type of *karāma*.

Al-Samālūṭī was not the only scholar that al-Jaʿfarī described as a knower of God or a spiritual master. He studied under a great many scholars whose great piety and spirituality he acknowledged, and he became very close to a handful of them. He described the scholars of al-Azhar of that age in these deeply reverent terms,

> When I came to al-Azhar I found a shaykh teaching at every pillar. Our tears used to flow from the lessons of the scholars, and from the brightness of their faces; they used to have a way of teaching and speaking that would make the hearts quiver. The scholars of al-Azhar had beautiful pronunciation, and special tones in their voices when they taught. And Shaykh al-Samālūṭī ﷺ used to read the *ḥadīth* as no one read it before him, so that you would feel as if it was the Messenger speaking.[74]

---

70. Al-Samālūṭī was a Mālikī jurist as well as a traditionist. He was appointed as a member of al-Azhar's Committee of Senior Scholars in 1920. He taught Qurʾānic commentary and *ḥadīth* in the mosque of Sayyida Zaynab and the mosque of al-Ḥusayn. He also authored works on *ḥadīth* and the jurisprudence of the four schools of law. He followed the Shādhiliyya path of Sufism.
71. *Awliyāʾ*: literally those who are near to God.
72. ʿAbd al-Ghanī l-Jaʿfarī, *al-Kanz al-tharī*, pp. 26–27.
73. Literally, unveiling.
74. Thābit, *Min aqṭāb al-umma*, p. 98.

With regard to al-Samālūṭī, he also says,

> I used to sit in the lesson of Shaykh al-Samālūṭī to the right of the chair that he would sit on. One time I said within my heart, "Is the Prophet ﷺ with the shaykh as he says?" So the shaykh said to me, "Yes, boy! Yes, boy! Yes, boy!"[75]

In that age, al-Azhar had not yet become a university but operated as a *madrasa*. Al-Jaʿfarī describes how he used to attend the lessons of Shaykh Yūsuf al-Dijwī in al-Azhar Mosque from after the dawn prayer until 7:30 am. At that point he would cross the road to the mosque of al-Ḥusayn to catch the last half hour of al-Samālūṭī's lesson. At 8:00 am he would return to al-Azhar Mosque once again for the beginning of the lessons in Islamic law. But during holidays when the lessons in al-Azhar stopped, he used to attend the lessons of al-Samālūṭī in their entirety.[76] He would also seek knowledge in other mosques outside al-Azhar and the Ḥusayn Mosque area, like the lessons of Shaykh al-Shabrāwī in al-Nūr Mosque, which was attached to Abdeen Palace.[77]

It also appears that the young student had already acquired knowledge in Dongola before coming to Egypt. This can be gleaned from the incident that he relates from the class of Shaykh Maḥmūd Khattāb al-Subkī (d. 1933). Though he was a Sufi of the Khalwatiyya *ṭarīqa*, the shaykh wanted to purify Sufism of many practices that he believed to be harmful innovations.[78] Al-Jaʿfarī relates,

---

75. ʿAbd al-Ghanī l-Jaʿfarī, *al-Kanz al-tharī*, pp. 40–41.

76. Ibid., p. 25.

77. More will be said of these lessons under the section on "Ṣāliḥ al-Jaʿfarī the Teacher."

78. In 1912 al-Subkī founded al-Jamʿiyya al-Sharʿiyya, a nonprofit Islamic organization that established Islamic schools with a reformist approach, and offered extensive medical, economic, and social services for the poor. Because of the reformist attitude of its founder, the organization became influenced by the Salafi movement even during his lifetime, though al-Subkī himself was known as a Sufi and a jurist of the Mālikī school. Al-Jaʿfarī studied Mālikī law with him and was among those who carried his body and placed it in the grave when he died. He often quoted him in his lessons to show that he did

> I attended his lesson where fifty-five students sat before him, having only been at al-Azhar for two months. When he ended the lesson and stood up to leave, I went to kiss his hand, but he did not allow me to. So I said to him, "Abū Dāwūd narrated in his *Sunan* in the section on the delegation of ʿAbd Qays that they threw themselves from on top of their riding animals and took the hand and foot of the Prophet ﷺ and kissed them. You do not have more fear of doing something questionable than the Messenger of God ﷺ!" So he looked at me carefully then he looked to the people around him, then said to me, "Where are you from?" I said, "From the lands of God ﷻ! I have been in al-Azhar for two months." Then he looked at the people around him and said, "Look at him! He has only been at al-Azhar for two months, and is addressing me with the *Sunan* of Abū Dāwūd, and in al-Azhar are those who have been there eighty years and do not know where to find the *Sunan* of Abū Dāwūd!" That was his answer, and I thank him, because he accepted the evidence, and after that, whenever I greeted him, he would extend his hand for me to kiss it. And so I thank him because he was convinced by the evidence, and I will bear witness to that for him on the Day of Rising in the presence of God ﷻ.[79]

As a student, al-Jaʿfarī used to ask many questions of his teachers, and it seems that they were impressed by his knowledge. He once said to his Shaykh al-Samālūṭī, "I ask you many questions, and you respond to my questions constantly. But my colleagues object to me and protest." The shaykh responded to him, "You ask, and we will answer. You must be able to bear the stings of the bees in order to get the honey!"[80] It also seems that he used to have dreams of the Prophet Muḥammad teaching him and discussing with him matters that he learned from his teachers. This emerges from the following story of a *karāma* that he relates about Shaykh ʿAlī l-Shāyib who taught him texts in theology and grammar. He says,

---

not have the same divisive opinions and attitudes that many of his followers developed.

79. ʿAbd al-Ghanī l-Jaʿfarī, *al-Kanz al-tharī*, pp. 25–26.
80. Ibid., pp. 27–28.

> One night I saw the Prophet ﷺ in my sleep telling me of a matter of learning that I had gotten wrong. So he got angry and called me "boy!" and that was part of a long discussion. So when I woke up in the morning and went to the lesson I said to myself while seated, "The Prophet ﷺ calls me 'boy.' Am I a boy?" The shaykh turned to me while teaching and said, "We only called you 'boy' because it is the custom of the Arabs, not because you are young!"

Al-Jaʿfarī commented on this, saying, "Shaykhs like this are called by the Sufis 'the people (i.e., knowers) of the hearts.' It is possible that they are the ones known as *al-muḥaddathūn* (those who are spoken to/receive news), among whom was our master ʿUmar ﵁ as mentioned in the *ḥadīth* in *Ṣaḥīḥ al-Bukhārī*."[81] He was referring to the saying of the Prophet, "There had been in the nations that came before you people who were inspired (*muḥaddathūn*, literally those who are spoken to/receive news). If there are any such people among my nation, then ʿUmar b. al-Khaṭṭāb is one of them." Muslim also narrated it, adding that the scholar Ibn Wahb (d. 197/818) explained *muḥaddathūn* to mean inspired.[82]

Among the most distinguished teachers that al-Jaʿfarī studied with was Shaykh Muḥammad Bakhīt al-Muṭīʿī (d. 1935), who had been the Mufti of Egypt from 1915 to 1920.[83] Al-Muṭīʿī died at 103 years of age and taught in al-Azhar Mosque until his death. Al-Jaʿfarī described some of the extraordinary things that he witnessed from this shaykh, such as the time when the shaykh was commenting on a Qurʾānic verse about patience, and wanted to give an example of patience. He said, "It is like when Dakhīlallāh curses Ṣāliḥ but Ṣāliḥ remains patient." What was extraordinary was that before coming to attend the shaykh's lesson, al-Jaʿfarī was cursed by his fellow student Dakhīlallāh.[84] Al-Jaʿfarī thus considered this to be another example

81. Ibid., p. 47. I have not found anything on this scholar.
82. *Ṣaḥīḥ al-Bukhārī*, vol. 2, p. 686; *Ṣaḥīḥ Muslim*, vol. 2, p. 1027.
83. He was a jurist from the Ḥanafī school of law. He became a judge in 1880 and then the Mufti of Egypt from 1915 to 1920. He authored many works and fatwas.
84. ʿAbd al-Ghanī l-Jaʿfarī, *al-Kanz al-tharī*, p. 41.

of a *karāma*. Al-Muṭīʿī used to begin all his lessons by reciting two verses of the Qurʾān: 2:32 and 6:59. Al-Jaʿfarī took this from him when he became a teacher and began all of his lessons by reciting the same two verses.[85]

Perhaps the most distinguished of al-Jaʿfarī's teachers was Yūsuf al-Dijwī (d. 1946), who was the most famous scholar of al-Azhar of his age, and the head of the scholars of the Mālikī school of law.[86] Despite being blind, he was considered not only the most knowledgeable person in Imam Mālik's school of jurisprudence, but one of the greatest—if not the greatest—scholars alive in his age. This earned him the honorific title "Shaykh al-Islam."[87] Al-Jaʿfarī studied Qurʾānic exegesis with him from the 47th chapter until the end, and then the *ḥadīth* collection *Ṣaḥīḥ al-Bukhārī*. He also relates that al-Dijwī took the *ṭarīqa* of Shaykh Aḥmad b. Idrīs from his own Shaykh Muḥammad al-Sharīf, and that he used to say, "The noble Aḥmad b. Idrīs was a great pole of spirituality (*quṭb*) unlike any other pole!"[88] About his relationship with this scholar al-Jaʿfarī relates,

---

85. Ibid., p. 42. The verses are *They said, "Exalted are You; we have no knowledge except what You have taught us. Indeed, it is You who is the Knowing, the Wise"* (2:32) and *And with Him are the keys of the unseen; none knows them except Him. And He knows what is on the land and in the sea. Not a leaf falls but that He knows it. And no grain is there within the darknesses of the earth and no moist or dry [thing] but that it is [written] in a clear record* (6:59).
86. Al-Dijwī was an expert on all the most important fields of Islamic science such as *ḥadīth*, Qurʾānic exegesis, jurisprudence, and the principles of the law. He used to publish his writings in the magazine *Nūr al-Islām*, later known as *Majallat al-Azhar*. After his death, his articles and fatwas were published in a large book. Cairo's Dār al-Baṣāʾir publishing house printed a 4-volume edition in 2006 that includes his biography.
87. Al-Ṭuʿmī, *al-Nūr al-abhar*, p. 135.
88. ʿAbd al-Ghanī l-Jaʿfarī, *al-Kanz al-tharī*, pp. 43–44. The term *quṭb* is used by the Sufis to signify the highest rank in the hierarchy of the Friends of God, a rank that is only held by one person at any time. It is most likely that al-Dijwī met Muḥammad al-Sharīf when the latter visited Cairo. Regarding this visit, refer to the section on "Ṣāliḥ al-Jaʿfarī the Teacher."

He ﷺ was once reading the *ḥadīth* of the questioning of the grave in *Ṣaḥīḥ al-Bukhārī*. I had studied the commentary of al-Kirmānī on *al-Bukhārī* and saw in it that the Prophet ﷺ appears to the one being questioned when the angel says to him, "What did you used to say about this man?"[89] After the lesson I kissed his hand and said to him, "Shaykh al-Kirmānī says that he appears to the one being questioned." He poked me in my chest and said to me, "I studied the commentary of al-Kirmānī and read that matter in it, so why did you not remind me of it in the lesson so that the people would hear it from me?"

He was once speaking about the vision of the Prophet ﷺ during sleep. He said, "Satan does not take his form, if he came in his original form, and the correct opinion is that he also does not take form in other than his original form." So I said to him, "Our shaykh the noble Aḥmad b. Idrīs ﷺ narrated in his book *Rūḥ al-sunna* that he said, "He who has seen me has truly seen me, for I appear in every form."[90] So he rejoiced greatly at this and said to me, "This *ḥadīth* is the evidence that Satan does not take his form, even if he were to come in other than his original form! You are blessed O Shaykh Ṣāliḥ! May God ﷻ benefit the Muslims by you!"[91]

Beside Yūsuf al-Dijwī, the other scholars mentioned above all died within five years of al-Jaʿfarī's arrival in Cairo. But the scholar with whom he had the closest relationship for a long time was the Mauritanian *ḥadīth* scholar Ḥabībullāh al-Shinqīṭī (d. 1944) who came to teach at al-Azhar after having taught for many years in Mecca.[92] Al-Jaʿfarī remained in his company as one of his closest

---

89. *Ṣaḥīḥ al-Bukhārī*, vol. 1, p. 250.
90. Ibn Idrīs, *Rūḥ al-sunna*, p. 275. Ibn Ḥajar al-ʿAsqalānī quoted a similar narration by Ibn Abī ʿĀsim (d. 287 AH) in his commentary on *Ṣaḥīḥ al-Bukhārī*. Ibn Abī ʿĀsim narrated on the authority of Abū Hurayra that the Prophet said, "He who has seen me has truly seen me, for I am seen in every form" (*Fatḥ al-bārī*, vol. 12, p. 384). Al-Muttaqī l-Hindī also attributed it to Abū Nuʿaym's *Ḥilyat al-awliyāʾ* (al-Muttaqī l-Hindī, *Kanz al-ʿummāl*, vol. 15, p. 384).
91. ʿAbd al-Ghanī l-Jaʿfarī, *al-Kanz al-tharī*, p. 46.
92. Al-Shinqīṭī studied the Qurʾān and Mālikī jurisprudence in Mauritania

students for fifteen years, and, when he passed away, buried him with his own hands. Al-Shinqīṭī was most famous for his work *Zād al-muslim*, a compilation of the *aḥādīth* that are found in the two most authentic collections of *ḥadīth*, *Ṣaḥīḥ al-Bukhārī* and *Ṣaḥīḥ Muslim*. He then wrote a commentary on *Zād al-muslim* called *Fatḥ al-Munʿim*. Al-Jaʿfarī used to teach the students at the mosque of al-Ḥusayn before al-Shinqīṭī arrived to give his lesson, and the shaykh would appoint him to teach his lessons in his place whenever he could not make it. This shows the great confidence that he had in al-Jaʿfarī's knowledge of *ḥadīth*. This relationship began when al-Jaʿfarī went to the shaykh's house to ask his permission to be his *ḥadīth* reciter, the person who reads the *aḥādīth* for him in the lessons before the shaykh explains them. He says,

> I went to his house near the citadel, intending in my heart to ask his permission to be his reciter for the texts of al-Bukhārī and Muslim. So when I arrived at his house and sat in the reception room, and that was the first time I ever visited him, he came to me smiling. When I greeted him and kissed his hand he said to me, "You are the one who, God willing, will be my reciter this year." Praise be to God I stayed with him until his death, and went into his grave, and buried him with my own hands.
>
> I used to give a lesson to the brothers who were present before his arrival at the mosque of al-Ḥusayn, and if anyone objected to me or gave me a hard time, he would whisper in my ear after coming and sitting on his chair, "They give you a hard time but

---

before moving to Morocco where he specialized in *ḥadīth*. He then moved to Medina, where he lived and taught for many years, and then to Mecca, where he lived and taught for an even longer period. He finally moved to Cairo where he became a teacher at al-Azhar until he passed away at the age of 66 years. He authored works on Qurʾānic recitation as well as several *ḥadīth* collections and commentaries. He also authored works in other sciences such as logic, eloquence, and Sufism—many of them in the form of poetic compositions. Among his works are a hagiography of the founder of the Qādirī *ṭarīqa*, Shaykh ʿAbd al-Qādir al-Jīlānī (d. 1166) and a compilation of the litanies and poems of the Qādirī *ṭarīqa*; this may mean that he was a follower of that spiritual path.

you are better than them" as if he was with me! Then in his lesson he would correct everything that I had erred in or missed in my lesson, as if he had been sitting with me listening to what I was saying, and this happened many times.

If he had any reason that he could not come, he would send me a student telling me to read the lesson in his place. One day, however, he sent me a letter written in his own handwriting, saying, "I have assigned to you the teaching of the lesson." This surprised me. Why did the shaykh change his custom from verbal authorization to a written one? Then the supervisor of the mosques came while I was giving the lesson and said, "Did the shaykh charge you to give the lesson?" So I said, "Yes." So he said, "And where is the assignment?" So I gave him the paper that was sent by the shaykh, which made him happy, and he prayed for goodness for me. So that was a *karāma* from him, may God have mercy on him and forgive him and give him residence in His most spacious gardens. He used to love me very much and say to me, "You are the blessing of the lesson! I give you authorization in all my scholarly authorizations and writings."

I stayed with him for fifteen years. He used to say to me, "Study well my commentary on *Zād al-muslim*, for I did not leave anything out of it, big or small!"[93]

Al-Jaʿfarī obtained the highest degree from al-Azhar, the ʿĀlimiyya, before the modernization of al-Azhar into a university with specialized degrees. This was a general undifferentiated degree that equaled a doctorate in modern terms. Al-Jaʿfarī stated that under the old system, students used to spend at least twelve years studying in al-Azhar before they obtained the ʿĀlimiyya, and it is most likely that he obtained it around his twelfth year there, in 1942.[94] After obtaining it he traveled back to Dongola to celebrate with his family and remained

93. ʿAbd al-Ghanī l-Jaʿfarī, *al-Kanz al-tharī*, pp. 42–44.

94. It was after 1940, when his father was still alive, because according to the chronology in his biography, he obtained it after his father passed away. It was also before his official appointment as a teacher in 1946. It was most likely more than a few years before then, as he used to teach of his own initiative before the appointment until he became very popular. Therefore it is very likely that he obtained it within

there for three months before returning to Cairo, where he found a job in al-Azhar Mosque.[95] In 1946 he was officially appointed as a teacher by the grand shaykh of al-Azhar. At that time, al-Azhar was being transformed into a modern university separate from the mosque, with classrooms, written examinations, and specialized degrees. Though he was a teacher in al-Azhar Mosque, al-Jaʿfarī wanted to enroll once again as a student to obtain the modern degree. He obtained a PhD, the modern ʿĀlimiyya, in 1953 from the Faculty of Sharīʿa, with a license to teach.[96]

Ṣāliḥ al-Jaʿfarī the Teacher

There is a remarkable trait that appears in al-Jaʿfarī's stories about his student years: his eagerness to teach others at every occasion. It is not clear where he acquired that confidence. Perhaps he was encouraged by a teacher or had a dream telling him to teach, or maybe it was his desire to emulate his spiritual master and role model Ibn Idrīs. One example is a time when Shaykh al-Shabrāwī, who used to teach in the mosque attached to Abdeen Palace, was late for class. Al-Jaʿfarī decided to sit in the shaykh's place and give the lesson in his place. When al-Shabrāwī arrived, he stood at a distance to hear his student teaching, overjoyed at his student's knowledge and teaching. When the lesson finished he came to him and said, "Mashāʾ Allāh, mashāʾ Allāh![97] You do not need to attend my lessons after today, for I realize now that you have the ability to sit and teach the people." Al-Jaʿfarī, however, said, "I can never do without your class, I only sat in your place until you came."[98] It has already been mentioned that al-Jaʿfarī was appointed by Shaykh al-Shinqīṭī to teach the *ḥadīth* lesson in his place whenever he could not come, and that al-Jaʿfarī used to give his own lesson to the students before

---

twelve years of his arrival, as per the number of years that he gave as a general rule (ʿAbd al-Ghanī l-Jaʿfarī, *al-Kanz al-tharī*, p. 38).

95. The nature of the job is not mentioned.
96. ʿAbd al-Ghanī l-Jaʿfarī, *al-Kanz al-tharī*, pp. 32–34.
97. An expression of admiration (literally, What God has willed).
98. ʿAbd al-Ghanī l-Jaʿfarī, *al-Kanz al-tharī*, p. 28.

al-Shinqīṭī's class. He does not mention having been appointed by the shaykh to give that lesson, and it is likely that he taught out of his own initiative.

In 1937 Shaykh Muḥammad al-Sharīf came from Dongola to Cairo. It was the year in which he passed away and he was very ill, so it is likely that he went for treatment. When he went to al-Azhar Mosque, he found a large crowd, some seated and some standing, surrounding his young student al-Jaʿfarī as he gave a lesson on the explanation and commentary on the shortest chapter of the Qurʾān. This was only al-Jaʿfarī's seventh year as a student in Cairo, and yet he had large crowds listening to his lessons. When the lesson finished, he told his listeners to get up and greet his shaykh, and when he kissed his hand the shaykh smiled at him and said what he used to say to him when he was a boy in Dongola, "Welcome, our shaykh!"

After al-Jaʿfarī obtained the old ʿĀlimiyya degree and found a job in al-Azhar Mosque, he took the opportunity to teach and to preach whenever he could. One of al-Jaʿfarī's famous students, Dr. Muḥammad Rajab al-Bayyūmī (d. 2011),[99] wrote that the shaykh's great zeal for guiding and teaching the people and the way that he preached tirelessly every day reminded those who saw him of the *salaf*, or the pious scholars of the earliest generations.[100] This, however, aroused the jealousy and anger of a small group of people, who accused him of overstepping his authority. This changed in 1946, however, according to al-Bayyūmī, when al-Azhar's eminent scholar Yūsuf al-Dijwī passed away. Al-Azhar's scholars and students all gathered to carry their teacher's bier to the grave, led by the Grand Shaykh of al-Azhar of the time, Muṣṭafā ʿAbd al-Rāziq.[101]

99. Al-Bayyūmī was chief editor of *Majallat al-Azhar* and one of Egypt's most famous writers and literary critics.

100. This description of al-Jaʿfarī comes up repeatedly when one reads about him or interviews those who knew him. He is very often compared to the people of the *salaf*, as if he was not of the twentieth century. The shaykh is also often described, in a surprisingly high number of instances, as a "kingly."

101. ʿAbd al-Rāziq held that position from 1945 until his death two years later in 1947.

Al-Bayyūmī, who at the time was a student in al-Azhar's Faculty of Arabic Language, described what happened when the mourners reached the grave. Al-Jaʿfarī stood up of his own initiative and gave a moving speech about his late teacher's great knowledge and his brave stance against both the secularists and certain Muslim reform movements.[102] Al-Bayyūmī wrote that the majesty of the situation and al-Jaʿfarī's sad voice so moved the souls of the listeners that the Grand Shaykh of al-Azhar immediately asked about him and then gave him an official appointment as a teacher in al-Azhar Mosque. Al-Bayyūmī added that this great honor silenced those who used to speak out against al-Jaʿfarī.[103] Al-Jaʿfarī continued to teach in al-Azhar on an almost daily basis until he passed away in 1979—a period of thirty-three years. If we were to count the years that he taught there prior to his official appointment, that would come out to at least forty-two years of teaching in al-Azhar Mosque out of the forty-nine years that he spent there.[104]

Al-Jaʿfarī had a small chamber, about three meters long by two meters wide, set up for him inside one of the teaching halls of al-Azhar Mosque. The hall that he chose was known as the Moroccan Hall, which used to be the wing that housed the students who came to al-Azhar from the Muslim West. He chose that hall because of his love of his Moroccan shaykh Ibn Idrīs. That small chamber, which was known as his *khalwa,* or enclosed place of seclusion, was his home for the rest of his life (some thirty-three years). He was known for never leaving al-Azhar Mosque except when he went to Mecca and Medina for pilgrimage (twenty-seven times), or to visit the tombs of the descendants of the Prophet and other friends of God who were buried in Egypt. In al-Azhar, he filled his time

102. Meaning, those who rejected many traditional Sunni practices such as *tawassul*: making the Prophet—whether through his intercession, or through God's love of him—a means for the fulfillment of one's needs. Al-Dijwī wrote many articles in defense of *tawassul* and other Sufi practices in al-Azhar's magazine, which was then known as *Nūr al-Islām* (see ʿAbd al-Ghanī l-Jaʿfarī, *al-Kanz al-tharī*, p. 46).

103. ʿAbd al-Ghanī l-Jaʿfarī, *al-Kanz al-tharī*, p. 33.

104. The earliest date we can be sure of is 1937 when his shaykh, Muḥammad al-Sharīf, came to Cairo.

with teaching as well as spiritual guidance, and the remembrance of God. He led a circle of remembrance on Thursday nights in the Moroccan Hall. He would only sleep a few hours between the noon and afternoon prayers, except on Fridays when he would give his most famous class. He did not sleep at all at night, but would spend his nights reading the Qurʾān or circling the courtyard of al-Azhar with a long prayer bead in his hand, repeating words or formulas of remembrance. He eventually became the imam of the mosque, in charge of leading the prayers and giving the Friday sermons.[105]

Al-Jaʿfarī had many regular classes at al-Azhar, such as his daily class after the sunset prayer, but his most famous class was the Friday lesson that he gave between the Friday prayers at noon and the afternoon prayer. This was a class of Qurʾānic commentary that was tailored for the general public who would stay after the Friday prayer to listen to him. Though they always began with a commentary on a Qurʾānic verse, they were mostly lessons on matters of the soul and spirituality, and focused a great deal on love of the Prophet Muḥammad and the Qurʾān. They were lessons that combined the Qurʾān, *ḥadīth*, jurisprudence, and Sufism. Among the greatest concerns that guided al-Jaʿfarī's topics and method was the rising influence of communist ideas in Egypt and much of the Arab world at the time. He considered it an obligation upon himself to respond to those ideas, and expressed concern that he would be questioned on the Day of Judgment if he did not do enough to stop or reverse the spread of this school of thought. He also stood against the ideas coming from new Muslim reform movements that were considered unorthodox by the traditional Sunni scholars of al-Azhar, ideas mainly associated with Salafī and Wahhābī schools of thought. Most notable at the time was the Salafī-influenced organization al-Jamʿiyya al-Sharʿiyya, founded by his own teacher Maḥmūd Khaṭṭāb al-Subkī. Al-Jaʿfarī would regularly quote him to show that his teacher was a traditional scholar, Mālikī in jurisprudence and Khalwatī in *ṭarīqa*, and that he did not hold the same divisive opinions that many of his followers held. Al-Jaʿfarī, however, rejected the use of labels such

105. Some of his Friday sermons have been collected and published in *Minbar al-Azhar*.

as "Wahhābī," and shunned them as causes of division among the Muslim community. Instead, he responded to individual opinions and attitudes, not to groups or organizations, always beginning by saying, "someone said to me," or "some people say" or "some people do," before proceeding to criticize that particular attitude or position and defend the traditional Sunni and Sufi views. At the same time he criticized many practices associated with the Sufism of the unlearned masses. He was very concerned with the preservation of unity among the Muslims. When he spoke on matters of jurisprudence, or when he answered questions and gave fatwas, he almost always gave not only the position of his own Mālikī school of law, but also the Shāfiʿī. Often he would also mention the Ḥanafī opinion, and many times also the Ḥanbalī. It is clear from some of his answers that he sometimes preferred positions from a school different to his own.[106]

Though aimed at the general public, his Friday lesson was known to attract the great scholars of al-Azhar, as well as people from all walks of life: the rich and poor, commoners and government or military officials. His lessons took place in the courtyard of al-Azhar Mosque and his audiences filled the courtyard. A man of tall stature and strong build, he would appear even grander when he stood on top of the chair in order to project his voice while giving lessons. It was only toward the end of his life when his body became weaker that he would sit on the chair. At the end of the lesson his audience would join him in reciting the poems that he composed in praise of the Prophet Muḥammad and his family.

The current shaykh of the Mālikī scholars of Egypt, Shaykh Aḥmad Ṭāhā Rayyān recalls,

> Shaykh Ṣāliḥ did not speak about jurisprudence too much, because his main concern was to elevate the Islamic spirit in the souls of the people, so that they would come to feel the spirit of the religion and taste its sweetness. He ﷺ would say beautiful and wondrous words about the love of God ﷻ, and

106. Transcripts from two years of his Friday lessons have been published in *Dars al-jumuʿa bi-l-Azhar* (10 volumes). See the third volume for his lesson on the preservation of the unity of the Muslims.

> raise the audience to a station in which they achieved love of God ﷻ and love of the Messenger of God ﷺ and of the Messenger's ﷺ family ﷺ. The message of the shaykh—and al-Azhar in general—was greater than teaching the people the rulings on the ritual purification or the ritual prayer, with all their importance in the religion, and their necessity on the Sufi path. He would quickly move on from these topics to guide the believer in his dealings with God ﷻ and the Messenger of God ﷺ.
>
> I have attended many lessons in commentary on the Qurʾānic chapter "Joseph" ﷺ. The shaykh would begin with a verse from that chapter and then speak about the Sufi spiritual states and stations that can be learned from this verse and from others. He would also tell the tales of the righteous, or speak from the knowledge which God ﷻ caused to overflow onto his heart, and the time would pass without us feeling it; the time between the Friday noon prayers and the afternoon prayer would end as if it were just minutes. . . . No one dared interrupt him, because in that state he was like a flowing river, not giving anyone the chance to ask questions, and people had no reason to ask, because everyone was in reception mode. The reception would continue for three hours or more, and questions, if any, would be at the end of the class.[107]

Another student recollects a time when al-Jaʿfarī was drawing out new meanings from a much beloved Qurʾānic verse (9:128) in a way that astounded the listeners. However, one listener "stood up and interrupted the shaykh with speech that had no basis in knowledge—speech that was a product of the imaginations and delusions of the commoners, driven out of their love of the Prophet ﷺ and his family." The listeners, he says, were in an uproar and angrily commanded the man to sit down. The shaykh, however, asked for the man to repeat what he said, then responded to him and corrected his mistake. He then turned toward his listeners and said to them that a scholar who holds an audience must be like a bridge over a stream: pedestrians, drivers, and animals all pass over

107. "Qaḍāyā wa dhikrayāt ḥawl al-taṣawwuf," *al-Ṭarīqa* 14 (2003), p. 24.

it. If the scholar cannot likewise bear everyone who comes to him, just as a bridge does, then he is not fit to teach. "Your brother did not know this one matter," said the shaykh to his audience. "Should we have left him in his ignorance or should we have corrected his information?"[108]

Those who attended al-Jaʿfarī's lessons often repeat that he always seemed to read their minds and answer any questions that they held, without them ever saying anything. Shaykh Aḥmad ʿAbd al-Jawād al-Dūmī, who was the head of al-Azhar's Department of Advocacy and Guidance, gives a remarkable example. He recalls that one Friday morning he came to al-Azhar Mosque and read the eighteenth chapter of the Qurʾān. When he came to the verse that described a dog extending its legs in *al-waṣīd*, he wished to determine the meaning of this word but the book with that information was at his house and he had no time to retrieve it before giving his lesson. He decided to look it up when he returned home later in the day. After the Friday prayers, he went to sit in al-Jaʿfarī's lesson, and found him commenting upon a chapter of the Qurʾān other than the one he had read in the morning. The shaykh, however, suddenly went quiet. "Why did the shaykh interrupt his lesson?" al-Dūmī asked himself. Al-Jaʿfarī then began to recite verses from the eighteenth chapter until he got to the same verse about the dog, and said, "The dog extended its legs in such-and-such a manner, and *al-waṣīd* means the front yard. Now, back to our lesson, my beloveds!" Al-Dūmī said that in his heart he addressed the shaykh, saying, "May God ﷻ reward you!" He comments on this incident, explaining, "That is from the light of God ﷻ." Al-Dūmī is referring here to the *ḥadīth* of the Prophet: "Beware of the insight of the believer for he sees with the light of God ﷻ."[109]

One of the most famous incidents among those reported by the attendees of his lessons occurred when al-Jaʿfarī was teaching one day in the winter season, and rain suddenly poured down from the

108. Muḥammad Sulaymān Ādam, "al-Shaykh Ṣāliḥ al-Jaʿfarī raḍī-Allāhu ʿanhu fī l-dhikrā l-thalāthīn li-raḥīlihi ila l-malaʾ al-aʿlā," *al-Ṭarīqa* 19 (2008), pp. 52–53.

109. *Sunan al-Tirmidhī*, vol. 2, p. 794.

skies all over the city. The shaykh said, "Is there no Friend of God among you to say, 'O God ﷻ, around us but not on us'?" Al-Jaʿfarī was referring to a famous miracle of the Prophet Muḥammad in which a bedouin came to the Prophet during a Friday sermon and asked him to pray for rain to quench the drought. The Prophet prayed for rain and suddenly clouds gathered over the city of Medina and rain poured down continuously for a week. During the following Friday sermon, either the same bedouin or another one stood up and pleaded, "We are drowned! Ask your Lord to stop it for us!" The Prophet smiled and then prayed, "O God ﷻ, around us but not on us." The clouds began to disperse to the right and left of the city and they continued to rain around the city but not on it, so that the city looked like it was inside a crown.[110] Al-Jaʿfarī had barely finished uttering those same words when the rain stopped just in the area of the lesson, and continued to pour down all around them.[111]

Among his most famous students are the following.

Muḥammad ʿAlawī l-Mālikī (d. 2004), the late *ḥadīth* master of Mecca.

Ali Gomaa, Grand Mufti of Egypt (2003–2013).

Aḥmad al-Ṭayyib, Grand Shaykh of al-Azhar (2010–present).

Aḥmad Ṭāhā Rayyān, current head of the Mālikī scholars of Egypt.

Abū Bakr Aḥmad al-Malibārī, General Secretary of the All India Muslim Scholars Association as well as the Sunni Cultural Centre, Calicut.

Murtaza bin Aḥmad, previously Mufti of Kerajaan Negeri Sembilan, Malaysia.

Aḥmad Babikr, Principal of Islamia School, London.

Muḥammad Ibrāhīm ʿAbd al-Bāʿith, the most famous *ḥadīth* scholar in Alexandria, Egypt.

Saʿd Jāwīsh, celebrated Egyptian *ḥadīth* scholar.

---

110. *Ṣaḥīḥ al-Bukhārī*, vol. 1, p. 193.

111. ʿAbd al-Ghanī l-Jaʿfarī, *Quṭūf min sīrat sayyidī l-shaykh Ṣāliḥ al-Jaʿfarī*, pp. 9–12.

Muḥammad Rajab al-Bayyūmī (d. 2011), famous professor of literature and rhetoric in al-Azhar who was a literary critic and an award winning Islamic author, poet, and playwright.

Ismāʿīl Ṣādiq al-ʿAdawī (d. 1998), who established Maḍyafat al-ʿAdawī, an institution that hosts lessons of religious learning near al-Azhar. He succeeded al-Jaʿfarī as the imam of al-Azhar Mosque.

Muḥammad Baryūn (d. 2012), Libyan scholar, educator, and publisher.

Among the things that were said of him as a scholar are the following:

> When Shaykh Muḥammad ʿAlawī l-Mālikī went to study in al-Azhar, his father ʿAlawi al-Mālikī, who was one of the most prominent scholars of Mecca, said to him, "Go to Shaykh Ṣāliḥ al-Jaʿfarī, for he is the scale of the scholars (*mīzān al-ʿulamāʾ*). They are to be measured according to him, and he is not to be measured according to anyone!"[112]

His colleague Shaykh ʿAbd al-Ḥalīm Maḥmūd (d. 1978), the most celebrated Grand Shaykh of al-Azhar (1973–1978) in recent memory, said about him, "Shaykh Ṣāliḥ is the Kaʿba of knowledge."[113]

Dr. ʿAbd al-Raḥmān al-Bīṣār, who held the title of the Grand Shaykh of al-Azhar from 1979 until his death in 1982, said about him,

> Shaykh Ṣāliḥ is al-Azhar by his presence in it and by his knowledge. Many visitors to al-Azhar from different countries found Shaykh Ṣāliḥ ﷺ representing al-Azhar with his knowledge, and so his presence at al-Azhar was a symbol of

112. From personal communication with Dr. ʿAṭiyya Muṣṭafā, one of the senior figures in the Jaʿfarī *ṭarīqa*, who heard it from al-Mālikī. ʿAlawī l-Mālikī (d. 1971) took the Idrīsī path from Aḥmad al-Sharīf al-Sanūsī (d. 1933) and passed it on to his son.

113. As related by Shaykh ʿAbd al-Ghanī l-Jaʿfarī to his students. He brought his eldest son Muḥammad Ṣaliḥ, a child at the time, to visit his grandfather in Cairo. Shaykh ʿAbd al-Ḥalīm Maḥmūd was there and he said to the young child, "You have come to visit the Kaʿba of knowledge. Shaykh Ṣāliḥ is the Kaʿba of knowledge."

> al-Azhar. His daily lesson was after the sunset prayer, and he would always teach on Islamic occasions, and he ﵀ was famous for his Friday lesson.[114]

Shaykh Ali Gomaa wrote,

> Shaykh Ṣāliḥ was one of the righteous men of al-Azhar, and among the great scholars of the Mālikī school. He had a famous lesson after Friday, and would guide people to that which is good. He was loved by the old and the young, the pious and the impious—God ﷻ made him loved and accepted by all. He revived the glorious deeds of the early scholars, and had beautiful character and was very accommodating of others. If you saw him you would remember the greatest scholars of the fourth Islamic century, like al-Juwaynī, al-Ghazālī and their like. If you entered upon him you would see light shining from his face, and he had a brown complexion. What made him special was that he loved the Prophet ﷺ and would send a great deal of blessings upon him night and day, and would counsel us to do so until we met our Lord. He ﵀ loved the Prophet ﷺ from the heart, and would frequently see him in his sleep. . . . He was a humble man who wanted little from this world.[115]

The Flood of Knowledge

He (i.e., Ibn Idrīs) ﵀ was asked one day about the *karāmāt* that will be given to those who take his Aḥmadiyya Muḥammadiyya *ṭarīqa*. He said, "It is knowledge which God ﷻ will cause to overflow into their hearts." He ﵀ also gave me the good tidings in a conversation that I had with him, saying, "God ﷻ will give you openings in knowledge that will benefit the brothers."[116]

With all its emphasis on the importance of knowledge and learning, it is no wonder that even the miracles associated with the shaykhs of this *ṭarīqa* are very often miracles about knowledge. When Ibn Idrīs moved to Zabīd, one of Yemen's greatest centers of

114. al-Jaʿfarī, *Dars al-jumuʿa bi-l-Azhar*, vol. 4, p. 4.
115. Ali Gomaa, *al-Dīn wa-l-ḥayā*, quoted in *al-Ṭarīqa* 18 (2007), p. i.
116. al-Jaʿfarī, *Fatḥ wa fayḍ*, p. 154.

learning, its Mufti ʿAbd al-Raḥmān b. Sulaymān al-Ahdal and the other respected scholars of the town used to attend his gatherings every morning and evening and ask him to resolve their most difficult inquiries. He once spent eleven—or according to another report, twelve—days giving one lesson in the morning and one lesson in the evening, explaining and commenting upon a single Qurʾānic verse, the one that begins with, *The Muslim men and the Muslim women . . .* (33:35). One of the scholars mentioned that his commentary was recorded in seventy notebooks.[117] Ibn Idrīs then said to them, "If God ﷻ extended our lives, and we spoke about the exegesis of this verse until the Day of Rising, and in each gathering we said something new, we would have done so."[118]

Likewise, the Yemeni scholar al-Ḥasan b. ʿĀkish wrote that he asked Ibn Idrīs to explain the verse, *The One who apportioned and then guided* (87:3). Ibn Idrīs gave lessons for three days on its meanings and then he said that if God were to prolong his life until the Day of Judgment, and were to prolong the openings of knowledge that He was bestowing upon him, he could have given a new understanding each day, and this only based on the outward and literal meaning of the verse, let alone its secrets.[119]

In his hagiography of Ibn Idrīs, al-Jaʿfarī refers to the story above, and then describes a similar incident that happened to Ibn Idrīs' son ʿAbd al-ʿĀli. He says that a scholar from Dongola related to him how ʿAbd al-ʿĀli would also give lessons every morning and night like his father. He used to teach according to the way of the Moroccans,

117. Dr. Yaḥyā Muḥammad Ibrāhīm found portions of these notes preserved in manuscripts in libraries in Upper Egypt and Sudan. He estimates that the full 70 notebooks would have amounted to 560 pages. See his *Madrasat Aḥmad b. Idrīs al-maghribī wa atharuhā fī l-Sūdān*. I am indebted to Dr. Knut S. Vikør for sending me a copy of one of these manuscripts.

118. There are two written reports about these lessons by Ibn Idrīs' students. One is Ibrāhīm al-Rashīd's *ʿIqd al-durr al-nafīs*, published by al-Jaʿfarī in *Aʿṭār azhār aghṣān ḥaẓīrat al-taqdīs*. The other has been translated by John Voll in, "Two Biographies of Aḥmad b. Idrīs al-Fāsī (1760–1837)."

119. O'Fahey, *Enigmatic Saint*, p. 199.

which was to have a reciter recite a verse to him, and then he would explain it. One time, the reciter, ʿAbdallāh Klamsīd, recited to him the verse, *Exalted is He who made the constellations in the heavens and made therein a sun and a shining moon* (25:61), and the shaykh explained it. The next day, a scholar asked the reciter to repeat the same verse to see if the shaykh could give a new commentary on it. The shaykh is said to have given a new and excellent explanation. When the third day came, it was ʿAbd al-ʿĀli himself who recited the same verse and then proceeded to give a new commentary on it that astounded the listeners. Shaykh Klamsīd kissed his hand and began to cry. ʿAbd al-ʿĀli said to him, "what makes you cry, our brother Shaykh ʿAbdallāh?" He said, "My master, I cry because you came to our town when I was already old, and I wish that I was still a strong young man so that I could receive this knowledge." The shaykh replied, "If I stayed with you as long as Noah stayed with his people I would have given you a new explanation every day."[120]

After narrating these stories about his spiritual predecessors, al-Jaʿfarī proceeded to give his own commentaries on these same verses. He gave twenty-eight explanations and examples for the verse, *The One who apportioned and then guided*, ranging from the simple to the sublime. He then gave a detailed spiritual commentary on 25:61, in which the heavens symbolize the soul, the sun symbolizes Islam in its exterior aspects, and the moon symbolizes one's interior faith, which took its light from the sun of the outward actions.[121]

In his Friday lessons as well, al-Jaʿfarī often explained the Qurʾān with a new depth that astounded his listeners. Dr. Bayyūmī described these lessons, and recalled in particular an incident in which, during a difficult era in Egyptian political history, al-Jaʿfarī moved from his original topic of discussion on almsgiving to speak about the verse,

> *Or do you think that you would enter the garden while yet the state of those who have passed away before you has not come upon you; distress and affliction befell them and they were shaken*

---

120. al-Jaʿfarī, *al-Muntaqā l-nafīs*, pp. 164–165. According to the Qurʾān and Bible, the Prophet Noah lived 950 years.

121. Verse 25:61 reads: *Blessed is He who has placed in the sky great stars and placed therein a [burning] lamp and luminous moon.* Ibid., pp. 165–171.

> *violently, so that the Messenger and those who believed with him said: When will the help of God come? Now surely the help of God is near!* (2:214).

Al-Bayyūmī wrote,

> God ﷻ poured out through his tongue dazzling meanings and precious words of wisdom, as if a spiritual supply was rising from the clashing of waves in his heart and flowing from his tongue. How many times did the shaykh, in his lessons, have such passionate leaps—we did not know from where they came! We have read what the people read—the books of Qurʾānic commentary and the works on *ḥadīth*—but we have never seen such a flowing and pulsating explanation from anyone who preceded him on this great verse. The shaykh was endowed with a sweetness of voice that made his listener imagine he was listening to music, not a person speaking![122]

Al-Jaʿfarī did not only teach in Egypt, but in many different parts of the Muslim world. In a poem that he wrote addressing his late father's soul, he thanked his father for giving him up as a gift to God and told him that it was because of his good intention that his son became a teacher and preacher not only in al-Azhar Mosque, but also in Mecca and Medina, the Sudan, and the Muslim West.[123] Al-Jaʿfarī went on pilgrimage every year from 1952 until he died in 1979, only missing it in 1962, when he spent time with his mother in Sudan instead.[124] Each year, after the pilgrimage, he would spend fifteen days visiting a different Muslim country.[125] Among those countries are Morocco, Libya, Palestine, Jordan, and Iraq. Al-Jaʿfarī's son ʿAbd al-Ghanī explained his father's travels as visits to the righteous scholars and friends of God, from whom he took knowledge and authorizations. Another reason for his travels was to find manuscripts of scholars to edit and publish.[126] From among

122. ʿAbd al-Ghanī l-Jaʿfarī, *al-Kanz al-tharī*, p. 75.

123. Ibid., p. 18.

124. Ibid., p. 19.

125. From personal communication with Dr. ʿAṭiyya Muṣṭafā, one of the senior figures in the Jaʿfarī *ṭarīqa*.

126. *al-Ṭarīqa al-Jaʿfariyya*, p. 37. Al-Jaʿfarī describes in his lessons his visit

those countries, his influence was most extensive in Sudan and Libya. In Sudan, he used to travel to different cities and villages, giving lectures and leading circles of remembrance; people would travel with him from one place to another. His lessons are said to have left a lasting effect on the memory of the Sudanese.[127] He captured the hearts of the people of Libya as well, and his poetry is extremely popular there.[128] There are now two centers of the Jaʿfariyya *ṭarīqa* in Libya.

Ṣāliḥ al-Jaʿfarī the Spiritual Guide

Al-Jaʿfarī dedicated his life to the legacy of his spiritual guide and role model, Aḥmad b. Idrīs, editing and publishing all that he could find of his works. He went to Morocco and the Muslim West in search of manuscripts, and contacted students and descendants of Ibn Idrīs in Yemen and Saudi Arabia.[129] In total he found and published eleven works of Ibn Idrīs, and wrote lengthy commentaries on two of them. He also published the hagiography of Ibn Idrīs, written by his student Ibrāhīm al-Rashīd, with whom he also published all of Ibn Idrīs' letters to his disciples that he was able to obtain.[130] In addition, al-Jaʿfarī compiled and published *al-Muntaqā l-nafīs*, his own biographical-hagiographical work about his master. He also often praised Ibn Idrīs in his Friday lessons, adding to his master's fame and popularity in Egypt and among the scholars and students of al-Azhar from all over the world. As an authorized shaykh in the *ṭarīqa*, he spread the Aḥmadiyya Muḥammadiyya as a representative of Ibn Idrīs.

He first began to receive students wishing to learn his path when,

---

to Libya and how it resulted in his publishing the biography of Libya's most famous friend of God, ʿAbd al-Salām al-Asmar.

127. Ibid.

128. From personal communication with Aḥmad al-Sanūsī, a young shaykh from the Sanūsī *ṭarīqa* in Libya. I also have a copy of al-Jaʿfarī's poem *al-Burda al-Ḥasaniyya al-Ḥusayniyya*, which was printed in Tripoli.

129. *al-Ṭarīqa al-Jaʿfariyya*, p. 71.

130. See Thābit, *Min aqṭāb al-umma*, pp. 124–125, for a list of the works of both shaykhs.

out of love for his shaykh, he decided to live in the Moroccan Hall of al-Azhar Mosque. Each year Moroccan pilgrims would visit Cairo on the way to Mecca, and the shaykh would celebrate and honor them. He used to give them lessons, but more importantly, he would recite to them his poetry of love and praise for the Prophet and they would repeat after him. He found in the Moroccan pilgrims a great longing and love for praise of the Prophet, and he began to cook meat for them and feed them in those gatherings. People began to experience visions in which they saw the souls of the Prophet's family attending the gatherings. Then, the shaykh narrates, God's victory and opening came, and people started traveling from all over the Islamic world to train in his spiritual path, with the authorization of Shaykh Aḥmad b. Idrīs. Eventually the pots of meat grew into large trays of food, and the shaykh would regularly feed all the disciples, students of al-Azhar, and guests that were present at those gatherings. The shaykh became an established spiritual master. People from everywhere flocked to him as disciples, and he held regular gatherings of remembrance inside al-Azhar Mosque itself.[131]

Al-Jaʿfarī taught that everyone who follows a spiritual path should consider the founder of that path—the one who composed its litanies—as his shaykh; the founder of the path and the author of its litanies would have been authorized as a spiritual guide by the Prophet himself. In most cases, that founder's soul was now in the intermediary realm (*barzakh*), which is connected to this physical world.[132] As for the living shaykh from whom one takes the path, the seeker must respect him, obey him, and think well of him, for he is the door or link to the founder of the path, and without him arrival becomes extremely difficult. All that is required of the living shaykh is that he is upright in acting upon the law—he does what is obligatory and abstains from what is forbidden. If this shaykh errs or commits a sin, as any human is capable of sinning, it will not

131. Fārūq Farrāj, "Iltiqāʾ al-arwāḥ al-zakiyya fi l-ḥadrat al-qudsiyya," *al-Ṭarīqa*, 19 (2008), p. 34.

132. It is the spiritual realm in which the souls reside until the Day of Resurrection. References to different aspects of life in this realm can be found in the commentaries on the following *aḥādīth*: 11–16, 32.

harm the seeker. The real guide for the soul of the spiritual seeker, however, is the shaykh who founded the path.[133]

Al-Jaʿfarī also taught that at the beginning of the path, the seeker is only able to perceive the guidance of his living shaykh who gives him instructions and guidance. As his soul becomes stronger, he begins to see the soul of the founder of the path in visions and receive guidance from him. The shaykh whose soul is in the intermediary realm, who has been freed from the limitations of the body, has much more knowledge of his disciple's states than his living representative. The guidance and spiritual upbringing that he gives his disciples is much more effective, and takes the seeker much farther than the guidance provided by the living shaykh.[134]

Al-Jaʿfarī thus counseled the seekers to look at their living shaykh with two eyes: an eye that sees him, and an eye that sees the founder of the path to whom he is connected.[135] The seeker must learn about the founder of the path, about his life and teachings, and must strive to follow in his footsteps. He must also recite his litanies and read his books so that his soul connects to the soul of the shaykh and receives its spiritual nourishment, light, and knowledge.[136]

Al-Jaʿfarī often repeated that the shaykh of his spiritual path is Aḥmad b. Idrīs and no one else, and that those who take the path from him must follow the way of Ibn Idrīs. More than anything, the way of Ibn Idrīs was the acquisition and teaching of knowledge. Al-Jaʿfarī wrote,

> Say to those who say, "We are upon the path of Shaykh Aḥmad b. Idrīs" ﵁: "If you understood the way of your shaykh, and knew his state, you would know that he was a shaykh of the Qurʾān and religious sciences, and that he spent a long time acquiring these sciences, and then spent a long time teaching them to the people. That is the way of your shaykh; if you want to be true Aḥmadīs then follow it![137]

133. al-Jaʿfarī, *al-Ilhām al-nāfiʿ*, pp. 58–59.
134. al-Jaʿfarī, *Dars al-jumuʿa bi-l-Azhar*, vol. 1, pp. 69–71.
135. al-Jaʿfarī, *al-Ilhām al-nāfiʿ*, p. 52.
136. Ibn Idrīs, *Shahd mushāhadat al-arwāḥ*, pp. 9–24.
137. al-Jaʿfarī, *Fatḥ wa fayḍ*, p. 153.

He also wrote,

> The Prophet ﷺ used to guide people through lessons of religious knowledge and the great Qurʾān. Our shaykh, my master Aḥmad b. Idrīs ؓ, followed him in that. He used to guide people by the noble Qurʾān and by knowledge and he remained upon that path until he met his Lord. I have asked God ﷻ to guide me and help me to follow the way of our shaykh, the scholar who possessed the most precious knowledge, Shaykh Ibn Idrīs ؓ.
>
> All the brothers have to help me by attending the lessons, and they must memorize part of the Qurʾān . . . for we have only the lessons and the memorization of the Qurʾān. So assist me with your strong determination, for I have only brought you together for this lesson in which there is the exegesis of the Qurʾān, the explanation of the prophetic *aḥādīth*, deep understanding of the religion and its jurisprudence, and the memorization and recitation of the Qurʾān. Worship is for God ﷻ alone, and the scholars are the guiding inheritors. He said, "The scholars are the inheritors of the prophets."[138]

Al-Jaʿfarī described the role of Ibn Idrīs as the guide for the souls of his followers, while the Prophet, in whose care they dwell, is the one who provides their souls with spiritual nourishment.[139] He also describes a spiritual inheritance derived from the soul of the shaykh himself:

> If you travel on the path of a shaykh and you love him, the state that he had in the world will transfer to you, meaning that your soul will do as he did. So if he was a scholar, then the soul would incline toward learning, and if he was in seclusion, then it would incline toward seclusion, and if he was in a state of divine pull and attraction, then it would incline toward that, and if he was busy with the recitation of the Qurʾān, teaching, and the acquisition of knowledge, then it would incline toward that. The life of the seeker in the world becomes like the life of his shaykh,

---

138. ʿAbd al-Ghanī l-Jaʿfarī, *al-Kanz al-tharī*, pp. 119–120. For the *ḥadīth* reference, see the commentary on *ḥadīth 27*.

139. al-Jaʿfarī, *Fatḥ wa fayḍ*, p. 98.

> and that is known as the station of inheritance. It comes about by loving the shaykh and reciting his litanies, and by following in his footsteps. The shaykh today, in the intermediate realm, dislikes those acts that he kept away from in his lifetime, and dislikes those who engage in them. We seek refuge in God ﷻ from that![140]

It seems, however, that al-Jaʿfarī began to feel that he would eventually have his own *ṭarīqa*. It has been mentioned that he used to compose poetry, and would recite it with his students after the Friday lesson and in the Thursday night gatherings of remembrance. Al-Jaʿfarī was a gifted poet, leaving behind twelve volumes of poetry. When his followers later published them according to theme, there were two volumes dedicated purely to spiritual guidance and affairs of the spiritual path, four volumes of poetry about love of God or in supplication to God, and six volumes of poetry about love of the Prophet and his family and descendants.[141] Even in the latter two categories, however, his poems often shifted to instructions to his students and followers. Al-Jaʿfarī's poems are very popular in Egypt, and some are recited in many other places in the Arab world. Of his four most popular poems, two are about love of the prophets, and two about love of the Prophet's family and descendants.[142] One

140. ʿAbd al-Ghanī l-Jaʿfarī, *al-Kanz al-tharī*, p. 177.

141. On the love of the Prophet's family and descendants in Islam, see *ḥadīth* 25 and its commentary.

142. The two on love of the Prophet are known as "al-Maqbūla" (i.e., the poem that has received prophetic acceptance), and "Ṣallā Allāhu ʿalā Ṭāhā." The first one is usually printed on its own with another popular poem about the same subject, on visiting the Prophet in Medina, called *Riyāḍ al-khuld* [The gardens of eternity]. The two on the love of the Prophet's family are two of his longest poems. One is an imitation of the famous poem *al-Burda* of al-Būṣīrī in praise of the Prophet, but his version focuses instead on the family and descendants of the Prophet; he composed it in 1934, at the young age of twenty-four. The second is *Rawḍat al-qulūb wa-l-arwāḥ* [The garden for hearts and souls]. These last two are also usually printed and sold on their own, and are very popular in Egypt and elsewhere in the Middle East and North Africa.

day, al-Jaʿfarī dreamt that Ibn Idrīs was chiding him for placing such importance on poetry of praise of the Prophet, saying to him, "We do not have poems of praise as part of our *ṭarīqa*." However, the Prophet then appeared in the dream and said to Ibn Idrīs, "This is the *ṭarīqa* of my son Ṣāliḥ."[143] Al-Jaʿfarī began to hint at the existence of his own path and litanies in some of his poetry. In one poem that summed up the principles and benefits of his path, he mentioned being the shaykh of the path, and being given his own litanies from the Prophet. In that poem also is the most famous verse that sums up his own path and that is written on a marble slab on his tomb,

> My path is the Qurʾān, knowledge, and *taqwā*,
> and praise for the Messenger of God,
> the one who abolishes misguidance.[144]

Al-Jaʿfarī, however, never clearly declared the establishment of his own independent branch of the Aḥmadiyya Muḥammadiyya. He prepared his litanies, but never revealed them during his lifetime. His followers believe that he was so deferential to his master Ibn Idrīs that he left the litanies to be discovered after his death. They have been arranged into a book of supplications and a book of blessings upon the Prophet; both books are divided into different portions for different days of the week. The book of blessings upon the Prophet contains 435 unique and individual formulas of blessings upon the Prophet, to which can be added another forty that are in a separate book that he composed early on in his life, and a few others scattered throughout the book of supplications. If one were to consider also the existence of six volumes of poetry expressing love of the Prophet and his family, one can only marvel at the force of a love that could express itself in so many ways.

Al-Jaʿfarī states in an autobiographical poem that he was given something that no friend of God was ever given before him, namely that whoever recites his blessings upon the Prophet regularly is

---

143. From personal communication with Dr. ʿAṭiyya Muṣṭafā, one of the senior figures in the Jaʿfarī *ṭarīqa*.

144. Thābit, *Min aqṭāb al-umma*, pp. 133–135. Refer to *ḥadīth* 39 and its commentary for a discussion on *taqwā*.

under the guardianship of the Prophet; he must surely mean even those who did not take his spiritual path, as those who have taken the path are meant to be under the Prophet's guardianship anyway. Furthermore, he said that he himself will serve whoever recites them just as a mother cares for her child—he will watch over him, protect him, and bring him near to him until his heart is flooded with lights.

With regard to his litanies, he says in the same poem that they suffice the seeker without his needing to go into spiritual retreats or seclusions, and will make he who recites them content with little of this world. There is a remarkable line in that poem in which he describes a future when people will take the oath of the spiritual path after his death through his successor, and that his soul will be present whenever that takes place.[145] This was interpreted as a hint at the appearance, after his death, of his own spiritual path.[146]

He also said,

> Know that this path of ours is built on the Book, the Sunna, the jurisprudence of the four schools of law, the creed of al-Ashʿarī,[147] and the way of Abū l-Qāsim al-Junayd[148] ﵁ in Sufism.
>
> This path is nothing but the close following of the Messenger of God ﷺ in sayings and actions, outwardly and inwardly.

The Jaʿfariyya Aḥmadiyya Muḥammadiyya

Al-Jaʿfarī said to his students at the end of his life that he had never intended for his son ʿAbd al-Ghanī (d. 1433/2012) to succeed him as the shaykh of the path, but instead wanted to designate as his successor his student of thirty-seven years, a scholar by the name of Muḥammad ʿAbd al-Bāqī. He said that the Prophet refused this strongly, however, and insisted that his son ʿAbd al-Ghanī take his

145. *al-Ṭarīqa al-Jaʿfariyya*, pp. 99–103.
146. Ibid., p. 116.
147. Died 324 AH/935–6 CE. Founder of the school of theology that bears his name. See "al-Ashʿarī, Abū'l-Ḥasan," in *Encyclopaedia of Islam*, 2nd edition.
148. Died 298 AH/910 CE. Considered the great early exemplar of Sufism.

place. In his last year before he died, like every year, al-Jaʿfarī met his son at the pilgrimage in Mecca, for ʿAbd al-Ghanī lived and worked in Sudan. There in Mecca, he told his son that he did not believe they would meet again, and said to him, "I leave the brothers in your trust. I leave the brothers in your trust. I leave the brothers in your trust, who have come together over the love of the Prophet ﷺ and his family."[149] ʿAbd al-Ghanī had lived his life in Sudan as a school teacher, principal, and then as technical supervisor of education in the Middle Region of Sudan. He later became the Executive Director of the Department of the Northern State. Throughout his life, he remained in close contact with his father through letters, and in 1943 he went to study in al-Azhar for a year in the presence of his father and took with him his mother and two sisters. When al-Jaʿfarī passed away in 1979, his son retired from his government position and left his life in the Sudan in order to fulfill the trust that he had been given.

When ʿAbd al-Ghanī arrived in Egypt, he began searching through his father's belongings for unpublished material. He collected all of his father's poems and published them; he also published his father's litanies and blessings on the Prophet. These litanies replaced those of Ibn Idrīs as the main invocations for the seekers. He decided to name his father's path the Jaʿfariyya *ṭarīqa*, or al-Jaʿfariyya al-Aḥmadiyya al-Muḥammadiyya in full, to recognize it as a branch or extension of the path of Ibn Idrīs. He also stressed the Shādhiliyya roots of Ibn Idrīs' path, most probably to show that this new path has old and firm roots. He had the *ṭarīqa* formally recognized by the Supreme Council of the Sufi Ṭarīqas in Egypt. He also appointed the scholar Muḥammad ʿAbd al-Bāqī, whom al-Jaʿfarī had first intended to be his successor, to give lessons in the shaykh's place. Under his leadership, more than sixty mosques and centers for the *ṭarīqa* were founded all over Egypt; these centers usually included bookshops, schools of Qurʾān memorization, and social and medical services for the wider community.[150] Outside Egypt, there are two centers

149. From personal communication with Dr. ʿAṭiyya Muṣṭafā, one of the senior figures in the Jaʿfarī *ṭarīqa*.

150. *Al-Ṭarīqa al-Jaʿfariyya*, pp. 83–98, and the biography of ʿAbd al-Ghanī

in Libya and another two in Malaysia. Followers of the Jaʿfariyya path meet every Sunday and Thursday nights for the congregational remembrance of God, followed by the recitation of the poetry of their shaykh. Al-Jaʿfarī replaced Ibn Idrīs as the main spiritual guide of the followers, and his son ʿAbd al-Ghanī passed on the path as a representative of his father, without claiming any special rank or role for himself beyond the preservation of his father's legacy and the care of his father's followers. The followers of the Jaʿfariyya path, however, believe that the son was a complete spiritual inheritor of his father, and a great but self-effacing friend of God. He passed away on the 19th of July 2012.

Social Activity

It seems that Muḥammad b. ʿAlī l-Sanūsī in particular infused a powerful work ethic into the path of his teacher Ibn Idrīs. When Ibn Idrīs left for Mecca, as we have said, he left al-Sanūsī behind as his main representative there, and put his followers in his care. Al-Sanūsī and the other students of Ibn Idrīs began building a *zāwiya* in Mecca on Jabal Abū Qubays. During the construction, a stranger came to ask al-Sanūsī a question:

> As al-Sanūsī was occupied, he called his student ʿAbd Allah al-Tuwātī over. Al-Tuwātī came in from the work site, all soiled and scruffy like a laborer, and gave a brilliant reply to the question the stranger asked. The latter marveled at that, and wondered why such a learned person was engaged in this kind of manual labor. Al-Sanūsī answered, "This is the kind of equality [between labor of the hand and the mind] that we all have or seek in our community."[151]

In the more than seventy *zāwiya*s that al-Sanūsī constructed in the Cyrenaica, the brethren farmed the lands in an effort to turn the desert green. One day a man came to ask al-Sanūsī about the science of alchemy, to which al-Sanūsī replied, "Alchemy is under

on the official website of the *ṭarīqa*, http://algaafary.com/temp/?page_id=59, accessed 8 March 2012.

151. Vikør, *Sufi and Scholar on the Desert Edge*, pp. 201–202.

the blade of the plough; it is the toil of the right hand and the sweat of the brow."[152] Each *zāwiya*'s community included people trained in various handicrafts like carpentry, blacksmith work, copper work, and the like. He encouraged the craftsmen to apply themselves to their trade and said to them, "Your good intentions and your performing the obligatory is all you need of the religion, and others are not better than you."[153] When some brethren complained that they did not have enough time to recite a great deal of litanies for their spiritual growth, he would say to them, "Do the people of booklets and prayer beads think they will reach God before us? No, by God, they will not reach before us!"[154] The network of *zāwiya*s and communities helped the followers in the Cyrenaica build a highly successful trade network. The *zāwiya*s were built across trade routes and were designed to accommodate visitors and traders; this helped promote the trans-Saharan trade. Their involvement and success in trade was such that "in some studies, the order appears almost as a commercial enterprise."[155]

These communities of the Aḥmadiyya Muḥammadiyya, which would later become known in that area as the Sanūsīyya, also helped revive the practice of Islam and the spread of the *sharīᶜa* in the deserts of the Cyrenaica and elsewhere. The *zāwiya*s were highly successful at creating peace between the tribes, at settling disputes, and at educating tribal members. Indeed young and prominent members of the most eminent tribes flocked to join the *zāwiya*s and take the path of Ibn Idrīs.[156] As one historian observed,

> In the place occupied by the lodge, compassion settles, the country flourishes, and settled people and the nomads benefit from it, because it is only founded for the Koran to be read and the *sharīᶜa* to be spread.[157]

152. Ibid., 202.
153. Aḥmad Ṣidqī Dajānī, *al-Ḥaraka al-sanūsiyya*, p. 161.
154. Ibid.
155. Vikør, *Sufi and Scholar*, p. 210.
156. Ibid., p. 207.
157. Ibid., quoting al-Ashhab.

Finally, there was the famous role of the Sanūsīyya in fighting against colonial invaders. Al-Sanūsī seemed to have foretold of the Italian colonization of Libya years before it happened. This is not simply a saying attributed later to al-Sanūsī, but a saying that was recorded in a letter by Muḥammad al-Shafiʿī who died in 1906, five years before the sudden Italian invasion. In this letter, al-Shafiʿī quotes al-Sanūsī's address to his students upon his arrival in the Cyrenaica from the Hijaz, "He to whom God will give a long life, will fight those who come this way" pointing at the sea.[158] Even Ibn Idrīs before him is said to have foretold of the *jihād* of his followers in the Cyrenaica when he traveled through Benghazi and Jabal al-Akhdar on the way to Egypt. He is reported to have said of Jabal al-Akhdar, "This is our land where our litanies will come to life. He who lives here will be blessed and he who dies here will die a martyr."[159]

Al-Sanūsī is also said to have foretold of the *jihād* of ʿAbd al-Qādir al-Jazāʾirī and his father against the French in Algeria. Al-Sanūsī received the young ʿAbd al-Qādir al-Jazāʾirī and his father in Mecca, in the same year in which the construction of the *zāwiya* in Jabal Abū Qubays was under way. In that encounter, al-Sanūsī is said to have counseled ʿAbd al-Qādir's father, saying, "You should take good care of our son, ʿAbd al-Qādir, because he will become one of the defenders of the sacred principles of Islam and will raise the banner of *jihād*."[160] When al-Sanūsī passed away, Ibn Idrīs' son ʿAbd al-ʿĀlī, who was raised under his care, left the Cyrenaica and left the leadership of the brethren there to al-Sanūsī's sons, and moved to Egypt and then Dongola. He must have carried with him the great work ethic that was stressed by his main teacher al-Sanūsī, as we see it in the writings of al-Jaʿfarī.

Al-Jaʿfarī developed a strong love and attachment for al-Sanūsī's grandson Aḥmad al-Sharīf al-Sanūsī (d. 1933). It was Aḥmad al-Sharīf, the warrior scholar, who led the Sanūsī brethren in their *jihād* against the colonial invaders—against the French invasion

158. Ibid., p. 216.

159. ʿAlī Muḥammad al-Ṣallābī, *al-Thimār al-zakiyya li-l-ḥaraka al-Sanūsīyya fī lībya* (Sharjah, UAE: Maktabat al-Saḥāba, 2001), vol. 1, p. 42.

160. O'Fahey, *Enigmatic Saint*, pp. 136–137.

of their territories in Chad, the British in Egypt and the Sudan, and the Italian colonizers in Libya. Though it is unlikely that they met, as al-Sharīf died in exile in Medina only three years after the young al-Jaʿfarī came to Egypt, al-Jaʿfarī considered him as one of his main spiritual teachers. He described this relationship in detail in a remarkable poem of fifty-four lines dedicated to him. In this poem al-Jaʿfarī states that he never again saw the likes of shaykh al-Sharīf, and portrayed him as a great knower of God. He also spoke of the spiritual instruction that he received from him in spiritual meetings, most likely in dream visions.[161] As for al-Sharīf's cousin and successor King Idrīs I of Libya (d. 1983), al-Jaʿfarī met him and took from him his chains of authorization in the Qurʾān and the books of *ḥadīth*, which go back to al-Sanūsī and from him to Ibn Idrīs.[162] The chains of Ibn Idrīs in the works of *ḥadīth*, especially in al-Bukhārī and Muslim, were considered to be among the loftiest and shortest in the world.

Hard work in one's profession is one of the most important principles of the Jaʿfarī *ṭarīqa*. Shaykh Ṣāliḥ al-Jaʿfarī emphasized this repeatedly in his lessons and poetry. In one poem he stressed that hard work is necessary to earn a living, just as weapons are necessary to scare off enemies, while the acquisition of religious knowledge is needed both for worship and to guide one in his dealings with others. Al-Jaʿfarī concludes these lines by instructing his students to farm, trade, and work hard in their craft to live prosperously. In another poem he states that God dislikes a jobless servant, and that those who do not seek the means of earning a living are sinful; he describes the way of hard work as "the way of the religion" and "the way of the early generations."[163] In one of the Shaykh's most important poems, which is known as "The Provision for the Path," he assures his followers that those who follow his path would find its blessings in their worldly lives, not just in spiritual matters. He said that whether they were farmers, traders, weavers or craftsmen,

161. Ṣāliḥ al-Jaʿfarī, *Dīwān al-Jaʿfarī*, vol 8, pp. 273–282.

162. Ṣāliḥ al-Jaʿfarī, *al-Sīra al-nabawiyya al-Muḥammadiyya*, p. 2. See also al-Jaʿfarī, *al-Muntaqā l-nafīs*, pp. 122, 213–214, and 217–218.

163. ʿAbd al-Ghanī l-Jaʿfarī, *al-Kanz al-tharī*, pp. 144–146.

the path would increase the blessings in their profit and the benefit of what they do.[164]

Under the direction of al-Jaʿfarī's son and successor ʿAbd al-Ghanī, these teachings were implemented at the level of the mosque. Each of the more than seventy mosque complexes for the *ṭarīqa* that were built in his lifetime included a hospital or clinic, or both, as well as a pharmacy, halls for social functions, and schools for Qurʾān memorization. These projects allowed followers of the Shaykh to earn a living while serving the community at large. Shaykh ʿAbd al-Ghanī put his middle son Ḥusayn in charge of an initiative which they called the Youth Awakening, to attract youth into the *ṭarīqa*. They built a youth center as part of the main mosque complex in Cairo to provide the youth with access to computers as early as the late 1980s or early 1990s. The young men of the path were taught elocution and encouraged to give public talks in large gatherings and to deliver Friday sermons. Every year at the annual celebration of the life and teachings of Shaykh Ṣāliḥ, the young children who memorized the Qurʾān in the *ṭarīqa*'s mosques across Egypt are honored. The facilities at the centers, such as the halls which are dedicated to social functions, are rented out at very low prices, and sometimes even given free to those in need, so that weddings or funerals can be held. In the gatherings of remembrance that take place in each of these mosques every Sunday and Thursday night, every attendee is fed, whether they are followers of the path, visitors, or the poor who come regularly for the free meal.

One of the more distinguished Jaʿfarī centers is in the town of Banī ʿAdī in Asyūṭ province, which the Egyptians call the "City of the Scholars" for having produced a great number of Egyptian luminaries. The Jaʿfarī mosque complex there includes a large library, a center for Qurʾān memorization, a hospital, a pharmacy, a dialysis clinic, a social welfare office, and a travel agency dedicated for pilgrimage trips to Mecca and Medina. Health checks, surgical operations, and dialysis are offered free to the poor, and at a discounted rate to those of limited means. Furthermore, the agent for the shaykh of the *ṭarīqa* there, a scholar by the name of Dr.

164. Ṣāliḥ al-Jaʿfarī, *Dīwān al-Jaʿfarī*, vol. 1, p. 16.

Muḥammad Sayyid Sulṭān, gives regular lessons in the mosque five days a week, and travels to al-Azhar Mosque in Cairo every Sunday to give another lesson there. Members of that center also established an Islamic school called Maʿhad Nūr al-Islām al-Azharī, which educates almost six hundred students. Buses from that school go to different towns around Banī ʿAdī, including the city of Manfalūṭ, to bring the children to the center. There they memorize the Qurʾān and gain a basic Islamic education, as well as skills such as elocution and the recitation of religious poetry. The school also emphasizes the learning of languages and computer skills.

It is this kind of service to the community and emphasis on organization and productivity that has gained the Jaʿfarī *ṭarīqa* respect as a model *ṭarīqa* in Egypt. Every mosque complex also contains a small bookshop to sell the books of the *ṭarīqa*, though the main bookshop in Cairo is quite large and one of the most popular Sufi bookshops in Egypt. In 1980 Shaykh ʿAbd al-Ghanī established a publishing house called Dār Jawāmiʿ al-Kalim for the sake of preserving the works of his father; it is dedicated to preserving and publishing works on Sufism and other Islamic sciences.

The Works of al-Jaʿfarī

Mention has been made above of the eleven works of Ibn Idrīs that al-Jaʿfarī edited and published, as well as Ibn Idrīs' letters, and the hagiography by his student al-Rashīd, and al-Jaʿfarī's own biographical work on his master. The biography and two other of the works above have received extensive commentaries and additions by al-Jaʿfarī, most notable among them being Ibn Idrīs' treatise on the four most important principles of the spiritual path. Al-Jaʿfarī's expansive commentary, entitled *al-Ilhām al-nāfiʿ li-kulli qāṣid*, is considered his most important work on spiritual guidance. He also wrote a commentary on parts of Ibn Idrīs' litanies, *al-Fuyūḍāt al-Jaʿfariyya bi-sharḥ al-awrād al-Idrīsiyya*, to which he added stories and visions about himself and his teachers. Other works include the following.

Dīwān al-Jaʿfarī—al-Jaʿfarī's poetry (12 volumes), including his poetic compositions. In following the path of the earliest scholars of Islam, or perhaps due to the influence of his Mauritanian teacher al-Shinqīṭī, he composed these works on religious knowledge and jurisprudence into poems for easy memorization. He wrote poems on theology, jurisprudence, *ḥadīth*, Qurʾānic exegesis, general Islamic knowledge, inheritance laws, Arabic grammar, and Sufism, all designed for memorization by the seeker of knowledge. The longest of these (436 lines) is a poetic adaptation of the entire text of the *Ājurrūmiyya*, the first-level text of Arabic grammar usually taught in al-Azhar and learned by heart by many students of knowledge.

Dars al-jumuʿa bi-l-Azhar—two years of transcripts from his Friday lessons (almost 104 lessons in 10 volumes)

Minbar al-Azhar—a small collection of his Friday prayer sermons

al-Fatāwā wa-l-ajwiba al-Jaʿfariyya—a very small collection of his fatwas, gathered from his lessons and other works

Fatḥ wa fayḍ wa faḍl min Allāh—this work on Islamic creed is his largest single work; in it he explains the traditional Sunni understanding of God and His prophets, followed by a defense of several understandings and practices that have been criticized by modern Muslim reform movements. It also includes a lengthy explanation of the benefits of remembering God with the Idrīsī formula, "There is no god but God, Muḥammad is the Messenger of God," as opposed to remembrance with only the first half, as is the practice of most other Sufi paths.

al-Sīra al-nabawiyya al-Muḥammadiyya—a *mawlid*, or a short prophetic biography that is designed to be read regularly, such as on Sunday and Thursday nights

Risāla fi-l-ḥajj wa-l-ʿumra—a short work on the jurisprudence of the great and the minor pilgrimage *al-Sirāj al-wahhāj fī qiṣṣat al-isrāʾ wa-l-miʿrāj*—a short work on the Prophet's Night Journey and Ascension

al-ʿAjab al-ʿujāb fī mā warada min aḥwāl al-mawtā baʿda dafnihim bi l-turāb—a short work on the states of the dead after they are buried

Miftāḥ mafātiḥ kunūz al-samāwāt wa-l-arḍ, a work on various supplications from the Idrīsī tradition for different occasions

Risālat al-kashf wa-l-bayān ʿan faḍāʾil laylat al-niṣf min Shaʿbān—a work by Shaykh Sālim al-Sanhūrī l-Mālikī (d. 1015/1606) on the virtues of the night of the 15th of the lunar month of Shaʿbān, which al-Jaʿfarī edited, annotated, and published.

al-Maʿānī l-raqīqa ʿalā l-durar al-daqīqa—A commentary on a small treatise by Aḥmad b. Idrīs, explaining three lines of poetry attributed to al-Junayd al-Baghdādī.

al-Fawāʾid al-Jaʿfariyya min anwār al-aḥādīth al-nabawiyya—al-Jaʿfarī's forty *ḥadīth* collection and commentary, the work translated in this book, was never edited in the original; rather the work was found after the shaykh's death.

al-Muntaqā l-nafīs fī manāqib quṭb dāʾirat al-taqdīs mawlāna al-sayyid Aḥmad b. Idrīs—a biography of Aḥmad b. Idrīs.

Aʿṭār azhār aghṣān ḥaẓīrat al-taqdīs fī karāmāt al-ʿālim . . . al-sayyid Aḥmad b. Idrīs—a combination of Ibrāhīm al-Rashīd's hagiography of Ibn Idrīs, and a collection of letters between Ibn Idrīs and his students.

Awrād al-ṭarīqa al-Jaʿfariyya—a collection of litanies.

al-Ṣalawāt al-Jaʿfariyya—formulas of sending blessings on the Prophet.

Shaykh Ṣāliḥ al-Jaʿfarī

Shaykh al-Jaʿfarī's Friday lesson at al-Azhar

Shaykh al-Jaʿfarī's Friday lesson at al-Azhar

Shaykh al-Jaʿfarī's Friday lesson at al-Azhar

Shaykh al-Jaʿfarī's Friday lesson at al-Azhar

Shaykh Muḥammad Bakhīt al-Muṭīʿī (d. 1935)

Shaykh Muḥammad Ḥabībullāh al-Shinqīṭī (d. 1944)

"Shaykh al-Islam" Yūsuf al-Dijwī (d. 1946)

Shaykh Muḥammad al-Sharīf al-Idrīsī (d. 1937)

Shaykh Muḥammad b. ʿAlī l-Sanūsī (d. 1859)

Shaykh al-Jaʿfarī with Shaykh ʿAbd al-Ḥalīm Maḥmūd (d. 1978)

Shaykh ʿAbd al-Ghanī (d. 2012)

JAʿFARĪ LESSONS FROM THE LIGHT OF THE PROPHETIC TRADITIONS

al-Fawāʾid al-Jaʿfariyya min anwār al-aḥādīth al-nabawiyya

Shaykh Ṣāliḥ al-Jaʿfarī

Translator's Note

There is a *ḥadīth* attributed to the Prophet Muḥammad that says, "Whosoever preserves for my community forty *ḥadīth* relating to their religion, God will raise him on the Day of Resurrection in the company of the jurists and scholars." Despite doubts about the authenticity of this *ḥadīth*, it has become a tradition among scholars to compose collections of forty prophetic *ḥadīth*, some revolving around particular themes, and others containing what the authors thought would be most beneficial to the people of their time. This work is of the latter type, reflecting the major issues of contention that were being debated in his time, and are still being debated today. It should also be noted that the scholars did not interpret the number forty literally, and so many of these collections might contain more or less traditions. For example, the most famous collection of forty *aḥādīth* ever written is that of al-Nawawī, consisting of forty-two *aḥādīth*. Furthermore, some scholars, including al-Nawawī, authored commentaries on their collections, and we see the same here with al-Jaᶜfarī. In fact, unlike al-Nawawī, al-Jaᶜfarī's work was clearly conceived with the commentary in mind, where the *aḥādīth* served as anchors for the ideas that he wanted to discuss. These ideas are summarized by the author's son, Shaykh ᶜAbd al-Ghanī l-Jaᶜfarī, in his introduction to the Arabic original. I have also taken the liberty of adding titles to the chapters.

Introduction

In the name of God, most merciful, bestower of mercy. Praise be to God the Lord of the worlds, most merciful in this life and the next. May God bless our master Muḥammad and his pure and good family. To proceed.

Our shaykh and imam, the knower of God most high, my master Ṣāliḥ al-Jaʿfarī who was an imam of the noble Azhar Mosque, wanted to explain forty *aḥādīth* from the *aḥādīth* of the Chosen One ﷺ, that are greatly needed by the people of this age. It is an age in which false schools of thought have multiplied, and corrupt beliefs have become widespread, popularized by those who follow their own desires, those who deny the life of the Prophet ﷺ and the rest of the prophets, and who forbid visiting him ﷺ and visiting (the tombs of) his family and the Friends of God and righteous men of his community.

He ﷺ also wanted these *aḥādīth* to contain that which instills in the reader the desire for the remembrance of God ﷻ and the desire to draw near Him by way of good works, and to act according to manners that refine the self and elevate the soul in the path of perfection.

Our shaykh ﷺ named the work *al-Fawāʾid al-jaʿfariyya min anwār al-aḥādīth al-nabawiyya* [Jaʿfarī lessons from the light of the prophetic traditions]. We praise God ﷻ who assisted us in the printing of this book, and whose grace and generosity enabled us to print it before the yearly celebration of the shaykh's birth, so that it could be one of his gifts to his children and followers on that great occasion.

We ask God most high to benefit everyone who reads it and contemplates its contents, and to give him of the shaykh's knowledge and guidance. We ask Him to direct us all to do good works and to follow the path of the people of light and perfection, and to avoid the people of error and misguidance. He 🕸 is most generous, compassionate, and merciful.

May God bless our master Muḥammad and his family with every glance and every breath, as many times as all that is contained in the knowledge of God.

The servant of His self-sufficient and perfect Lord,

ʿAbd al-Ghanī Ṣāliḥ al-Jaʿfarī
Shaykh of the Jaʿfariyya Ṭarīqa

Ḥadīth 1

Love

عَنْ أَنَسٍ رَضِيَ اللهُ عَنْهُ ، عَنِ النَّبِيِّ صَلَّى اللهُ عَلَيْهِ وَسَلَّمَ ، قَالَ : «ثَلَاثٌ مَنْ كُنَّ فِيهِ وَجَدَ حَلَاوَةَ الْإِيمَانِ ، أَنْ يَكُونَ اللهُ وَرَسُولُهُ أَحَبَّ إِلَيْهِ مِمَّا سِوَاهُمَا ، وَأَنْ يُحِبَّ الْمَرْءَ لَا يُحِبُّهُ إِلَّا لِلَّهِ ، وَأَنْ يَكْرَهَ أَنْ يَعُودَ فِي الْكُفْرِ كَمَا يَكْرَهُ أَنْ يُقْذَفَ فِي النَّارِ»

On the authority of Anas b. Mālik ﵁, the Prophet ﷺ said,

> Whoever possesses these three things will find the sweetness of faith: That God and His Messenger are more beloved to him than anything other than them, that he loves someone only for the sake of God, and that he hates to return to disbelief just as he would hate to be thrown into the fire.[1]

Linguistically, faith (*īmān*) means to believe. As a technical term, the Prophet ﷺ explained, "To believe in God, His angels, His books, His messengers, the last day, and divine apportionment—the good and the bad of it,"[2] "the sweet and the sour of it."[3]

1. Narrated by Bukhārī, Muslim, and others. See *Ṣaḥīḥ al-Bukhārī*, vol. 1, p. 9.
2. Narrated by Bukhārī, Muslim, and others. The wording here is that of Muslim, vol. 1, pp. 23–24.
3. This is an addition in the narration of al-Nasāʾī in *al-Sunan al-kubrā*,

The Prophet ﷺ mentioned the sweetness of faith and named three causes for it, the first being, "That God and His Messenger are more beloved to him than anything other than them." This sentence means two things: First, that faith happens by believing in God ﷻ and in His Messenger ﷺ. And second, that faith becomes sweet by loving God ﷻ and His Messenger ﷺ.

The Proof of Islam, Shaykh al-Ghazālī, wrote a wonderful and greatly beneficial treatment of this subject in the fourth volume of his book *Iḥyāʾ ʿulūm al-dīn,* in the section, "On Love of God ﷻ." He wrote, "Love has causes, and they are blessings, and we do not find as many blessings from anyone as we do from God ﷻ, and so we should love Him more than anything." Indeed there is a *ḥadīth* that says, "Love God ﷻ for the blessings He gives you."[4]

One of the greatest signs that indicate a servant's love of his Lord is obedience. As a Sufi poet once said,

> You show that you love God but you disobey Him,
> that, I swear, is wondrous logic!
> Had your love been true you would obey Him,
> for the lover is obedient to the beloved.

Another said,

> Your beauty is in my eye, Your mention in my mouth,
> and Your love is in my heart.
> So how could You possibly be absent from my sight?

God's love of His servant is better than the servant's love of his Lord, just as God's remembrance of His servant is better than the servant's remembrance of his Lord.

As for the cause of God's love of the servant, it is His servant's following of His Prophet ﷺ. He ﷻ said, *Say* (*to them O Muḥammad*), *"If you love God then follow me, and God will love you"* (3:31).

As for the cause of God's ﷻ remembrance of His servant, it is His servant's remembrance of Him. He ﷻ said, *Remember Me, I shall*

"Kitāb al-ʿilm, Bāb tawqīr al-ʿulamāʾ," and Ibn Ḥibbān in his *Ṣaḥīḥ*.

4. Narrated by al-Tirmidhī in his *Sunan*, vol. 2, p. 963.

remember you (2:152), and He 🌸 said, *The remembrance of God is greater* (29:45).

Some said that it means that God's remembrance of His servant is greater than the servant's remembrance of Him. This is shown by the fact that the servant remembers and calls upon his Lord while being in need of Him, while God remembers His servant, though He needs him not.

The meaning of the servant's remembrance of God is his saying, "There is no god but God," "glory be to God," and so on. The meaning of God's remembrance of His servant is to forgive him and have mercy on him, and to look at him with the eye of care and gentleness so that if he were poor, He would make him rich, and if he were defeated, He would give him victory, and if he were sick, He would cure him, and if he were far, He would bring him near. Beyond all this there are many secrets and lights that come to those men and women who remember God often, may God make us among them. Amen.

Love is not diminished a bit, even if the lover is cut down or injured in the battles of life. The [Prophet's] Companions 🌸 only increased in faith and acceptance of God's will with regard to whatever injuries befell them. God 🌸 said in His book,

> *If you are hurting, they too are hurting, but you hope to receive from God that which they do not hope for* (4:104).

God thus affirmed that they had great hope and expectations along with their pain.

It says in the *al-Futūḥāt al-makkiyya*, "A lover said: If You cut me piece by piece, I would only increase in love of You!" Meaning, my love would not decrease because of it. This is the saying of a female lover; it is said that it is the saying of the famous Rābiʿa al-ʿAdawiyya, whose rank and spiritual state rose above that of the great men. She 🌸 divided love into types and explained them, and that is a remarkable way to explain love. She said,

> I love you two loves: the selfish love,
> and a love because You are worthy of it.

As for my selfish love, that is
my remembrance of You, and nothing else!
As for the one You are worthy of, it is
Your lifting the veil so that I see You!
And no praise in this or that is mine,
but in both the praise is Yours.

On the same topic the maidservant of ʿAttāb al-Kātib said,

O Beloved of the hearts, who have I but You?
have mercy today on a visitor that has come to You.
You are my desire, my goal, my happiness
my heart refuses to love any other than You!
O my hope, my master, my support
my longing has gone too long, when will I meet You?
I seek not the bliss of the gardens of paradise,
no, I only want them to see You!

Another lover said,

Your bliss or torment for me are the same
they will not affect my love of You
My love is in that which You choose for me
and Your love of me is like creating me anew!

Shaykh Ibn ʿArabī ﷺ wrote in the *al-Futūḥāt al-makkiyya*,

They say that a male swallow courted a female swallow that he loved in the dome of Solomon—upon our Prophet Muḥammad and upon him be the best peace and blessings—and Solomon ﷺ was under the dome. He said to her, "My love for you is so strong that if you told me to demolish this dome over Solomon's head I would." Solomon ﷺ called him over and said to him, "What is this that I heard from you?" He said, "O Solomon! Do not be quick in punishing me! The lover has a tongue that only lovers speak with, and I love this female, and thus said what you heard. There is no blame laid upon passionate lovers, for they speak with the tongue of love, not with the tongue of knowledge and intellect." Our master Solomon ﷺ laughed, showed him mercy, and did not punish him.

The Greatest Shaykh also said in *al-Futūḥāt al-makkiyya*,

> I learned from my teachers this poem of our lady Rābiʿa
> al-ʿAdawiyya,

> They all worship You out of fear of the fire
> seeing salvation as a great boon!
> Or to live in the gardens, enjoy their bliss
> and drink from their pure rivers.
> For me there is no share in the gardens or fire
> I seek no alternative for my Beloved.
> You have penetrated deep into my heart,
> I am thoroughly infused with Your love.

This speech of Shaykh Muḥyī l-Dīn [Ibn ʿArabī] 🌿 explains the states of the lovers. The nature of love is like the tasting of the tongue. With the tongue, one can taste the sweetness of the honey that he rightfully owns, as well as the sweetness of the honey that he stole from others. Likewise, he who directs love to something forbidden is a lover, and he who directs love to something licit is a lover. The highest level of love is that which is for God and His Messenger 🌿, and it is the goal of the Sufis, may God 🌿 be pleased with them all.

The Sultan of the Lovers, my master ʿUmar Ibn al-Fāriḍ 🌿 said,

> The Beloved of my heart! Love is my intercessor with You.
> if You so wish, with it the rope is connected.

He says,

> If her name is mentioned in a neighborhood,
> all become drunk—and there is no shame on them nor
> blame!

He also says,

> If that name but enter a man's mind,
> gladness shall dwell with him and grief depart.

That is because for such people, there is no worry, grief or sadness in the presence of love and spiritual witnessing of God. He 🌿 said,

In that let them rejoice! It is better than what they gather! (10:58)[5]

Their happiness in God makes them forget all other than Him, and their pleasure in His remembrance makes them give up any ephemeral pleasures, shallow adornments, or fleeting shadows. Ibn al-Fāriḍ ﵁ says,

> I witness the reality of Your beauty, and so becomes pleasurable to me
> my submission and self-abasement in my love of You!

For they find pleasure in submission, in humbling themselves and being broken, in asceticism, seclusion, longing, remembrance, ecstasy, and crying in hearing the Qurʾān and poems of prophetic praise, and in visiting pure and good places like the Kaʿba, the Station of Abraham ﵇, ʿArafāt, Muzdalifa, Mina, and in the visit of the Chosen One ﷺ and praying in the Noble Rawḍa, and everything that ignites the fire of passion and sends the soul a reminder that brings longing. That is because the soul loves God ﷻ by its original nature, but this love needs igniting like a trigger. This needs great preparation and a big struggle. It is said to the untruthful lover what Ibn al-Fāriḍ ﵁ said,

> You came to houses that cannot be entered from the back,
> and their gates will not open to a knocking from the likes of you!

He ﵁ also said,

> Some people attempted to face love but turned away
> they claimed to swim the oceans of love but did not get wet!

My master ʿAbd al-Raḥīm al-Buraʿi ﵁ said,

> Leave love to the lover whose tears are blood.
> Bewildered, remembrance brings him into existence and out of it.
> Love is only for a people who are known for it
> for they have engaged love until they could bear it!

---

5. It could also be understood as "He is better."

He also said,

> Was it a perfumed breeze, or did the love of Medina flare
> and revive my heart, so it answered the call of the beloved!
> Not every breeze comes from the Hijaz—far be it!
> and not every light fills East and West!

Imam al-Būṣīrī ﷺ said,

> Is it from remembering your neighbors in Dhī-Salam
> that the tears flowing from your eyes are mixed with blood?

Such are the people of love: their love produces jewels of meaning, pearls of rhetoric, and phrases that express their love, their longing, and their state, in poetry and in prose.

Ḥadīth 2

Drawing Near

عَنْ أَبِي هُرَيْرَةَ قَالَ : قَالَ رَسُولُ اللهِ صَلَّى اللهُ عَلَيْهِ وَسَلَّمَ إِنَّ اللهَ قَالَ :
« مَنْ عَادَى لِي وَلِيًّا فَقَدْ آذَنْتُهُ بِالحَرْبِ ، وَمَا تَقَرَّبَ إِلَيَّ عَبْدِي بِشَيْءٍ
أَحَبَّ إِلَيَّ مِمَّا افْتَرَضْتُ عَلَيْهِ ، وَمَا يَزَالُ عَبْدِي يَتَقَرَّبُ إِلَيَّ بِالنَّوَافِلِ
حَتَّى أُحِبَّهُ ، فَإِذَا أَحْبَبْتُهُ كُنْتُ سَمْعَهُ الَّذِي يَسْمَعُ بِهِ ، وَبَصَرَهُ الَّذِي
يُبْصِرُ بِهِ ، وَيَدَهُ الَّتِي يَبْطِشُ بِهَا ، وَرِجْلَهُ الَّتِي يَمْشِي بِهَا ، وَإِنْ سَأَلَنِي
لَأُعْطِيَنَّهُ ، وَلَئِنْ اسْتَعَاذَنِي لَأُعِيذَنَّهُ »

On the authority of Abū Hurayra ﵁ who said: the Messenger of God ﷺ said,

> God said: Whoever shows enmity to a friend of Mine, then I have declared war on him! My servant does not draw near to Me with anything more loved by Me than the religious duties I have imposed upon him, and My servant continues to draw near to Me with supererogatory works until I love him. When I love him I am his hearing with which he hears, his seeing with which he sees, his hand with which he strikes and his foot with which he walks. Were he to ask something of Me, I would surely give it to him, and were he to ask Me for refuge I would surely grant him it.

Narrated by al-Bukhārī.[1]

· ❁ · ❁ · ❁ ·

---

1. *Ṣaḥīḥ al-Bukhārī*, vol. 3, p. 1319.

Know O servant of God that it is impossible for the Real, Transcendent is He, to be apart from something, or for something to be apart from Him; or to be connected to something, or something be connected to Him. He does not draw near to anything in a physical, sensory way. Free is He, Transcendent, from all the characteristics of originated beings.

If you know that, then know that scholars have two opinions on the Qurʾānic verses and prophetic *aḥādīth* that are ambiguous in meaning: The scholars of the earliest generations simply believed in them while distancing their apparent meaning from that which does not befit the Real 🌸. The later scholars interpreted them. My master Ibrahīm al-Laqqānī 🌸, said in his work *Jawharat al-tawḥīd*, "And every text that gives the illusion of anthropomorphism, interpret it, or leave its meaning to God, but keep it free from that." This *ḥadīth* is from the ambiguous kind.

The meaning of "I am his hearing" is that he hears from God, not from any other, because all else has disappeared from him.

The meaning of "I am his seeing with which he sees" is that He sees the acts of God, dressed in His marvelous creation and wondrous wisdom. When the night darkens, he is reminded of what the heedless have forgotten, and *When the dawn breathes* (Q. 81:18), he is reminded of that which preoccupies those who are in heedless play. When the earth is covered in its green blanket he is reminded of the greenery of paradise and its different colored fruits remind him of God's great favors. The shaking of the trees when the wind blows reminds him of the shaking of the souls out of desire to meet the Real 🌸 in every moment. Different colors remind him of the different layers of the Earth, and the different seasons remind him of how planets change according to their orbits. He sees nothing without seeing God before it, and does not see any action as coming from a created being. He is drowned in the ocean of, *Is there any creator other than God?* (Q. 35:3), rejoicing at the glad tidings in, *God is the creator of all things* (Q. 39:62), thinking of the clarification and detailed exposition in the unambiguous Qurʾān, *God has created you and what you make* (Q. 37:96).

Since the apparent meaning of this *ḥadīth* is impossible in regard to God ﷻ, I interpreted it, and said by the grace of my Lord ﷻ:

> "I am his hearing. . . ." means, My love will be in his hearing, sight, and all his limbs.

This is because the love of the heart, if it increases, travels to all the limbs, and its increase is caused by God's love of His servant, which makes the divine love flow in all his parts. Everything, then, revolves around God's love of you, not your love of Him; yet it is by your love of Him ﷻ that you worship Him, and by your worship of Him that He loves you. So do not forget love and its causes, and make the extra devotions your wine, until you see what you desire! Ibn al-Fāriḍ ؓ said,

> And my extra devotions are my wine,
> and the Beloved my night companion.

Spiritual states come one after another, there where the stations of the men compete! So do not neglect your horse at the race, and do not let an obstacle keep you from rising!

Ḥadīth 3

God's Friends

عَنِ ابْنِ عَبَّاسٍ رَضِيَ اللهُ عَنْهُمَا أَنَّ النَّبِيَّ صَلَّى اللهُ عَلَيْهِ وَسَلَّمَ قَالَ :

« أَوْلِيَاءُ اللهِ الَّذِينَ إِذَا رُءُوا ذُكِرَ اللهُ »

On the authority of Ibn ʿAbbās ﵄,[1] the Prophet ﷺ said,

> The friends of God are those who, when they are seen, God is remembered.

Quoted by the noble Aḥmad b. Idrīs in *Rūḥ al-sunna*. It is the narration of al-Ḥakīm al-Tirmidhī as mentioned by al-Suyūṭī in *al-Jāmiʿ al-ṣaghīr*.[2]

· ✿ · ✿ · ✿ ·

"When they are seen, God is remembered" because the natural disposition of the human is such that if he sees one of the Friends of God, that person's state or speech would remind him of God ﷻ. That is because the soul knows the Friends of God, whether they are alive or dead, and has a feeling when it meets their souls in the

1. Ibn ʿAbbās is short for "ʿAbdallāh, son of ʿAbbās," referring to the cousin and uncle of the Prophet. Convention is to say "may God be pleased with them" after "Ibn ʿAbbās" to encompass both son and father.
2. Al-Ḥakīm al-Tirmidhī, *Nawādir al-usūl*, vol. 4, p. 80. It was narrated by al-Nasāʾī in *al-Sunan al-kubrā*, "Kitāb al-tafsīr" of Sūrat Yūnus, thus, "The Messenger of God ﷺ was asked, 'Who are the friends of God?' He said, 'Those who, when they are seen, God is remembered.'"

world of the living or in the world of the intermediary life. The recognition might be from both sides if both were Friends of God.

"When they are seen, God is remembered" and that is because of the attachment of their souls to God ﷻ and their nearness to Him, so they are like the one that delivers musk—if you come close to him you smell a beautiful scent that reminds you of the beautiful smelling one ﷺ, and that is why when you smell such a scent you say, "O God send blessings upon our master Muḥammad!"

Likewise are the Friends of God—they remind you of God ﷻ by what they have of divine attraction that pulled them to God; scents that made them smell beautiful; gnosis that made them know Him; nearness that made them rare; light that shines from them; a secret that has flown to them, effusions that effused over them from the source of effusions; and words that you hear from them, like wine. You will often see them lined up in rows, in prayer. Sometimes you see them while awake and sometimes in your sleep. They traversed the world of the physical and so the physical retreated before them and the norms were ripped apart for them. If you were to visit them in any state, before or after their death, you would gain the most treasured gifts. Their breaths are perfumed, their gazes spiritual, and their states Muḥammadan. He who sits with them shall not suffer,[3] and their disciple will be elevated because of them.

3. In reference to *ḥadīth* 34 of this book.

Ḥadīth 4

God's Fortress

عَنْ عَلِيٍّ بْنُ أَبِي طَالِبٍ سَيِّدُ الأَوْلِيَاءِ قَالَ : أَخْبَرَنَا سَيِّدُ الأَنْبِيَاءِ مُحَمَّدُ بْنُ عَبْدِ اللهِ صَلَّى اللهُ عَلَيْهِ وَسَلَّمَ ، قَالَ : أَخْبَرَنِي جِبْرِيلُ سَيِّدُ المَلَائِكَةِ ، قَالَ : قَالَ اللهُ سَيِّدُ السَّادَاتِ : إِنِّي أَنَا اللهُ لا إِلَهَ إِلا أَنَا ، مَنْ أَقَرَّ لِي بِالتَّوْحِيدِ دَخَلَ حِصْنِي ، وَمَنْ دَخَلَ حِصْنِي أَمِنَ مِنْ عَذَابِي

On the authority of our master ʿAlī (may God be pleased with him and ennoble his countenance) who said, the Messenger of God ﷺ said: God ﷻ said,

> I, I am God, there is no god but I. He who admits to My unity enters My fortress, and he who enters My fortress is secure from My punishment.

Narrated by al-Shīrāzī, and quoted by al-Suyūṭī in *al-Jāmiʿ al-ṣaghīr*.[1]

Similarly there is al-Sumbulī l-Madanī's narration on the authority of Jaʿfar al-Ṣādiq on the authority of Muḥammad al-Bāqir, on the authority of ʿAlī Zayn al-ʿAbidīn, on the authority of al-Ḥusayn b. ʿAlī, on the authority of ʿAlī b. Abī Ṭālib ؓ that the Prophet ﷺ said,

1. Al-Suyūṭī, *al-Jāmiʿ al-ṣaghīr*, p. 376. Al-Suyūṭī said it is authentic. Al-Shīrāzī's *Alqāb al-muḥaddithīn* is no longer extant and al-Suyūṭī did not quote any chains in his *Jāmiʿ*. We therefore took the wording of the chain of transmission from Muḥammad ʿAqīla in his *al-Fawāʾid al-jalīla*, with his chain of transmission back to al-Suyūṭī and from him back to al-Shīrāzī. (See ʿAqīla, *al-Fawāʾid al-jalīla*, pp. 91–92).

لَا إِلَهَ إِلَّا اللهُ حِصْنِي ، فَمَنْ قَالَهَا دَخَلَ حِصْنِي ، وَمَنْ دَخَلَ حِصْنِي
أَمِنَ عَذَابِي

I was told by Gabriel ☙, who said, "God ❀ says, 'No god but God' is My fortress, and he who says it enters My fortress, and he who enters My fortress is secure from My punishment."[2]

I say, by the grace of God and His assistance and inspiration, the saying of he who absolves himself of any power or might to the power and might of God, for there is no power or might except by God ❀, that several things are to be taken from this.

First, that he who says it with his tongue and heart enters the fortress of God ❀. In other words, His protection.

Second, that he who says it is secure from God's punishment in this world and the next, except for punishments related to the rights of Islam. So if he kills he is killed, and if he steals his hand is cut off, and if he drinks an intoxicant he is lashed eighty times. If he slanders someone by saying that someone is such and such, and describes him

2. I suspect that "al-Sumbulī l-Madanī" is a typographical error and should be either Sunbul al-Makkī (d. 1803) or Muḥammad ʿĀbid al-Sindī al-Madanī (d. 1841). This ḥadīth was narrated thus by Abū ʿUthmān Saʿīd b. Muḥammad al-Baḥīrī (d. 451 AH) in the ninth part of his Fawāʾid, which is in manuscript form, and has been copied into online ḥadīth databases such as that of islamweb.net. Al-Baḥīrī's contemporary, colleague, and teacher al-Ḥākim, author of al-Mustadrak, also narrated it in his history of Nishapur, Tārīkh Nīsābūr, and likewise al-Quḍāʿī in Musnad al-Shihāb, thus: "'No god but God' is My fortress, and whoever enters it is secure from My punishment." Abū Nuʿaym narrated it in the Ḥilya thus: "I, I am God, there is no god but I, so worship Me. Whoever from among you comes to Me with the testimony of 'There is no god but God,' with sincerity, enters My fortress, and whoever enters My fortress is secure from My punishment (Ḥilyat al-awliyāʾ, vol 3, p. 192).

with something unfitting like adultery, and does not come with four witnesses, then he is lashed eighty times, which is the punishment for slander. If he does not receive these punishments in this life then he will receive them on the Day of Rising, unless he has repented sincerely—because repentance erases everything, even murder—or has performed pilgrimage, because pilgrimage erases all sins except for the rights that are due to people. When a person returns from pilgrimage he has to return these rights to their owners. As for what he owes of missed obligatory acts of worship such as prayer, fasting, or alms-giving, he has to make up for it all.

The opinion that obligatory acts of worship that are purposely neglected cannot be made up goes against the four schools of law as shown in the following *ḥadīth* in the *Muwaṭṭa*ʾ of Imam Mālik ﵀. "The Prophet ﷺ said, 'He who forgot a prayer should pray it when he remembers it.' Then he recited the saying of God ﷻ, *Establish the prayer for My remembrance*" (20:14).[3]

The scholars said that if it is incumbent upon the one who forgot a prayer to make up what he missed, then surely it would be even more incumbent upon the one who missed his prayer intentionally. According to the Mālikīs ﵃, he who has many prayers to make up has to make them all up at a minimum of five times a day [along with the ones prescribed for that day], and if he does not then he is blameworthy.

Third, that he who remembers God by repeating, "There is no god but God," should keep in mind the meaning of the *ḥadīth*, "[he] is secure from My punishment." He should assure himself of safety and security as long as the remembrance goes on.

Fourth, that security from punishment necessitates that one be distanced from its causes, which are acts of disobedience, and that one is assisted in doing the acts that bar it, and they are acts of obedience. So let the one who remembers God with this formula have the good tidings that he will be distanced from acts of disobedience and guided to acts of obedience. That is why

3. It could also mean "upon remembering Me," which is how it is understood in this *ḥadīth*.

remembrance performed with this phrase takes the *nafs* (the ego) from the state in which it commands to evil and transforms it to the state in which it blames itself for wrongdoing.

Ḥadīth 5

Under His Shade

عَنْ أَبِي هُرَيْرَةَ رَضِيَ اللهُ عَنْهُ ، عَنِ النَّبِيِّ صَلَّى اللهُ عَلَيْهِ وَسَلَّمَ قَالَ :
« سَبْعَةٌ يُظِلُّهُمُ اللهُ تَعَالَى فِي ظِلِّهِ يَوْمَ لَا ظِلَّ إِلَّا ظِلُّهُ ، إِمَامٌ عَدْلٌ
وَشَابٌّ نَشَأَ فِي عِبَادَةِ اللهِ ، وَرَجُلٌ قَلْبُهُ مُعَلَّقٌ فِي الْمَسَاجِدِ ، وَرَجُلَانِ
تَحَابَّا فِي اللهِ اجْتَمَعَا عَلَيْهِ وَتَفَرَّقَا عَلَيْهِ ، وَرَجُلٌ دَعَتْهُ امْرَأَةٌ ذَاتُ مَنْصِبٍ
وَجَمَالٍ فَقَالَ : إِنِّي أَخَافُ اللهَ ، وَرَجُلٌ تَصَدَّقَ بِصَدَقَةٍ فَأَخْفَاهَا حَتَّى
لَا تَعْلَمَ شِمَالُهُ مَا تُنْفِقُ يَمِينُهُ ، وَرَجُلٌ ذَكَرَ اللهَ خَالِيًا فَفَاضَتْ عَيْنَاهُ »

On the authority of Abū Hurayra ﵁, the Messenger of God ﷺ said,

> There are seven whom God will shade in His shade on a day when there is no shade but His shade: a just ruler, a youth who grew up worshiping God, a man whose heart is attached to the mosques, two men who love each other for the sake of God, they meet upon that and part upon it, and a man who was invited by a woman of position and beauty and said 'I fear God,' and a man who gave in charity and hid it so that his left hand would not know what his right hand had spent, and a man who remembered God while alone and so his eyes overflowed.

Narrated by al-Bukhārī, Muslim, al-Tirmidhī, al-Nasāʾī, and Aḥmad.[1]

---

1. *Ṣaḥīḥ al-Bukhārī*, vol. 1, p. 127.

The "just ruler" is the ruler who fully fulfills the rights of the Creator and the created, and brings himself to account before he is brought to account before the All-Knowing King. He raises the banner of justice and quashes the banner of injustice and darkness, so that he is in this world a soldier of God, and in the next will be in gardens of bliss.

The "youth who grew up worshiping God" overcomes his desires in order to worship his Lord, and God ﷻ proudly displays him to the noble angels, saying, "Look, My angels, how My servant went against his desires and escaped to Me from what is forbidden." When he grows old, God will write for him the reward of what he used to do as a youth before he became old and lost his strength.

The "man whose heart is attached to the mosques" is the one who prays his five prayers in congregation, even when his body suffers from pains and tiredness. He goes to the mosque, walking speedily, leaving his preoccupations and comforts. Good tidings will be his—after his effort and tiredness when he wins eternal bliss.

The "two men who love each other for the sake of God" with a pure heart and sincerity, respect, and dignity. Each helps his companion in the affairs of his religion without cheating and without ceasing. Each is happy for his companion's happiness and sad for his sadness. He gives his companion priority over himself in times of severity and pain, and does not leave his companion during difficulty or mock him. To love for the sake of God is to see a person doing the acts of one who loves God, and then to love him because of these acts.

"A man who was invited by a woman of position and beauty" to fornicate with her, but remembered the fire and its torment, "so he said: I fear God." He forbade himself from coming near her, and imprisoned his evil-commanding self and locked the door. Let him have good tidings of his security in this world from afflictions, and in the next from the torment of the fire.

"A man who gave a charity and hid it" out of fear of the resulting reputation, or of hypocrisy, and was content with Him, who knows what is in the earth as He knows what is in the sky. "His left hand would not know what his right hand had spent" of charity, and so

God grants him victory, happiness, and honor. So struggle against yourself to be under this noble shade!

"A man who remembered God while alone"—i.e., in times of seclusion—"so his eyes overflowed" with tears from the majesty of God and in sorrow over what he missed (of good acts). The clouds of mercy and blessings descend upon him from God, and on the Day of Rising: '*Peace,' a word from a Merciful Lord* (36:58).

In this *ḥadīth* there is instruction and guidance to the human to be just in all his states, for justice is the opposite of oppression, and he who oppresses himself with acts of disobedience is not just. Justice is not unique to the ruler alone, but is incumbent upon every Muslim man and woman.

This *ḥadīth* directs the youth to worship because Satan says to them, "do what you want, then when you grow old, repent and worship God." *He makes them promises and raises false hopes* (Q. 4:120). That is why the Prophet ﷺ instilled in the youth a desire for worship and obedience.

The Prophet ﷺ also urged that dealings between people are done for God. The Muslim is the brother of the Muslim—he does not oppress him, belittle him, or act with him hypocritically; he does not love him except for the sake of God who created him.

The Prophet ﷺ directed us to the fear of God ﷻ and the constant awareness of God ﷻ, because God ﷻ is with us wherever we are and He hears our speech and sees us. One of the supplications of the Prophet ﷺ, as narrated in an authentic *ḥadīth*, is, "O my Lord, O He who hears my speech and sees my location." If He is like that then we must have awareness of Him watching us while we are in seclusion as well as when we are among people, and must not do anything that angers Him.

The Prophet ﷺ also urged us to spend on the poor and needy for the cause of God, and on those who struggle for the cause of God.

So good tidings will be for the one who has these characteristics or one of them, for he will be under the shade of the Powerful, the Forgiver, on the Day of Rising.

Ḥadīth 6

Fear and Hope

عن ابن عمر رضي الله عنهما قال: سمعت رسول الله صلى الله عليه وسلم يقول: « إِنَّمَا يُسَلَّطُ عَلَى ابْنِ آدَمَ ما خَافَهُ ابْنُ آدَمَ ، وَلَوْ أَنَّ ابْنَ آدَمَ لَمْ يَخَفْ إِلا اللَّه لَمْ يُسَلَّطْ عَلَيْهِ غيره ، وَإِنَّمَا وكل ابْنُ آدَمَ لِمَنْ رَجَا ابْنَ آدَمَ ، وَلَوْ أَنَّ ابْنَ آدَمَ لَمْ يَرْجُ إِلا اللَّه لَمْ يَكِلْهُ إِلَى غَيْرِهِ »

On the authority of Ibn ʿUmar 🌿[1] who said, I heard the Messenger of God 🌿 say,

> Only that which the son of Adam fears will be given mastery over him, but if the son of Adam fears nothing save God, God will not give anything mastery over him. The son of Adam is only entrusted to whomever he puts his hopes in, but if the son of Adam puts his hopes only in God, then God will not entrust him to anything but Himself.[2]

Fear of God 🌿 is one of the greatest characteristics. God singled out only His messengers, prophets, and the elect among His friends to have this trait.

---

1. Ibn ʿUmar is short for ʿAbdallāh son of ʿUmar. Muslims convention-ally say "may God be pleased with them both" when Ibn ʿUmar is mentioned.

2. Narrated by al-Bayhaqī in the *Sunan* and al-Suyūṭī in *Jamʿ al-jawāmiʿ* (original footnote). Narrated by al-Ḥakīm al-Tirmidhī in the *Nawādir*, vol. 3, p. 80. Part of it is in the *Musnad* of Aḥmad.

He ﷺ said, "The most God-fearing and most knowledgeable of God among you is I."[3] God ﷻ said, *They fear their Lord above them* (16:50).

God gave security to His messengers, prophets, and the elect among His friends from fearing anything but Him, as He did for His angels as well, for they fear none but Him. Since the fear of God is one of the greatest characteristics, God rewards the one who possesses it with security in this world and with fear of none but Him. Likewise, He punishes the one who fears other than Him by bringing about his punishment earlier, in this life, by allowing those whom he fears beside God to gain mastery over him.

The Sufis tell a story that clarifies this for us. They say that someone went to visit a righteous man in the desert and slept that night in his place of residence. When he woke up from his sleep, he went to do the ritual ablution at a nearby spring and found a lion there. Frightened, he ran back. The righteous man asked him, "What has happened?" He replied, "There is a lion!" The righteous man stood up and went with him to the lion, grabbed its ear, and said to it, "Did I not forbid you from appearing to my guests?" Then the lion left. The righteous man said to the guest, "You feared something other than God, so the lion scared you! We feared God, so the lion feared us!"

If the servant has this characteristic, which is the fear of God alone without a partner, then he enters the divine protection that my master Shaykh Aḥmad b. Idrīs ؓ referred to in his saying,

> Safeguard me, my Lord, with the most protective veil of impregnable might, behind the covers of greatness and grandeur, in the presence of Your essence, from all things other than You, so that even if all trials and afflictions pursued me incessantly, they would not be able to reach me, because of my being safeguarded by You in a presence in which affliction is unimaginable.[4]

---

3. *Ṣaḥīḥ al-Bukhārī*, p. 9. Another *ḥadīth* in *Ṣaḥīḥ al-Bukhārī* states, "I am the most knowledgeable of God among people, and the most fearful of Him," vol. 3, p. 1245.
4. This, and the following supplications of Shaykh Aḥmad b. Idrīs are

This safeguarding occurs in the presence of Lordly security on the carpet of divine proximity.[5] He ﷻ said, *He secured them against fear* (106:4). Meaning: When they feared Him alone and no other, He made them secure against fearing anything other than Him. He knew that they were being sought by what is other than Him, so He let them enter His protection and brought down around them the covers of greatness and grandeur. Whoever is surrounded by these covers is respected and venerated by others.

In one *ḥadīth* there is the supplication, "O God, make me thankful, make me patient, and make me small in my eyes and great in the eyes of the people."[6]

In another *ḥadīth* there is also, "O God, make me humble to you, make me beloved to You, and make me great in the eyes of people."[7]

These two *aḥādīth* allude to the covers of greatness and grandeur.

He knew that they were being sought by what is other than Him, so He safeguarded them behind the most protective veil of impregnable might. He ﷻ said, *When you (O Muḥammad) recite the Qurʾān, We put an invisible barrier between you and those who do not believe in the life to come* (17:45).

Perhaps it is this veil to which my master Aḥmad referred to as "the most protective veil of impregnable might." The servant receives it by way of prophetic inheritance. This veil with its impregnability is also characterized with might, which is protection from enemies and victory over them. My master ʿAbd al-Qādir al-Jīlānī said in one of his supplications, "He who seeks greatness through Your greatness is great; he will experience no subjugation or abasement. He who seeks greatness without Your greatness is abased and weak."

Similarly, having fear of the loss of sustenance, instead of fear of the Sustainer, will lead to its loss as well as worrying about how to

---

from his litanies.

5. "Carpet" is a term often used by Sufis as a metaphor for an honored station.

6. Narrated by al-Bazzār in his *Musnad*. See al-Haythamī's *Kashf al-astār*, vol. 4, p. 61.

7. Narrated by Ibn Lāl, and copied from him by al-Suyūṭī in *al-Jāmiʿ al-ṣaghīr* (see al-Nabahānī, *al-Fatḥ al-kabīr*, vol. 1, p. 246) and al-Muttaqī l-Hindī in *Kanz al-ʿummāl*.

obtain it. The Sufis see this as a flaw just like fear of creation. That is why my master ʿAlī Abū l-Ḥasan al-Shādhilī ﷺ says, "O God I seek refuge in you from fear of creation, and worrying over sustenance, and draw near to me!" He asked for nearness after the removal of fear from what is other than God, because both cannot be found together. My master Aḥmad b. Idrīs ﷺ said, "Let me stand beyond the beyond, without a veil, in the presence of Your name 'the All-Encompassing,' in the station of audition, so that I am delighted by the pleasure of the divine address."[8]

The delight at hearing the Speaker does not happen except after the removal of fear, and one is not addressed if there is fear of other than God, because of the presence of what is other than God in the heart. That is why God ﷻ says, *When he said to his companion: Grieve not! God is with us!* (Q. 9:40) Here, the Prophet ﷺ is forbidding his Companion Abū Bakr ﷺ from fearing anything other than God, for this causes grief. Then he is transporting him to the company of God, which causes security and happiness. It is as if the Prophet ﷺ is saying to our master Abū Bakr al-Ṣiddīq ﷺ "Do not fear what is other than God, because we are in the presence of God ﷻ."

8. The author wrote an explanation of this supplication from the litany of Shaykh Aḥmad b. Idrīs in another of his works. He said, "The beyond" is a station in which the intellect can (still) imagine, and in that is the witnessing of what is other than God ﷻ. "Beyond the beyond" is a station in which the intellect does not imagine, and it is the station of divine witnessing without veils and without any type of imagination. Here, you will necessarily witness His name "The All-Encompassing," because if you speak He hears you, and so you will witness that He hears you from all directions, a [type of] hearing greater than what your mind can imagine. "The station of audition" is to hear the Qurʾān from within you, with your soul, and the soul hears it from all of its directions, and there will be a conversation with the divine, which produces great joy for the soul. The Prophet ﷺ said, "He who wants to converse with God should read the Qurʾān." It was narrated by al-Daylamī in *al-Firdaws*. That is what is meant by conversation with the divine, and it has different levels, the highest of which is what happened to the Messenger of God ﷺ. Know, my brother, that this can only be understood by tasting, not from reading, so if you want it, go for it, from your soul to your soul. (*Fatḥ wa fayḍ*, pp 25–26.)

When our master Moses ﷺ saw the snake and feared it, God ﷻ said to him, *Do not be afraid. The messengers fear not in My presence* (27:10). Meaning: There is no fear of other than Him for those who are in His presence are witnessing Him (with the heart).

My master Aḥmad b. Idrīs ﷺ said, ". . . So that everyone who looks at me intending harm fears my power."

The gnostic does not fit this description until he removes all fear of anything other than God ﷻ, and his becoming firm in the fear of God ﷻ. Then God will surround him with a majesty that makes everyone who looks at him intending harm shake with fear. For example, a man entered upon the Prophet ﷺ and shook and trembled with fear. The Prophet ﷺ said to him, "Be calm! I am not a king! I am but the son of a woman from Quraysh who used to eat dried meat."[9]

My master Aḥmad b. Idrīs ﷺ said, "So that I find the pleasure of the Qurʾānic revelation from me to me."[10] This pleasure does not happen except after the removal of fear from what is other than God, and then the heart finds rest, and feelings of *uns*[11] and pleasure come about.

Fear of what is other than God ﷻ does not happen to the knower of God ﷻ because he is in the presence of *uns*, nearness, and love, feeling *waḥsha* from what is other than Him ﷻ, and feeling *uns* in Him. My master Ibn al-Fāriḍ ﷺ said,

---

9. Narrated by Ibn Māja, p. 484, Ibn Saʿd, and al-Ṭabarānī.
10. Refer to the footnote above on the station of audition.
11. The meaning of *uns* and its opposite (*waḥsha*): When you are alone, and you do not like being alone, you feel bored, lonely, maybe cold, uncomfortable or scared, then you are feeling "*waḥsha.*" This word comes from "*waḥsh*" which means a far away, desolate place like a desert. *Waḥsh* also means a wild beast such as a wolf. The opposite of *waḥsha* is *uns*. So if there is someone, or something, who makes you feel happy, content and warm, and takes away your loneliness and coldness, then that person is giving you *uns*. He, or it, is your *anīs*. Animals that are domesticated, and become house pets, are described as *anīs* because they have a familiarity with you: a relationship. The word *insān* (human) is also related to it, which is the opposite of the *waḥsh*. However, some people begin to feel *waḥsha* around other people, and find their *uns* in God.

> I felt *uns* in the *waḥsh* (beast) because my *waḥsha* is from the *ins* (human)

As for his saying, "I felt *uns* in the *waḥsh,*" it does not conform to its apparent meaning, because he did not find *uns* except in God. Rather he meant, I lived in the desert of the wild animals, escaping from the possibility of my heart leaning toward *uns* in people. He who escapes from the *uns* of humans will escape even more from what is other than it. In this is a declaration of not fearing anything but God, and that is why the righteous man lived in the proximity of the wild beasts and did not fear them, and God took charge of preserving him. One should know, however, that the *sharīʿa* does not allow anyone to go to the forests of the wild animals, yet He who took charge of the affairs of our master Joseph ﵇ in the depths of the well, and rescued our master Jonah ﵇ from the darkness, and rescued His intimate friend Abraham ﵇ from the fire, and decreed the safety of His beloved ﷺ in the cave, is capable of protecting His loved ones if their spiritual state drives them into the deserts and mountains.

Al-Ghazālī ﵀ said that one of the righteous men of spiritual states was walking in the desert and fell into a hole from which he could not get out. A group of men passed by but he felt too ashamed of God ﷻ to ask them to save him. After a while, the man saw a hand reach down to him, so he held on to it, and when he was pulled out of the hole, he was surprised to see that the one who reached out to him was a lion! God ﷻ had inspired it to save the man from his plight, and then it left and continued on its way. The man said, "How great and transcendent is He who saved me from death with death!"

This righteous man reached this rank and was honored with this miracle only because he was not afraid of anything but God; the love of God was firmly rooted in his heart. Thus the saying of God ﷻ holds true for him, *For them there is no fear nor do they grieve* (10:62). That is because they feared God and nothing else. Fear of what is other than God is only because of seeing other than God.

"*Nor do they grieve*" because they see the Beloved with them, and grief is only at the veiling of the Beloved.

God ﷻ said, *Satan is your enemy, so take him for an enemy* (35:6). My master Abū l-Ḥasan al-Shādhilī ﵁ said, "There are those who understood from this verse: 'And the All-Merciful is your Lover so take Him as a Beloved.' They therefore busied themselves with the Beloved and the Beloved sufficed them and protected them from the harm of the enemy." That is because of their lack of fear of the enemy, their *uns* and trust in the Beloved, and because they heard the call of the Real ﷻ, *So do not fear them and fear Me if you are believers* (3:175). In this there is a call to the masses and to the elect:

The call to the elect is: ". . . If you believe in Me, witness Me, and love Me. . . . For fear of Me cannot be combined with these descriptions."

My master ʿAlī Wafā said: "He who found You did not miss a thing, and he who missed You missed everything. Ignorant is he who does not see that You are watching over him, and at a loss is the trade of he who does not receive a share from Your love. When did You disappear so that people would need a guide to You? You are enough for me, and the best guardian."

Ḥadīth 7

Deep Understanding

عَنْ مُعَاوِيَةَ قَالَ : قَالَ رَسُولُ اللهِ صَلَّى اللهُ عَلَيْهِ وَسَلَّمَ : « مَنْ يُرِدِ اللهُ بِهِ خَيراً يُفَقِّهْهُ فِي الدِّينِ »

On the authority of Muʿāwiya ﷺ who said, the Messenger of God ﷺ said,

> Whoever God wills good for, He gives him *fiqh* (deep understanding) of the religion.[1]

Narrated by al-Bukhārī and others.[2]

Having *fiqh* in the religion means that one learns the things that God made obligatory for him to do, and knows the things that God ﷻ forbade so that he may avoid them. He who performs the obligatory as is required and desists from the forbidden is among the people of paradise.

Fiqh in the [Arabic] language means understanding; [In its technical meaning,] scholars have defined it as the legal rulings that are acquired from their specific proofs.

The Qurʾān and the Sunna are general proofs. As for His ﷻ saying, *Perform the prayer* (24:56), that is a specific proof; so is his ﷺ saying,

1. In the narration of the Companion Ibn Masʿūd there is the addition, "and He inspires him to do what is right." It was narrated by Aḥmad b. Ḥanbal in *Kitāb al-zuhd* and Abū Nuʿaym in his *Ḥilya*, vol. 3, p. 269.
2. *Ṣaḥīḥ al-Bukhārī*, vol. 1, p. 21.

"Actions are according to intentions"—from this we understand that all actions need an intention.

It is obligatory upon he who does not know the rulings to imitate an imam from among the *mujtahids*[3] who deduced the specific injunctions from their general proofs. As for him who says, "I do not follow the imams," he is more ignorant than the donkey of Umm ʿAmr:

> And if the donkey goes off with Umm ʿAmr,
> then she will never return, and nor will the donkey!

Imam Ibrāhīm al-Laqqānī said in his rhymed treatise *Jawharat al-tawḥīd*,

> Mālik and the rest of the imams
> likewise Abū l-Qāsim,[4] are the guides of the community.
> It is obligatory to imitate a scholar from among them,
> the scholars have said so in clear speech.

A man said to me, "I do not imitate a school of law, but act according to the Qurʾān and Sunna." I said to him, "I ask you by God, do you have the Qurʾān and Sunna memorized?" He said, "No, it is not obligatory." I said to him, "Then you are among those about whom God said, *Who does greater wrong than someone who fabricates a lie against God?* (6:21). You have fabricated a lie against God ﷻ, and claimed to memorize His Book, while you are ignorant of it; and you have fabricated a lie against the Prophet ﷺ and claimed that you act according to the Sunna, while you are ignorant of the Sunna."

Some people speak with audacity toward God ﷻ because He veiled Himself from them, and had they seen Him they would have crumbled like the mountain.[5]

You must believe in a correct creed that you learn from the scholars, and know your Prophet ﷺ and know his worth according to God ﷻ.

---

3. The jurists who have the ability to deduce rulings from the texts of the Qurʾān and Sunna.
4. Al-Junayd.
5. Reference to 7:143, *But when his Lord appeared to the mountain, He rendered it level.*

Ḥadīth 8

Circles of Knowledge

عَنْ أَبِي وَاقِدٍ اللَّيْثِيِّ : أَنَّ رَسُولَ اللهِ صَلَّى اللهُ عَلَيْهِ وَسَلَّمَ بَيْنَمَا هُوَ
جَالِسٌ فِي الْمَسْجِدِ وَالنَّاسُ مَعَهُ إِذْ أَقْبَلَ نَفَرٌ ثَلَاثَةٌ ، فَأَقْبَلَ اثْنَانِ إِلَى
رَسُولِ اللهِ صَلَّى اللهُ عَلَيْهِ وَسَلَّمَ وَذَهَبَ وَاحِدٌ ، قَالَ : فَوَقَفَا عَلَى رَسُولِ
اللهِ صَلَّى اللهُ عَلَيْهِ وَسَلَّمَ ، فَأَمَّا أَحَدُهُمَا فَرَأَى فُرْجَةً فِي الْحَلْقَةِ فَجَلَسَ
فِيهَا ، وَأَمَّا الْآخَرُ فَجَلَسَ خَلْفَهُمْ ، وَأَمَّا الثَّالِثُ فَأَدْبَرَ ذَاهِبًا ، فَلَمَّا فَرَغَ
رَسُولُ اللهِ صَلَّى اللهُ عَلَيْهِ وَسَلَّمَ قَالَ : « أَلَا أُخْبِرُكُمْ عَنِ النَّفَرِ الثَّلَاثَةِ ،
أَمَّا أَحَدُهُمْ فَأَوَى إِلَى اللهِ فَآوَاهُ اللهُ، وَأَمَّا الْآخَرُ فَاسْتَحْيَا فَاسْتَحْيَا اللهُ
مِنْهُ ، وَأَمَّا الْآخَرُ فَأَعْرَضَ فَأَعْرَضَ اللهُ عَنْهُ »

On the authority of Abū Wāqid al-Laythī ﵁, who said, the Messenger of God ﷺ was seated in the mosque surrounded by people. Three people came, and two of them approached the Messenger of God ﷺ and stood near him, while the third walked away on his own. One of the two found an empty space in the circle and sat in it; as for the other, he sat behind them. As for the third, he turned away and left. When the Messenger of God ﷺ finished (what he was talking about), he said,

> Shall I not tell you about the three men? As for one of them, he betook himself to God, so God took him in. As for the other, he

was too ashamed, so God was ashamed of him. And as for the other, he turned away, so God turned away from Him.[1]

Narrated by al-Bukhārī, Muslim, al-Tirmidhī, and al-Nasāʾī.[2]

·✿·✿·✿·

The commentators on the *ḥadīth* said that the Prophet ﷺ called the gathering of religious knowledge the gathering of God, and said that he who turned away from it, turned away from God. This shows the great value of the gatherings of knowledge and scholars.[3]

O people, you must listen to religious knowledge and study it, because it is the light with which humans find their guidance. Our Master ʿAlī (may God be pleased with him and ennoble his face) said, "People are dead, but the people of knowledge are alive." We must strive as much as we can to read from the great Qurʾān, even

1. The attribution of "taking in," "being ashamed of," and "turning away from and leaving" God is a type of metaphor or similitude known as *mushākala*, where an expression used for one object (in this case, each of the three men) is repeated for another (in this case God), but with a different meaning. The meaning is as follows: As for one of them, he joined the gathering of His Messenger, and so God rewarded him by joining him to, and including him among the people of His pleasure, and covered him in His mercy and goodness. As for the second, he was too ashamed to push himself into the circle so God forgave him for not joining it. As for the third, because he stayed away from the gathering of guidance and the place of descent of mercy, God became displeased with him and denied him great bounties. (Footnote from the original). The author, dictating from memory, only quoted from the *ḥadīth* the words of the Prophet, so I have added to it the beginning of the *ḥadīth*, which was put in a footnote by the publishers along with the explanation above.
2. *Ṣaḥīḥ al-Bukhārī*, vol. 1, p. 20.
3. In his main book dedicated to spiritual guidance, the author writes, "The meaning of fleeing to God ﷻ is to enter into circles of knowledge, as per the *ḥadīth*, 'As for one of them, he went to God, so God took him in.' It is also by having shaykhs who take the seeker to God ﷻ. He who has a shaykh should flee to him when he faces the evil whispers [of satan]." (*al-Ilhām al-nāfiʿ*, p. 51).

if only a little bit, because when the human is buried in his grave having memorized the Qurʾān, it will illuminate it for him like the Sun; and if he had not memorized the Qurʾān, it will illuminate for him according to the amount he had memorized. He ﷺ said, "The carriers of the Qurʾān are the people of God and His elect."[4]

He ﷺ said, "May God have mercy upon my successors." Someone said, "Who are your successors, O Messenger of God?" He said, "They are those who will come after I am gone, who will narrate my *aḥādīth* and my Sunna, and teach them to the people."[5]

He ﷺ also said, "May God enlighten the face of the one who hears what I say, memorizes it, and conveys it to others."[6]

He ﷺ also said, "The virtue of a man of knowledge over a worshiper is like the virtue of the full moon at night over the stars."[7]

O people, you must learn religious knowledge, for with it you will escape from the darknesses of ignorance, and with it you will know your Lord, and with it you will know your law. God ﷻ revealed to our master Abraham ﷺ, "O Abraham, I am most knowledgeable, and I love everyone who is knowledgeable."[8]

4. *Sunan Ibn Māja*, p. 36.
5. al-Suyūṭī, *al-Jāmiʿ al-ṣaghīr* (see al-Nabahānī, *al-Fatḥ al-kabīr*, vol. 1, p. 233).
6. Narrated by Aḥmad, al-Tirmidhī, and Ibn Ḥibbān (original footnote). This is the wording of Ibn Māja in his *Sunan*, p. 49.
7. Narrated by Abū Dāwūd in his *Sunan*, vol. 2, p. 620, and al-Tirmidhī, Abū Nuʿaym, and many others.
8. Mentioned by Ibn ʿAbd al-Barr (original footnote), and al-Subkī in *Ṭabaqāt al-Shāfiʿiyya al-kubrā*, vol. 6, p. 288.

Ḥadīth 9

Prayer

عَنْ مَالِكٍ ، عَنِ ابْنِ شِهَابٍ ، أَنَّ عُمَرَ بْنَ عَبْدِ الْعَزِيزِ أَخَّرَ الصَّلَاةَ يَوْمًا ، فَدَخَلَ عَلَيْهِ عُرْوَةُ بْنُ الزُّبَيْرِ ، فَأَخْبَرَهُ أَنَّ الْمُغِيرَةَ بْنَ شُعْبَةَ أَخَّرَ الصَّلَاةَ يَوْمًا وَهُوَ بِالْعِرَاقِ ، فَدَخَلَ عَلَيْهِ أَبُو مَسْعُودٍ الْأَنْصَارِيُّ ، فَقَالَ : مَا هَذَا يَا مُغِيرَةُ ؟ أَلَيْسَ قَدْ عَلِمْتَ أَنَّ جِبْرِيلَ نَزَلَ فَصَلَّى ، فَصَلَّى رَسُولُ اللهِ صَلَّى اللهُ عَلَيْهِ وَسَلَّمَ (يعني الظهر)، ثُمَّ صَلَّى فَصَلَّى رَسُولُ اللهِ صَلَّى اللهُ عَلَيْهِ وَسَلَّمَ (يعني العصر)، ثُمَّ صَلَّى فَصَلَّى رَسُولُ اللهِ صَلَّى اللهُ عَلَيْهِ وَسَلَّمَ (يعني المغرب)، ثُمَّ صَلَّى فَصَلَّى رَسُولُ اللهِ صَلَّى اللهُ عَلَيْهِ وَسَلَّمَ (يعني العشاء)، ثُمَّ صَلَّى فَصَلَّى رَسُولُ اللهِ صَلَّى اللهُ عَلَيْهِ وَسَلَّمَ (يعني الصبح)، ثُمَّ قَالَ : بِهَذَا أُمِرْتُ.

On the authority of Mālik, on the authority of Ibn Shihāb, that ʿUmar b. ʿAbd al-ʿAzīz delayed the prayer one day. ʿUrwa b. al-Zubayr came to him and told him that al-Mughīra b. Shuʿba once delayed the prayer when he was in Iraq, so Abū Masʿūd al-Anṣārī came to him and said, "What is this O Mughīra? Did you not know that Gabriel descended and prayed and the Messenger of God ﷺ prayed—meaning the noon prayer. Then he prayed again and the Messenger of God ﷺ prayed—meaning the afternoon prayer. Then he prayed again and the Messenger of God ﷺ prayed—meaning the sunset prayer. Then he prayed again and the Messenger of God ﷺ

prayed—meaning the night prayer. Then he prayed again and the Messenger of God ﷺ prayed—meaning the dawn prayer. Then he—meaning Gabriel ﷺ—said, 'I was commanded to do this.'" Narrated by al-Bukhārī in the section on the times of the prayer.[1]

We learn from this [narration] that the times of prayer must be observed, and that they are of great importance in the eyes of God ﷻ. That is why Gabriel ﷺ was commanded to descend to the Prophet ﷺ to make clear to him the times of the five prayers.

God ﷻ revealed in the Qurʾān a harsh warning for those who let the times of prayer slip away and pray them at times other than their set times. He ﷻ said, *So wayl to those who pray, who are unmindful of their prayers* (107:4–5). *Wayl* means either a painful punishment, a valley in hell, or a well in hell. This warning is for those who miss the set times of prayer, so what about those who neglect the prayers altogether?

1. *Ṣaḥīḥ al-Bukhārī*, vol 1, pp. 105–106.

Ḥadīth 10

The Joy in Prayer

عَنْ أَنَسٍ ، أَنّ النَّبِيَّ صَلَّى اللهُ عَلَيْهِ وَسَلَّمَ قَالَ : « حُبِّبَ إِلَيَّ مِنَ الدُّنْيا النِّسَاءُ ، وَالطِّيبُ ، وَجُعِلَ قُرَّةُ عَيْنِي فِي الصَّلَاةِ »

On the authority of Anas b. Mālik ﵁, who said: the Messenger of God ﷺ said,

> Of this world I was made to love women and perfume; and the joy of my eyes was made to be in the prayer.[1]

Narrated by Shaykh Aḥmad b. Idrīs, Imam Aḥmad, al-Nasāʾī, al-Ḥākim, and al-Bayhaqī.[2]

The scholar and Sufi Shaykh Aḥmad b. ʿAṭāʾillāh al-Sakandarī l-Mālikī ﵀ said,

> The joy in witnessing is according to the extent of knowledge of the witnessed. The eyes of the Prophet ﷺ did not find joy except in God ﷻ, and that is why he said "in the prayer" and did not say "the prayer."[3]

1. The expression, "joy of my eyes" (*qurrat ʿayni*) means "the thing that I love most" or "the thing that gives me the most satisfaction, joy, or pleasure."
2. *Sunan al-Nasāʾī*, vol 2, p. 649.
3. The Prophet said *fi* and not *bi*, meaning that what gave him the greatest satisfaction and joy was not the prayer itself but what is found within it. Al-Sakandarī is saying that this is the spiritual witnessing of God.

Prayer is the beloved of the souls, and in it is intimate conversation between the soul and its beloved. In it descend the effusions of the conversations and divine self-disclosures. In it is the wedding celebration of the souls, and the descent of that which delights it, of comforts and beautiful scents. The eyes have every right to find their joy in it, because in it is nearness to their Lord.

You must, O brother, come to the obligatory prayer and the non-obligatory prayer, to attain by them what those who pray to their Lord with reverence and humility obtained—for they obtained from their Lord the success of the successful ones and the repentance of the humble worshipers.

Al-Qasṭalānī said,

> The prayer was called *ṣalāt* for the following reasons:
>
> First, that it takes one (*tūṣil*) to paradise. It is related that ʿAlī ﷺ said, "Do you know why the *ṣalāt* was called *ṣalāt*?" They said, "No, O Commander of the Believers!" He said, "Because it takes the one who performs it to paradise."
>
> Second, that it is from *al-ṣila* (connection) because when the servant performs it he is connected to his Lord, and when he leaves it he is cut off. It has been related on the authority of Jābir ﷺ that the Messenger of God ﷺ said, "Between the servant and between disbelief is the leaving of the prayer." Narrated by Muslim and Ibn Māja.
>
> Third, that it is from *taṣliya,* which means to straighten metal by putting it in the fire. That is because it makes the human upright and improves and corrects his heart and mind.
>
> Fourth, that it was called *ṣalāt* because of God's *muwāṣala* (continual exchange and communication) with His servant by promising him His blessings upon doing it, as He ﷻ said, *And order your people to pray and pray steadfastly yourself. We are not asking you for provision, We provide for you* (20:132).
>
> And fifth, it was called *ṣalāt* because it takes the one who neglects it to the fire. He ﷺ said, "If a servant performs the prayer and does not complete its bowing and prostration, it

is wrapped as the worn-out robe is wrapped and then thrown on his face." Narrated by al-Suyūṭī.[4]

4. Al-Suyūṭī, *al-Jāmiʿ al-ṣaghīr*, where he attributes it to al-Ṭayālisī (see al-Nabahānī, *al-Fatḥ al-kabīr*, vol. 1, p. 69).

THE BOOK OF
GENESIS

1 IN the beginning God created the
heaven and the earth.
2 And the earth was without form, and
void; and darkness *was* upon the face of
the deep. And the Spirit of God moved
upon the face of the waters.
3 And God said, Let there be light: and
there was light.
4 And God saw the light, that *it was*
good: and God divided the light from
the darkness.
5 And God called the light Day, and
the darkness he called Night. And the
evening and the morning were the first
day.
6 ¶ And God said, Let there be a firmament in the midst of the waters, and
let it divide the waters from the waters.
7 And God made the firmament, and divided the waters which *were* under the
firmament from the waters which *were*
above the firmament: and it was so.
8 And God called the firmament Heaven.
And the evening and the morning were
the second day.
9 ¶ And God said, Let the waters under
the heaven be gathered together unto
one place, and let the dry *land* appear:
and it was so.
10 And God called the dry *land* Earth;
and the gathering together of the waters called he Seas: and God saw that
it was good.
11 And God said, Let the earth bring
forth grass, the herb yielding seed, *and*
the fruit tree yielding fruit after his
kind, whose seed *is* in itself, upon the
earth: and it was so.
12 And the earth brought forth grass,
and herb yielding seed after his kind,
and the tree yielding fruit, whose seed
was in itself, after his kind: and God
saw that *it was* good.
13 And the evening and the morning
were the third day.
14 ¶ And God said, Let there be lights
in the firmament of the heaven to divide
the day from the night; and let them be
for signs, and for seasons, and for days,
and years:
15 And let them be for lights in the
firmament of the heaven to give light
upon the earth: and it was so.
16 And God made two great lights; the
greater light to rule the day, and the
lesser light to rule the night: *he made*
the stars also.
17 And God set them in the firmament
of the heaven to give light upon the
earth,
18 And to rule over the day and over the
night, and to divide the light from the
darkness: and God saw that *it was* good.
19 And the evening and the morning
were the fourth day.
20 And God said, Let the waters bring
forth abundantly the moving creature
that hath life, and fowl *that* may fly
above the earth in the open firmament
of heaven.
21 And God created great whales, and
every living creature that moveth, which
the waters brought forth abundantly, after their kind, and every winged fowl
after his kind: and God saw that *it was*
good.
22 And God blessed them, saying, Be
fruitful, and multiply, and fill the waters in the seas, and let fowl multiply
in the earth.

are faithful and true: and the Lord God
of the holy prophets sent his angel to
shew unto his servants the things
which must shortly be done.
7 Behold, I come quickly: blessed *is* he
that keepeth the sayings of the prophecy of this book.
8 And I John saw these things, and
heard *them*. And when I had heard
and seen, I fell down to worship before
the feet of the angel which shewed me
these things.
9 Then saith he unto me, See *thou do it*
not: for I am thy fellowservant, and of
thy brethren the prophets, and of them
which keep the sayings of this book:
worship God.
10 And he saith unto me, Seal not the
sayings of the prophecy of this book:
for the time is at hand.
11 He that is unjust, let him be unjust
still: and he which is filthy, let him be
filthy still: and he that is righteous, let
him be righteous still: and he that is
holy, let him be holy still.
12 And, behold, I come quickly; and
my reward *is* with me, to give every
man according as his work shall be.
13 I am Alpha and Omega, the beginning and the end, the first and the last.
14 Blessed *are* they that do his com-
mandments, that they may have right
to the tree of life, and may enter in
through the gates into the city.
15 For without *are* dogs, and sorcerers,
and whoremongers, and murderers, and
idolaters, and whosoever loveth and ma-
keth a lie.
16 I Jesus have sent mine angel to testify
unto you these things in the churches. I
am the root and the offspring of David,
and the bright and morning star.
17 And the Spirit and the bride say, Come.
And let him that heareth say, Come.
And let him that is athirst come. And
whosoever will, let him take the water
of life freely.
18 For I testify unto every man that
heareth the words of the prophecy of
this book, If any man shall add unto
these things, God shall add unto him the
plagues that are written in this book:
19 And if any man shall take away from
the words of the book of this prophecy,
God shall take away his part out of the
book of life, and out of the holy city,
and *from* the things which are written
in this book.
20 He which testifieth these things saith,
Surely I come quickly. Amen. Even so,
come, Lord Jesus.
21 The grace of our Lord Jesus Christ *be*
with you all. Amen.

Ḥadīth 11

Miracles

بَيْنَمَا رَسُولُ اللهِ صَلَّى اللهُ عَلَيْهِ وَآلِهِ وَسَلَّمَ جَالِسٌ وَأَسْمَاءُ بِنْتُ عُمَيْسٍ قَرِيبَةٌ مِنْهُ إِذْ رَدَّ السَّلامَ ، ثُمَّ قَالَ : « يَا أَسْمَاءُ ، هَذَا جَعْفَرُ بْنُ أَبِي طَالِبٍ مَعَ جِبْرِيلَ وَمِيكَائِيلَ وَإِسْرافِيلَ سَلَّمُوا عَلَيْنَا فَرُدِّي عَلَيْهِمُ السَّلامَ ، وَقَدْ أَخْبَرَنِي أَنَّهُ لَقِيَ الْمُشْرِكِينَ يَوْمَ كَذَا وَكَذَا قَبْلَ مَمَرِّهِ عَلَى رَسُولِ اللهِ صَلَّى اللهُ عَلَيْهِ وَآلِهِ وَسَلَّمَ بِثَلاثٍ أَوْ أَرْبَعٍ ، فَقَالَ : لَقِيتُ الْمُشْرِكِينَ فَأَصَبْتُ فِي جَسَدِي مِنْ مَقَادِيمِي ثَلاثًا وَسَبْعِينَ بَيْنَ رَمْيَةٍ وَطَعْنَةٍ وَضَرْبَةٍ ، ثُمَّ أَخَذْتُ اللِّوَاءَ بِيَدِي الْيُمْنَى فَقُطِعَتْ ، ثُمَّ أَخَذْتُ بِيَدِي الْيُسْرَى فَقُطِعَتْ ، فَعَوَّضَنِي اللهُ مِنْ يَدَيَّ جَنَاحَيْنِ أَطِيرُ بِهِمَا مَعَ جِبْرِيلَ وَمِيكَائِيلَ أَنْزِلُ مِنَ الْجَنَّةِ حَيْثُ شِئْتُ ، وَآكُلُ مِنْ ثِمَارِهَا مَا شِئْتُ » ، فَقَالَتْ أَسْمَاءُ : هَنِيئًا لِجَعْفَرٍ مَا رَزَقَهُ اللهُ مِنَ الْخَيْرِ ، وَلَكِنْ أَخَافُ أَنْ لا يُصَدِّقُ النَّاسُ ، فَاصْعَدِ الْمِنْبَرَ فَأَخْبِرْ بِهِ ، فَصَعِدَ الْمِنْبَرَ فَحَمِدَ اللهَ وَأَثْنَى عَلَيْهِ ، ثُمَّ قَالَ : « يَا أَيُّهَا النَّاسُ ، إِنَّ جَعْفَرًا مَعَ جِبْرِيلَ وَمِيكَائِيلَ لَهُ جَنَاحَانِ عَوَّضَهُ اللهُ مِنْ يَدَيْهِ سَلَّمَ عَلَيَّ » ، ثُمَّ أَخْبَرَهُمْ كَيْفَ كَانَ أَمْرُهُ حَيْثُ لَقِيَ الْمُشْرِكِينَ ، فَاسْتَبَانَ لِلنَّاسِ بَعْدَ الْيَوْمِ الَّذِي أَخْبَرَ رَسُولُ اللهِ صَلَّى اللهُ عَلَيْهِ وَآلِهِ وَسَلَّمَ أَنَّ جَعْفَرًا لَقِيَهُمْ فَلِذَلِكَ سُمِّيَ الطَّيَّارُ فِي الْجَنَّةِ

On the authority of Ibn ʿAbbās ﵁, who said,

> While the Prophet ﷺ was sitting, and Asmāʾ bt. ʿUmays was near him, he suddenly returned the greeting of peace and said, "O Asmāʾ, this is Jaʿfar b. Abī Ṭālib with (the angels) Gabriel, Michael, and Israfil, and they have greeted us, so return their greeting. He told me that he fought the polytheists three days ago and said, 'I was injured on the front of my body seventy-three times, between stabs, blows, and strikes. I then held the banner with my right hand, but it was cut off, so I held the banner with with my left hand, but it was cut off; so God gave me two wings in their place, with which I fly with Gabriel and Michael. I descend from paradise to any place I want, and eat of its fruits whatever I want.'" Asmāʾ said, "Congratulations to Jaʿfar for the good that God gave him! I fear, though, that the people will not believe me, so climb the pulpit and tell the people of it." So he climbed the pulpit, and thanked God and praised Him, then said, "Jaʿfar is with Gabriel and Michael—God gave him two wings instead of his hands—and he came and greeted me." Then he told them about what happened to him when he fought the polytheists. The next day after the Messenger of God ﷺ told the people, they received the news that Jaʿfar had fought the polytheists. This is why he was called "the flyer in paradise."

Narrated by al-Ḥākim.[1]

Ibn ʿAsākir also narrated through Ibn Isḥaq, who said, I was told by al-Ḥusayn b. ʿAbdallāh b. Abbās that the Messenger of God ﷺ said after the killing of Jaʿfar, "Jaʿfar passed by me tonight, following

1. al-Ḥākim, *al-Mustadrak ʿalā l-saḥīḥayn*, vol. 3, p. 232. Ibn Saʿd also narrated on the authority of ʿAbdallāh b. al-Mukhtār ﵁ who said, the Messenger of God ﷺ said, "Jaʿfar b. Abī Ṭālib passed by me tonight among a group of angels. He has two wings covered in blood, and their primaries are white" (*Kitāb al-ṭabaqāt al-kabīr*, vol. 4, p. 36). Primaries are the largest flight feathers along the outer edge of a bird's wing.

a group of angels, and he had two wings whose front sides were covered in blood. They were going to Bīsha, a town in Yemen."[2]

Ibn ʿUdayy also narrated the *ḥadīth* of ʿAlī b. Abī Ṭālib (may God ennoble his face) that the Messenger of God ﷺ said, "I recognized Jaʿfar among a company of angels, going to give the people of Bīsha the good tidings of rain."

O believing brother, have you read the *ḥadīth* of the martyr, our master Jaʿfar "the flier" b. Abī Ṭālib ؓ? For if you have read it and understood it, then you have understood something strange and wondrous! I only wanted to show you God's great favor upon the ones He loves, and how He breaks for them the norms, to transport you to think about the virtue of the Seal of the Prophets and Messengers ﷺ. If his cousin the martyr, our master Jaʿfar, flies with the angels and comes from paradise to this world to give glad tidings of rain to the people of a town in Yemen, and that is after having been killed and buried under the sand. . . . Did it not reach you that he who is under the sand is in paradise, and that God ﷻ testified to the fact that he is alive? How did he come back to this world and come to fly with the noble angels?

This *ḥadīth* is supported by the *aḥādīth* about the Night Journey, and in which God ﷻ brought all the prophets and messengers, God's peace and blessings upon them all, together for our Prophet ﷺ and that he led them in prayer. This matter is called a miracle by the scholars, and the matter of our master Jaʿfar ؓ is called a *karāma*.[3] The existence of the miracles and the *karāmāt* has been established by the Book, the Sunna, and consensus. The scholars said, "Every miracle for a prophet can be a *karāma* for a friend of God."

---

2. Also by Ṭabarī in his *Tārīkh*, p. 432.
3. Literally, an honorific gift. The term used for the miracles of the friends of God.

Ḥadīth 12

The Prophets Are Alive

عَنْ أَنَسِ بْنِ مَالِكٍ رَضِيَ اللهُ عَنْهُ ، قَالَ : قَالَ رَسُولُ اللهِ صَلَّى اللهُ عَلَيْهِ وَسَلَّمَ : « الأَنْبِيَاءُ أَحْيَاءٌ فِي قُبُورِهِمْ يُصَلُّونَ »

On the authority of Anas b. Mālik ﵁ who said, the Messenger of God ﷺ said,

> The prophets are alive in their graves, praying.

Narrated by al-Bayhaqī, and al-Suyūṭī attributed it in *al-Jāmiʿ al-ṣaghīr* to Abū Yaʿlā l-Mawṣilī in his *Musnad*, and its commentator said, "It is an authentic *ḥadīth*."[1]

·❁·❁·❁·

The author of *Naẓm al-mutanāthir min al-ḥadīth al-mutawātir*[2] said, "Among that which reached the level of *tawātur*[3] from the Prophet ﷺ is the lives of the prophets ﵈ in their graves.

Al-Suyūṭī said in *Mirqāt al-suʿūd*, the commentary on the *Sunan*

---

1. Nūr al-Dīn al-Haythamī wrote that it was narrated by both Abū Yaʿlā and al-Bazzār, adding that, "the narrators in Abū Yaʿlā's chain are all trustworthy" (al-Haythamī, *Majmaʿ al-zawāʾid*, vol. 8, p. 211). Al-Bayhaqī's narration is in his book *Mā warada fī ḥayāt al-anbiyāʾ baʿda wafātihim* (Beirut: Muʾassassat Nādir, 1989).
2. "Arranging together what was scattered of the widely-reported *aḥādīth*," and the author is imam Muḥammad b. Jaʿfar al-Kattāni.
3. A *mutawātir ḥadīth* is a *ḥadīth* that was so widely reported by so many sources, either in the same words or in meaning, that it could not have been fabricated and must be true.

of Abū Dāwūd, "The life of the Prophet ﷺ in his grave, him and the rest of the prophets, is known to us with certainty, because of all the evidence that we have that supports it, and the reports that give evidence reached the level of *tawātur.*"

Ibn al-Qayyim said in *Kitāb al-rūḥ*, quoting Abū ʿAbdallāh al-Qurṭubī,

> It was authentically related from the Prophet ﷺ that the earth does not eat the bodies of the prophets, and that he ﷺ met with the prophets on the night of the Night Journey and Ascension in Jerusalem, and then in the sky, especially with our master Moses. He ﷺ also told us that no Muslim greets him without God having returned his soul to him so that he returns the greeting . . . and other things from the whole of which it becomes certain that the death of the prophets only means that they became unseen to us, even though they are alive and present, and that is like the state of the angels, for they are alive and present, but we do not see them. . . .

The Qurʾān gave evidence of the life of the Prophet ﷺ and the life of all the prophets and messengers for they are also alive after their death. That is in God's saying, *Think not of those who have been killed in God's way as dead. Nay, they are alive . . .* (3:169). This verse indicates the life of all the prophets by way of implication,[4] and that is because the prophets are more deserving of this excellent state than the martyrs. It also indicates the life of our Prophet ﷺ by its general application, and that is because God combined for him prophethood, the role of messenger, and martyrdom, as authentically reported.

He ﷺ said, "God forbade the earth from consuming the bodies of the prophets."

It was related by Aws b. Aws as part of a long *ḥadīth*, and was narrated by:

1. Abū Dāwūd
2. Imam Aḥmad

---

4. What the scholars call *Mafhūm al-muwāfaqa*: Implication, harmonious meaning, or *a fortiori* reasoning.

3. al-Nasāʾī
4. Ibn Māja
5. al-Dārimī
6. al-Bayhaqī in *Kitāb al-daʿawāt al-kabīr*
7. Ibn Khuzayma
8. Ibn Ḥibbān in his *Ṣaḥīḥ*
9. al-Ṭabarānī in *al-Kabīr*
10. Saʿīd b. Manṣūr in his *Sunan*
11. Ibn Abī Shayba
12. al-Ḥākim, and he declared it to be authentic.

Al-Nawawī ﵀ also declared it to be authentic.[5]

Abū Yaʿlā narrated from Abū Hurayra ﵁ who said, I heard the Messenger of God ﷺ say, "By Him in whose hand is my soul, Jesus the son of Mary will descend. Then, when he stands at my grave and says, 'O Muḥammad!' I will answer him."[6]

In his work *al-Tadhkira,* Imam al-Qurṭubī, the great *ḥadīth* master of al-Andalus, commented on the *ḥadīth* of the blowing of the horn that will cause everyone's death, quoting his shaykh,

> Death is not ceasing to exist, but a transition from one state to another. Proof is that the martyrs, after their death, are alive and receiving sustenance; they are happy and rejoicing, and these are characteristics of those who are alive in this world, and if they are established for the martyrs then prophets have more right to that.
>
> It has also been authentically related that the earth does not consume the bodies of the prophets, and that he ﷺ met the prophets on the night of the Night Journey in Jerusalem and in the sky, and saw Moses ﵇ standing in prayer in his grave, and he ﷺ said that he returns the greeting of everyone who greets him, and other things from which it becomes certain that their

---

5. The author then wrote, "I have, by the grace of my Lord, composed the names of the narrators of this *ḥadīth*, due to their multitude, into poetry to make it easier to memorize them." This was followed by six lines of poetry.

6. Abū Yaʿlā l-Mawṣilī, *Musnad Abī Yaʿlā l-Mawṣilī*, 14 vols (Beirut: Dār al-Maʾmūn li-l-Turāth, 1989), vol. 11, p. 462.

> death only means that they become unseen to us, even though they are alive and present, and none of our kind sees them except those that God singled out with *karāma.*[7]

Al-Bayhaqī said in *Dalāʾil al-nubuwwa*, "The prophets are alive with their Lord like the martyrs."

Shaykh Taqī l-Dīn al-Subkī said in his work *Jamʿ al-jawāmiʿ*,

> The lives of the prophets and martyrs in the grave is like their lives in this world, and Moses' prayer in his grave testifies to that, for the prayer requires a living body, and so do the descriptions that were mentioned about the prophets on the night of the Night Journey: all are descriptions of the bodies. Though their life is real, that does not necessitate that their bodies are like they were in their previous life in needing food and drink. As for types of realization like knowing and hearing, there is no doubt that these are established for them and all the dead.

Ibrāhīm al-Laqqānī said in the commentary on *Jawharat al-tawḥīd*, "The prophets are alive in their graves after their death."

Imam Badr al-Dīn b. al-Ṣāḥib said in his *Tadhkira*,

> "Section on his life ﷺ after his death in the intermediary realm":
>
> The Law-Giver gave both clear and implied evidence of this. From the noble Qurʾān is His saying ﷻ, *Think not of those who have been killed in God's way as dead. Nay, they are alive with their Lord, receiving sustenance* (3:169). For this state, being the life in the intermediary realm after death, happens to the normal members in the Muslim community, but the martyrs will be in a higher and better state than those who do not have that rank—especially in the intermediary realm. No one in the community has a rank higher than the Prophet ﷺ, nay they (i.e., the martyrs) only achieved this rank by following him and being purified by him.[8]

---

7. See the commentary on *ḥadīth* 11.
8. This passage and the one below, from Badr al-Dīn b. al-Ṣāḥib's *Tadhkira*, are copied from al-Suyūṭī's *Tanwīr al-ḥalak.* However in the print that I have of this work (see bibliography) it says "by his blessings" instead of "by following him and being purified by him"

In it he also said,

> He ﷺ said, "I passed by Moses the night I was taken on the Night Journey, at the red sand hill, and he was standing in his grave in prayer."[9]
>
> This is clear in establishing life for Moses ﷺ, for the Prophet described him as being in prayer and standing, and such things are not descriptions that souls are described with—only bodies are so described. By specifying that the prayer was in the grave he provides evidence of that, for if that life was a description of the soul alone, the specification of the grave would not have been necessary, for no one ever said that the souls of the prophets are imprisoned in the graves with the bodies. The souls of the martyrs and believers are in paradise.

Al-Laqqānī said in his short commentary,

> We believe with certainty in the return to life of every dead person in his grave, and in the bliss or torment of the grave, and these are conditions that require life but do not require a body. As for the traditions proving the life of the prophets, they necessitate the existence of a body and the power of influence in the world, without the need of the norms of the world, and that is why Abū l-Ḥasan al-Ashʿarī ﷺ said, "The Prophet ﷺ (even) now possesses the role of messenger."

Al-Bārizī ﷺ was asked, "Is the Prophet ﷺ alive in his grave?" He answered, "Yes, he is alive."

The Shaykh of the Shāfiʿī school (of his age), Abū Manṣūr ʿAbd al-Qādir b. Ṭāhir al-Usūlī l-Baghdādī said in his response to certain questions,

> The greatest scholars of theology from among our companions said that our Prophet Muḥammad ﷺ is alive after his death, and that he is given good tidings of his community's acts of obedience, and is sad at the disobedience of those who disobey,

---

(p. 78). The three words, "blessings," "following," and "purification" look very similar in Arabic.

9. *Ṣaḥīḥ Muslim*, vol. 2, p. 1016.

> and that when people of his community send blessings upon him, it reaches him.

He also said,

> The bodies of the prophets do not decompose, and the earth does not consume any part of them, and our master Moses died in his time, and our Prophet said that he saw him praying in his grave, and mentioned in the *ḥadīth* of the Ascension that he saw him in the fourth heaven, and saw Adam and Abraham. If this is authenticated for us, then we say, based upon it, that our prophet became alive after his death, and that he is (still) in his role of prophethood.

The great *ḥadīth* master al-Bayhaqī said in *Kitāb al-iʿtiqād*,

> The prophets had their souls returned to them after they died, and they are alive with their Lord, and our Prophet saw a group of them and led them in prayer, and confirmed—and his reports are true—that our blessings upon him are presented to him, and that our greetings reach him, and that God forbade the earth from consuming the bodies of the prophets. . . .

He then said, "I have also written a book that proves that they are alive."[10]

He said after that, "O God, let us live according to the Sunna of this noble Prophet, and let us die in his faith, and unite us with him in this world and the next, for You are capable of all things."

The supplication of this shaykh is in harmony with what our shaykh said in his 'Ṣalāt ʿAẓīmīyya,' "Unite me with him in the same way that You united the soul and the self, outwardly and inwardly, in the waking and in sleep."[11]

The Shāfiʿī scholar ʿAfif al-Dīn al-Yāfiʿī said,

> Certain states come to the Friends of God in which they see the realms of the heavens and the Earth, and they see the prophets

10. See the first footnote in this chapter.
11. It continues, "In this world before the next, O Great One!" The Ṣalāt ʿAẓīmīyya is the formula of blessings upon the Prophet that the Prophet gave to Ibn Idrīs.

> alive, as the Prophet ﷺ saw Moses ﷺ in his grave. It has been accepted that what is possible for the prophets as a miracle is possible for the Friends of God as a *karāma*, with the condition of the absence of a challenge,[12] and only the ignorant denies that. The sayings of the scholars proving that the prophets are alive are many, so let this much suffice us.

The stories of the gnostics are well known and widespread, like when my master Aḥmad al-Rifāʿi stood at the noble grave and recited his two famous lines of poetry, and the noble hand came out and shook his hand.

I say by the grace of God ﷻ, among the things that prove that he ﷺ is alive in his body and soul is the saying of God ﷻ, *God would not send them punishment while you are in their midst . . .* (8:33). The pronoun "*while you are*" refers to the soul, the body, and the existence of life. It becomes necessary by his existence as he is, that destroying punishments are prevented. They have indeed been prevented from them, and he is indeed among them, as is clear in the saying of God ﷻ, *When you are with them, and establish the prayer for them* (4:102). Meaning, with them in your body and soul.

God ﷻ said, *Those who pledge loyalty to you are actually pledging loyalty to God* (48:10). The pledge of loyalty does not work without the admission of the two testimonies[13] when he ﷺ was in the midst of his Companions ﷺ. Now that he has gone to the highest Companion, the pledge of loyalty has stayed the same. If he had not been alive after death, and if his role as messenger ﷺ did not remain as it was, the pledge of loyalty would have changed.[14] Islam is also not completed or accepted except with the mention of his name, which means that the mention of his name ﷺ is a means for the acceptance of Islam and faith.

God ﷻ said, *Obey God and obey the Messenger* (4:59; 47:33). This command remains until the Day of Rising, for obedience

12. I.e., a challenge to produce a miracle, as in the case of the prophets.
13. "I bear witness that there is no god but God, and I bear witness that Muḥammad is the messenger of God."
14. Meaning that it would have changed to ". . . and I bear witness that Muḥammad *was* the Messenger of God."

is obedience, and the Messenger ﷺ is the Messenger, and the obedience to him that was obligatory when he was in the midst of his Companions is the obedience to him that is obligatory now. He who denies the first has rejected Islam, and he who denies the second has rejected Islam. The first obedience was to a living messenger, in his body and soul. Today he ﷺ still has his role as messenger and he has our obedience, and they are better than life, and they require the existence of life, so contemplate what I said that perhaps you might be guided.

God ﷻ said, *So how will it be, then, when We bring from every people a witness, and bring you as a witness against these?* (4:41). Does *"these"* here refer just to his Companions or to the entire community? No, what is meant is the entire community, including the Companions and the rest, until the Day of Rising, as he ﷺ is the witness of the community.

God ﷻ said, *God—and His Messenger—has more right that they should please Him* (9:62). The pleasure of God ﷻ is by the obedience to God ﷻ, and the pleasure of the Prophet ﷺ is by the obedience to God ﷻ. So let the obedient one believe that God ﷻ is pleased with him now, and that His Prophet ﷺ is pleased with him now.

God ﷻ said to His Prophet ﷺ, *We sent you not but as a mercy to the worlds* (21:107). This mercy continues until now, and until the time that God wills.

God ﷻ said, *Whoever does good, whether male or female, is a believer. We will most certainly make him live a happy life, and We will most certainly give them their reward for the best of what they did* (16:97). God ﷻ made His Prophet ﷺ live the best life in this world, because it is the life of a prophet and messenger, a life of struggle and worship. He also made him live after death, and rewarded him for the best that he used to do ﷺ; so if the reward was better, the life would be better. Good rewards begin from the moment of the removal of the soul; He ﷻ said, *Those whom the angels cause to die in a good state, saying: Peace be on you: enter the garden for what you did* (16:32). He ﷻ also said, *The angels descend upon them, saying: Fear not, nor be grieved, and receive good news of the garden which you were promised* (41:30). He ﷺ

said, *O soul at peace: return to your Lord, well-pleased and well-pleasing* (89:27–28).

This is all of the good reward—the best reward—at the time of dying. As for the time after death, the Prophet ﷺ said, "The grave is either a garden from the gardens of paradise or a pit from the pits of the fire."[15] The imam of the prophets and messengers ﷺ is the best of people after death, and the highest and best of them in the garden of the grave, and the best of them in reward, for he ﷺ was the best of them in works, in obedience, in struggle, nightly worship, worship, and recitation of the Qurʾān, and the one who remembered the Lord of the worlds the most.

Ibn Ḥajar al-Haythamī said,

> The proofs and texts reached the level of *tawātur*
> to the extent that the author cannot count what he says
> That the Chosen One is alive and tender
> like the moon, and he does not wane
> And the earth consumed not his body,
> nor any of his flesh, and I will establish what I say.

These lines are from a long poem that was commented upon by our shaykh the *ḥadīth* scholar Ḥabībullāh al-Shinqīṭī.

The great *ḥadīth* scholar ʿAbd al-ʿAẓīm al-Mundhirī mentioned in his book *al-Targhīb wa-l-tarhīb*, in the section on the 'Ṣalāt al-Ḥāja' [prayer of need] that ʿUthmān b. Ḥanīf taught a man who needed something from our master ʿUthmān b. ʿAffān during the days of his caliphate, the *ḥadīth* of the blind man in which there is *tawassul*[16] by him ﷺ. That was after the death of the Prophet ﷺ. From this the life of the Prophet ﷺ after death is known, because our master ʿUmar and other Companions told us that they used to do *tawassul* by the Prophet in his lifetime, and their *tawassul* by him after his death is proof of his life with his Lord ﷺ.

God also made the sending of blessings and peace upon His Prophet obligatory in his life and after his death ﷺ. The scholars have agreed that it is obligatory to send peace and blessings on him

15. Narrated by al-Tirmidhī in his *Sunan*, vol. 2, p. 629.
16. Making the Prophet a means of the acceptance of a request.

at least once in one's life. Al-Ṭaḥāwī said that sending peace and blessings upon him is obligatory every time he is mentioned, and this was accepted by al-Ḥalīmī among the Sḥāfiʿīs because of the saying of the Prophet ﷺ, "May the nose of the man who does not send blessings upon me if I am mentioned in his presence be covered in dirt." Narrated by al-Tirmidhī and al-Ḥākim, from Abū Hurayra.[17]

17. "May his nose be covered in dirt" is an ancient Arab expression, based on the understanding that the nose is a symbol of one's pride. This is *ḥadīth* 31 in this book.

Ḥadīth 13

The Two Graves

عَنْ سَعِيدٍ المَقْبُرِيِّ ، عَنْ أَبِيهِ ، أَنَّهُ سَمِعَ أَبَا سَعِيدٍ الخُدْرِيَّ رَضِيَ اللهُ عَنْهُ ، أَنَّ رَسُولَ اللهِ صَلَّى اللهُ عَلَيْهِ وَسَلَّمَ قَالَ : « إِذَا وُضِعَتِ الجَنَازَةُ وَاحْتَمَلَهَا الرِّجَالُ عَلَى أَعْنَاقِهِمْ ، فَإِنْ كَانَتْ صَالِحَةً قَالَتْ : قَدِّمُونِي ، وَإِنْ كَانَتْ غَيْرَ صَالِحَةٍ قَالَتْ : يَا وَيْلَهَا أَيْنَ يَذْهَبُونَ بِهَا ؟ يَسْمَعُ صَوْتَهَا كُلُّ شَيْءٍ إِلَّا الإِنْسَانَ وَلَوْ سَمِعَهُ صَعِقَ »

On the authority of Abū Saʿīd al-Khudrī ﷺ who said, the Messenger of God ﷺ said,

> When the body is laid out and carried on the shoulders of men, if it was righteous it says, "take me forward!" and if it was not righteous it says, "Woe to it! Where are they taking it?" Everything except man hears its voice. If he were to hear it, he would be struck down.

This *ḥadīth* was narrated by al-Bukhārī in, "Section on men rather than women carrying the *jināza*."[1]

·❁·❁·❁·

The word "*jināza*" is sometimes used for the dead person, and sometimes for the bier. For example, they say "the washing of the *jināza*," and the "burying of the *jināza*," meaning the dead person.

---

1. *Ṣaḥīḥ al-Bukhārī*, vol. 1, p. 246.

An example of the usage of the word "*jināza*" for the bier is the saying of the poet,

The biers frighten us as they go
then we go back to play as they come back
Like the fright of the sheep from a wolf's assault
and when he leaves, they return to their grazing

What is meant by the word in this verse of poetry is the bier on which the dead is carried. Ibn Ḥajar deduced that "*jināza*" in this *ḥadīth* either means the dead person himself or the bier. He said, "It is possible that he ﷺ meant by the *jināza* the dead person himself, and by laying him out, putting him on the bier. It is also possible that he meant the bier."

The "world of the unseen" is the one that we cannot know with our five senses. Al-Qurṭubī said in the beginning of his commentary on the verse, *Those who believe in the unseen* (2:3), The "unseen" is what is absent to us. The poet said,

In the unseen we believe, but before Muḥammad
our people prayed to the idols.

The soul is from the world of the unseen, and that is why it cannot be known or perceived by the five senses. Two things can be done by a dead person after his soul leaves: his speech on the bier while he is being carried on men's shoulders, and his reply when he is questioned in the grave; both are from the unseen.

There are different opinions concerning the speech while he is carried atop shoulders. The strongest in my view is what was said by al-Ḥasan b. Baṭṭāl al-Mālikī in his commentary on *Ṣaḥīḥ al-Bukhārī,* and which was also said by Ibn Ḥajar: that this speech is by the soul only and that it is therefore from the world of the unseen. The soul cannot be seen, nor its speech heard, except in sleep; but not in a waking state.

As for the dead person's reply to the questioning in the grave, it has been reported that it is by the soul and the body, but in the way of the world of the unseen, so that it cannot be seen or heard. This means that if a person dug up the grave, or if we left the dead with his grave open, and the angels came to him and questioned him, we would not see or hear anything. Even if a person stayed inside the grave with the dead, and the angels came to him and questioned him, the living would not hear or see anything, because the world of the unseen cannot be seen.

It is reported in the *ḥadīth* that "the grave is either a garden from the gardens of paradise or a pit from the pits of the fire."[2] This saying needs an explanation, for we believe in it, but if we dug up the grave and opened it on the dead, we would not see a paradise or a fire.

Know that the grave is two graves: a grave for the body, and that is the one we bury it in, and a grave that is created by the angels. If the dead person is of the people of paradise, the angels make his grave a garden from the gardens of paradise, but if he is of the people of the fire, they make his grave a pit from the pits of the fire. This is from the world of the unseen and cannot be perceived. He ﷻ said, *From it We created you, and into it We shall return you, and from it We shall take you out again* (20:55). This refers to the bodies, not the souls, for the souls are not of the Earth, and are not buried in it, and do not come out of it.

My master Aḥmad Zarrūq al-Maghribī l-Mālikī said, "We believe in the world of the unseen and do not tire ourselves in trying to imagine it with our minds, for they cannot know it," or words to this effect.

Everything that is done by the dead after the exiting of their souls, if it appears to us, is a breaking of the norms. It was narrated that one of the [students of the Prophet's] Companions swore never to laugh until he knew that he was one of the people of paradise. When he died he remained smiling while on the washing bed until they finished washing him.[3]

---

2. Narrated by al-Tirmidhī in his *Sunan*, vol. 2, p. 629.
3. The author said that it was a Companion of the Prophet, but I was only able to find such a story for Rabʿī b. Ḥarrāsh, a student of the Companions of the Prophet. His story is narrated by Ibn Abī l-Dunyā, al-Ṭabarānī in *al-Awsaṭ*, Ibn Abī Ḥātim in *al-Jarḥ*, al-Bayhaqī in *Dalāʾil al-nubuwwa*, and Abū Nuʿaym in his *Dalāʾil al-nubuwwa* and his *Ḥilya*. See Ibn Abī l-Dunyā, *Man ʿāsha baʿd al-mawt*, pp. 20–21.

If the dead person knew that he was of the people of paradise he would say to the people carrying his bier, "Take me forward! Take me forward!" because he is happy and pleased. If, however, it is other than that, he would say, "O my punishment!" Because he knows that he is of the people of punishment, so he does not want to go to his grave, because he knows of the punishment that awaits him there.

A beneficial point: know that the dead will be in bliss even before he is taken out of his house, because of the beautiful address of the angels, as God ﷻ said, *Those whom the angels cause to die in a good state, saying, "Peace be on you. Enter the garden for what you did"* (16:32). He ﷻ also said, *the angels descend upon them, saying, "Fear not, nor be grieved, and receive good news of the garden which you were promised"* (41:30). This speech is a type of bliss, because the dead will rejoice at it greatly. As for him who is from the people of the fire, he will feel grief for the saying of the angels to those like him, *Give up your souls! Today you will be repaid with a humiliating punishment* (6:93). God ﷻ says, *If only you were to see the angels as they take the souls of the disbelievers, striking their faces and backs, saying, "Taste the punishment of the fire!"* (8:50). The disbeliever, then, tastes the punishment of the fire before he is taken out of his house.

Al-Bukhārī ﵀ narrated that the Prophet ﷺ said, "The believer will have his place in paradise revealed to him, and so he will love to meet God ﷻ, and God will love to meet him."

Perhaps it is these things that make the believer say, "take me forward!" and make the disbeliever say, "O my punishment!" because the unseen is only known to God ﷻ. Thus we know that the dead person realizes, from the time before leaving his house, whether he is of the people of paradise or the people of the fire.

The Messenger of God ﷺ said, "Everything except man hears its voice. If he were to hear it, he would be struck down." Struck down means that he would faint or that he would die from the terribleness of what he hears. We ask God ﷻ to make us of those who say, "Take me forward! Take me forward!" Amen.

Ḥadīth 14

The Destined Abode

عَنْ عَبْدِ اللهِ بْنِ عُمَرَ رَضِيَ اللهُ عَنْهُمَا ، أَنَّ رَسُولَ اللهِ صَلَّى اللهُ عَلَيْهِ وَسَلَّمَ قَالَ : « إِنَّ أَحَدَكُمْ إِذَا مَاتَ عُرِضَ عَلَيْهِ مَقْعَدُهُ بِالْغَدَاةِ وَالْعَشِيِّ ، إِنْ كَانَ مِنْ أَهْلِ الجَنَّةِ فَمِنْ أَهْلِ الجَنَّةِ ، وَإِنْ كَانَ مِنْ أَهْلِ النَّارِ فَمِنْ أَهْلِ النَّارِ ، فَيُقَالُ هَذَا مَقْعَدُكَ حَتَّى يَبْعَثَكَ اللهُ يَوْمَ الْقِيَامَةِ »

On the authority of Ibn ʿUmar ﵄ who said: the Messenger of God ﷺ said,

> When one of you dies, he is shown his destined place morning and evening. If he is one of the people of the garden, it is among the people of the garden. If he is one of the people of the fire, it is among the people of the fire. He is told, "This is your place until God raises you up on the Day of Rising."

Agreed upon.[1]

·❁·❁·❁·

In this *ḥadīth* is proof that the dead man has a strong level of perception and realization, even in his grave, and that the believer sees his place in paradise, and the disbeliever sees his place in the fire.[2]

---

1. al-Bukhārī in his *Ṣaḥīḥ*, vol. 1, p. 258, and Mālik, Muslim, and others.
2. The Qurʾān likewise speaks of the souls of the people of Pharaoh being shown their final destination while still in the intermediary realm

This *ḥadīth* supports the *ḥadīth* that the actions of the Muslims will be presented to the Prophet ﷺ. The *ḥadīth* was narrated by al-Bazzār with a chain whose narrators are all from the men of the authentic collections, on the authority of Ibn Masʿūd ؓ who said, the Messenger of God ﷺ said,

> "My life is good for you as you will relate about me and it will be related to you. When I die, my death will be good for you too, as your actions will be presented to me. If I see goodness I will praise God, and if I see what is bad I will seek God's forgiveness for you."[3] This is a *ḥadīth* with a complete chain back to the Prophet, and it has another chain that stops at Bakr b. ʿAbdallāh al-Muzanī, and others.[4]

As for the presentation of the actions to relatives, it was narrated by Imam Aḥmad, al-Ḥakīm al-Tirmidhī in *Nawādir al-usūl*, as well as Ibn Mandah, that the Messenger of God ﷺ said, "Your actions

---

before the coming of the Hour: *They will be brought before the fire morning and evening, and on the Day the Hour comes it will be said: "Throw Pharoah's people into the worst torment"* (40:46).

3. It is narrated in al-Bazzār's *Musnad*. Al-Haythamī said, "All the men in its chain are those whose narrations are in the most authentic collections." See al-Haythamī's *Kashf al-astār* (vol. 1, p. 397), which is a collection of the unique narrations from al-Bazzār's *Musnad* that are not found in the six major collections. It seems, however, that in some editions of al-Bazzār's *Musnad* itself, the wording is "You will relate about me and I will relate to you."
4. It is narrated by Ibn Saʿd in *Kitāb al-ṭabaqāt al-kabīr*, vol. 2, p. 174. This *ḥadīth* is classified as *mursal*, which means that al-Muzanī did not name the Companion—or Companions—of the Prophet who taught it to him. Traditionists accept the *mursal aḥādīth* of some early followers of the Companions and reject others. Many of the earliest scholars of Islam considered *mursal aḥādīth* to be even more authentic than the others, based on the fact that certain scholars would only say "The Prophet said . . ." without mentioning the Companion who narrated it because it was narrated by many Companions and they are absolutely sure of its authenticity. Imams Mālik and Abū Ḥanīfa and according to one narration, Aḥmad b. Ḥanbal, accepted *mursal aḥādīth* as proofs. This particular *mursal ḥadīth* from al-Muzanī is considered authentic (*mursal ṣaḥīḥ*) by the traditionists.

are presented to your dead relatives and clans. If they see goodness they will rejoice at it, and if it is other than that they will say, 'O God do not let them die until you guide them as you guided us!'" In a narration by al-Ṭayālisī, "If it was other than that they would say, 'O God inspire them to work in obedience to you!'" Al-Ḥakīm al-Tirmidhī also narrated in his *Nawādir* from the *ḥadīth* of ʿAbd al-Ghafūr b. Abd al-ʿAzīz, from his father, from his grandfather who said, the Messenger of God ﷺ said, "Actions are presented to God on Mondays and Thursdays, and presented to the prophets, fathers, and mothers on Fridays. They will rejoice at their good works and their faces will increase in whiteness and brightness. So fear God and do not hurt your dead."

As for the presentation of the actions to non-relatives, Ibn al-Mubārak and Ibn Abī l-Dunyā narrated from the Companion Abū Ayyūb that [the Prophet] ﷺ said, "Your actions are presented to the dead, so if they see goodness they will rejoice, and if they see what is bad they will say, 'O God, let them repent from this and replace their bad actions with good ones.'"[5]

5. Narrated by Ibn al-Mubārak in *al-Zuhd*, and Ibn Abī l-Dunyā in *al-Manāmāt* (See *al-Manāmāt*, pp. 20–21).

Ḥadīth 15

Visiting Graves

أخبرنا عبد الرزاق عَنْ مَعْمَرٍ ، قَالَ : أَخْبَرَنَا عَطَاءٌ الخُرَاسَانِيُّ ، قَالَ : حَدَّثَنِي عَبْدُ اللهِ بْنُ بُرَيْدَةَ ، عَنْ أَبِيهِ ، قَالَ : قَالَ رَسُولُ اللهِ صَلَّى اللهُ عَلَيْهِ وَسَلَّمَ : « إِنِّي كُنْتُ نَهَيْتُكُمْ عَنْ زِيَارَةِ الْقُبُورِ ، فَزُورُوهَا ، فَإِنَّهَا تُذَكِّرُ الآخِرَةَ »

On the authority of ʿAbd al-Razzāq, on the authority of Maʿmar who said, we were told by ʿAṭāʾ al-Khurasānī, who said, I was told by ʿAbdallāh b. Burayda from his father, who said, the Messenger of God ﷺ said, "I had previously forbidden you from visiting graves, but do visit them for they remind of the next life!"[1]

·❁·❁·❁·

This is the *ḥadīth* that abrogates all that was said before it in forbidding the visiting of graves for men and women. The saying of the Prophet ﷺ "visit them" is a command from him to visit the graves of all Muslims, men and women, whether they were near or

1. This narration is in ʿAbd al-Razzāq al-Ṣanʿānī's *Muṣannaf*, vol. 3, pp. 569–570. Muslim narrated the first portion of it, "I had previously forbidden you from visiting graves, but do visit them," through the same chain in his *Ṣaḥīḥ*, p. 383. The editors of the Arabic added the following footnote: Aḥmad b. Ḥanbal narrated on the authority of Abū Saʿīd al-Khudrī, who said, the Messenger of God ﷺ said, "I had previously forbidden you from visiting graves but do visit them, for in them is a lesson."

far. This command from him 🌺 is to establish it as a recommended practice (*sunna*).[2] The Muslims are in agreement that this *ḥadīth* establishes the visiting of graves as a *sunna* for both men and women.

On the authority of Zayd b. Thābit 🌺 who said, the Messenger of God 🌺 said, "Visit the graves but do not say reprehensible things." It was narrated by al-Ṭabarānī in *al-Ṣaghīr*.[3] The narration of Abū Saʿīd al-Khudrī adds, "... but do not say that which angers the Lord." It was narrated by al-Bazzār.[4]

---

2. The Sunna (with a capital 's') is the lofty and noble way or practice of the Prophet and is sometimes used to refer to the corpus of prophetic *aḥādīth*. Some of the commands or practices of the Prophet are obligatory upon all Muslims, and are known as *farḍ*. The commands or practices of the Prophet that are recommended but are not obligatory are called *sunna* (with a lowercase 's'). They both carry rewards but the obligatory practices usually carry more reward than the non-obligatory ones.

3. Al-Suyūṭī attributed it to Ibn Māja in *al-Jāmiʿ al-ṣaghīr* (see al-Nabahānī, *al-Fatḥ al-kabīr*, vol. 2, p. 144). It was also narrated by Abū Yaʿlā and others in this wording, and in similar wording by al-Nasāʾī.

4. al-Haythamī, *Kashf al-astār*, vol. 1, p. 407.

Ḥadīth 16

Greeting the Dead

أخبرنا عبد الرزاق قَالَ : أَخْبَرَنَا ابْنُ جُرَيْجٍ ، قَالَ : أَخْبَرَنَا ابْنُ أَبِي مُلَيْكَةَ ، أَنّ النَّبِيَّ صَلَّى اللهُ عَلَيْهِ وَسَلَّمَ قَالَ : « ائْتُوا مَوْتَاكُمْ فَسَلِّمُوا عَلَيْهِمْ ، وَصَلُّوا عَلَيْهِمْ فَإِنَّ لَكُمْ فِيهِمْ عِبْرَةً »

On the authority of ʿAbd al-Razzāq, who said, we were told by Ibn Jurayj, who said we were told by Ibn Abī Mulayka that the Prophet ﷺ said, "Go to your dead, greet them, and make supplications for them, for in them is a lesson for you."[1]

In this *ḥadīth* there is a command to visit the graves, which supports and strengthens the first *ḥadīth* that commanded their visitation. The first one told of benefits enjoyed by the living when they visit the dead, it reminds of the next life and brings tears to the eyes.[2] One narration adds, "for they help detach you from the world."[3]

1. ʿAbd al-Razzāq al-Ṣanʿānī, *al-Muṣannaf*, vol. 3, p. 570. See the similar narration by Aḥmad quoted in the footnote to *ḥadīth* 15.
2. The author is referring to the narration by Aḥmad on the authority of Anas, "I had previously forbidden you from visiting graves, but then it appeared to me that it softens the heart, brings tears to the eyes, and reminds one of the hereafter. So visit them, but do not say reprehensible things!"
3. Ibn Māja narrated on the authority of Ibn Masʿūd, "I had previously forbidden you from visiting graves, but do visit them for they help

In this *ḥadīth* he ﷺ showed that in visiting the graves is a lesson, warning, and reminder for the living.

He ﷺ commanded that we greet them (i.e., those who are buried in the graves), because they can hear the greeting and reply to those who greet them. He ﷺ also commanded us to pray for them, because the dead benefit from the prayers of the living made for their sake. This has been established by the great Qurʾān. God ﷻ said, *Those who came after them say, "Our Lord, forgive us our sins, and the sins of our brothers who believed before us"* (59:10). Likewise, there are many *aḥādīth* in the Sunna, including this one.[4] The meaning of "and make supplications for them" (*ṣallū ʿalayhim*) is to pray for them.

It is also narrated in Ibn Māja's *Sunan* on the authority of ʿĀʾisha ﷺ that the Messenger of God ﷺ permitted the visiting of graves.[5]

detach you from the world and remind you of the next life" (*Sunan Ibn Māja*, p. 228).

4. The word Sunna here refers to the corpus of prophetic *aḥādīth*.
5. *Sunan Ibn Māja*, p. 228.

Ḥadīth 17

Reciting Yā Sīn for the Dead

عَنْ مَعْقِلِ بْنِ يَسَارٍ ، أَنَّ رَسُولَ اللهِ صَلَّى اللهُ عَلَيْهِ وَسَلَّمَ ، قَالَ :

« اقْرَءُوا عَلَى مَوْتَاكُمْ يس »

On the authority of Maʿqil b. Yasār ﷺ, the Messenger of God ﷺ said,

Recite Yā Sīn over your dead.

[Narrated by Abū Dāwūd, al-Nasāʾī in *al-Sunan al-kubrā*, and Ibn Ḥibbān in his *Ṣaḥīḥ*.][1]

·❁·❁·❁·

The Prophet ﷺ also said, "Yā Sīn is for whatever it is recited for, so recite it over your dead."[2]

This is a clear text and *ḥadīth* that commands the recitation of Yā Sīn, which is a chapter of the Qurʾān, over the dead. If it is permissible to recite Yā Sīn then, by way of analogy, it is permissible to recite other chapters.

---

1. The narration of Abū Dawūd in his *Sunan* is in the section on "Recitation beside the dead," p. 543. Al-Nasāʾī also narrated it thus, "Yā Sīn is the heart of the Qurʾān . . . read it over your dead." Similarly, Ibn Māja narrated, "Read it beside your dead," and explained: "Meaning Yā Sīn" (*Sunan Ibn Māja*, p. 212).
2. The intended meaning is that the recitation of this chapter of the Qurʾān will help fulfill the intention, need, or supplication of the reciter. On this tradition see Mulla ʿAlī l-Qārī's *al-Asrār al-marfūʿa*, p. 394.

This opinion was chosen by Shaykh al-Shawkānī in his book *Nayl al-awṭār*. He refuted the opinion of Shaykh Muḥibb al-Dīn al-Ṭabarī ☙, who said that it refers to those who are dying. He said that the *ḥadīth* says, "on your dead," and the dead are different from the dying, so why did he divert its meaning from the real to the metaphorical without there being any accompanying evidence for that?

I am most pleased with the saying of al-Shawkānī because it is the reality and what is known from the *ḥadīth*, and what the people of the earlier and the later generations have acted upon. May God guide me and guide you to following the clear and authentic Sunna, out of love of the Messenger of God ☙.[3]

---

3. Al-Shawkānī states in *Nayl al-awṭār* that it was Ibn Ḥibbān in his *Ṣaḥīḥ* who, after narrating this *ḥadīth*, said that it meant those who are dying and not those who were already dead. Al-Shawkānī stated that Muḥibb al-Dīn al-Ṭabarī agreed with Ibn Ḥibbān's opinion in one of his works and refuted the same opinion in another of his works. Al-Shawkānī then proceeded to refute the opinion of Ibn Ḥibbān in the manner explained by the author (*Nayl al-awṭār*, vol. 4, p. 29).

Ḥadīth 18

Charity for the Dead

عَنْ ابْنِ عَبَّاسٍ أَنَّ رَجُلًا قَالَ : يَا رَسُولَ اللهِ ، إِنَّ أُمِّي تُوُفِّيَتْ أَفَيَنْفَعُهَا إِنْ تَصَدَّقْتُ عَنْهَا ؟ قَالَ : « نَعَمْ » قَالَ : فَإِنَّ لِي مَخْرَفًا فَأُشْهِدُكَ أَنِّي قَدْ تَصَدَّقْتُ بِهِ عَنْهَا

On the authority of Ibn ʿAbbās ﵄, who said,

> A man said, "O Messenger of God, my mother died, so will it benefit her if I give in charity on her behalf?" He (the Prophet) said, "Yes." He (the man) said, "Then I have an orchard, and I make you my witness that I have given it in charity on her behalf!"

Narrated by Abū ʿĪsā l-Tirmidhī in his *Sunan*.[1]

·❁·❁·❁·

The great *ḥadīth* master al-Suyūṭī ﵀ said,

> They have differed on the arrival of the reward of reciting the Qurʾān for the dead. The majority of the scholars of the earliest generations and three of the four imams believe in its arrival, and our Imam al-Shāfiʿī and some scholars went against that because of His saying ﷻ, *For man is only what he strives for* (53:39).
>
> (The first group) found the following evidence for its arrival:

1. *Sunan al-Tirmidhī*, vol. 1, p. 189. Also narrated by Abū Dāwūd, al-Nasāʾī, and Aḥmad, and in a different wording by al-Bukhārī.

An analogy can be made with supplications, charity, fasting, pilgrimage, and the freeing of slaves.[2] This is because there is no difference in the moving of the reward from one person to another, be it the reward of pilgrimage, charity, an endowment, a supplication, or the recitation of the Qurʾān.

The narration of Abū Muḥammad al-Samarqandī on the virtues of [Sūrat al-Ikhlās],[3] on the authority of ʿAlī, that the Prophet ﷺ said, "He who passes by the cemetery and recites [Sūrat al-Ikhlās] eleven times then gives its reward to the dead as a gift, will be given of reward as much as the number of the dead."

The narration of Abū l-Qāsim Saʿd b. ʿAlī l-Zanjānī in his *Fawāʾid* on the authority of Abū Hurayra (may God be pleased with him) who said, the Messenger of God ﷺ said, "He who enters the cemetery then recites the Opening of the Book, [Sūrat al-Ikhlās] and [Sūrat al-Takāthur][4] then says, 'I give the reward of what I recited of Your speech to the people of the cemetery of the believing men and women,' they will be his intercessors to God (Exalted is He)."[5]

What was narrated by al-Khallāl's companion [Abū Bakr ʿAbd al-ʿAzīz] with his chain to Anas, that the Messenger of God ﷺ said, "When someone enters the cemetery and recites Sūrat Yā Sīn, God will make things easier for them [i.e., the dead], and he will receive as many good deeds as the people in it."[6]

Even though these *aḥādīth* are weak, together they show that there is an origin for it. The fact is that the Muslims have always, even until now, in every land and every age, come together and recited the Qurʾān for their dead without anyone's disapproval. This constitutes a consensus on the matter.

---

2. The arrival of the reward of each of these for the dead has been well established by the Qurʾān or Sunna.
3. Chapter 112 of the Qurʾān.
4. Chapter 102 of the Qurʾān.
5. Chapters 1, 112, and 102 of the Qurʾān.
6. Abū Bakr ʿAbd al-ʿAzīz b. Jaʿfar (d. 363 AH), a well known Ḥanbalī jurist who was known as "al-Khallāl's companion" because he was the student of the famed Ḥanbalī jurist and traditionist Aḥmad b. Muḥammad al-Khallāl (d. 311 AH).

Al-Mubārakfūrī said in his commentary on al-Tirmidhī's *Sunan*,

> All of the above was mentioned by the great *ḥadīth* master Shams al-Dīn b. ʿAbd al-Wāḥid al-Maqdisī l-Ḥanbalī in a volume he authored on the matter.

Al-Shawkānī ﷺ said in *Nayl al-awṭār*,

> The truth is that the general application of, *For man is only what he strives for,* becomes limited by the following exceptions: charity by the offspring, pilgrimage by the offspring and others, and the freeing of slaves by the offspring, because all of this is in the *ḥadīth*. It also becomes limited by the following exceptions:
>
> The prayer that is performed by the offspring, because of what al-Daraquṭnī narrated, that "A man said, 'O Messenger of God, I had parents to whom I would do acts of goodness in their lives, so how do I act with goodness toward them after their death?' He ﷺ said, 'One of the types of good acts toward them is to perform the prayer for them, along with your prayer, and to fast for them, along with your own fasting.'"
>
> Fasting performed by the offspring as mentioned in the previous *ḥadīth* and also the *ḥadīth* of Ibn ʿAbbās that was narrated by al-Bukhārī and Muslim that "a woman said, 'O Messenger of God, my mother died with an unfulfilled vow to fast.' He ﷺ said, 'If your mother had a debt and you repaid it for her, would that settle it for her?' She said, 'Yes.' He said, 'Then fast.'"
>
> Fasting performed by someone other than the offspring, because of the *ḥadīth* of ʿĀʾisha ﷺ that the Messenger of God ﷺ said, "If anyone dies owing some fasting, his guardian should fast on his behalf."[7]
>
> The recitation of Yā Sīn by the offspring or others, because of the *ḥadīth*, "Read Yā Sīn over your dead."[8]
>
> A supplication from an offspring or others, because of the *ḥadīth*, "Or a righteous son who prays for him,"[9] and, "ask

---

7. *Ṣaḥīḥ al-Bukhārī*, vol. 1, p. 365.
8. This is *ḥadīth* 17 of this book.
9. This is *ḥadīth* 19 of this book.

forgiveness for your brother and ask for him to be given a firm footing,"[10] and other *aḥādīth.*

Every good action that the son does for his parents is in fact accepted for them because of the *ḥadīth*, "The person's son is part of what he strived for."

It has been said that an analogy could be based on all these things that are in the textual evidences, and so the dead person receives the reward of everything that someone else did (for him).

This is a summary of what al-Shawkānī said in *Nayl al-awṭār*, taken from the commentary of al-Mubārakfūrī on al-Tirmidhī's *Sunan.*

Translator's Note

The two quotes above, by al-Suyūṭī and al-Shawkānī, are taken from al-Mubārakfūrī's commentary on al-Tirmidhī's *Sunan*. In that same work al-Suyūṭī's passage is longer, and gives the interpretations of some of the earliest scholars of Islam on the verse, *For man is only what he strives for.* He quoted a certain al-Ḥusayn b. Faḍl's opinion that men only receive what they worked for by way of God's justice, but can receive more than that by way of God's favor and grace, who gives more to His servants as He wills. Others, he said, maintained that the letter *lām* in "*li-l-insān*" does not mean "for" but "on/against" (ᶜ*alā*), and so man can get rewards from the works of others for him, but cannot be punished for their bad acts. Al-Suyūṭī also quoted a great scholar from among the students of the Prophet's Companions, al-Rabīᶜ b. Anas, who said that what is meant by "man" here is the disbeliever. The believer, said al-Rabīᶜ, will have what he strived for, and what others did for him. He also quoted ᶜIkrima the servant of Ibn ᶜAbbās, one of the four greatest scholars of his generation, who said that this verse only applies to the people of Abraham and Moses, but not for the community of Muḥammad, for the latter have what they work for

10. Narrated by Abū Dāwūd in the *Sunan*, vol. 2, p. 558, al-Ḥākim in *al-Mustadrak*, al-Bazzār in his *Musnad*, and al-Bayhaqī in al-*Sunan al-kubrā.*

and what is done for them. This is because the verse is preceded by, *Has he not been told what was written in the scriptures of Moses and Abraham* (53:36).[11]

11. al-Mubārakfūrī, *Tuḥfat al-aḥwadhī*, vol. 3, p. 340.

Ḥadīth 19

Reaping Rewards after Death

عَنْ أَبِي هُرَيْرَةَ أَنَّ رَسُولَ اللهِ صَلَّى اللهُ عَلَيْهِ وَسَلَّمَ قَالَ : « إِذَا مَاتَ الْإِنْسَانُ انْقَطَعَ عَنْهُ عَمَلُهُ إِلَّا مِنْ ثَلَاثَةٍ ، إِلَّا مِنْ صَدَقَةٍ جَارِيَةٍ ، أَوْ عِلْمٍ يُنْتَفَعُ بِهِ ، أَوْ وَلَدٍ صَالِحٍ يَدْعُو لَهُ »

On the authority of Abū Hurayra (رضي الله عنه), the Prophet ﷺ said,

> When a person dies his works are cut off from him except for three: a continuing charity, knowledge that benefits, or a righteous son who prays for him.

Narrated by al-Bukhārī [in *al-Adab al-mufrad*] and Muslim.[1]

This means that when the son of Adam dies, his own works for himself and for others are cut off because of death, and if he is still alive, his works for himself and for others are not cut off, because of life.

In this is evidence that the dead benefit from the works of the living, because its literal meaning is that if the son of Adam dies, his works of prayer, pilgrimage, fasting, and charities[2] are cut off because of his death. Its implied meaning, therefore, is that the works of the living for the dead are not cut off, because the living can still do works.[3]

1. *Ṣaḥīḥ Muslim*, vol. 2, p. 700.
2. I.e., charities that do not continue after his death.
3. Here the author wants to say that there has been a great and widespread

The first work (of others) that the dead benefit from is the funeral prayer, for the Prophet ﷺ prayed over those who died. Al-Bukhārī has in his *Ṣaḥīḥ*, a section entitled "On reciting the Opening of the Book in the funeral prayer over the dead." Imam al-Shāfiʿī ؓ acted upon this *ḥadīth* and so the followers of the Shāfiʿī school read the "Fātiḥa" [Opening of the book] after the first *takbīr* ("Allāhu akbar") of the funeral prayer. The funeral prayer is like sustenance for the traveler. If the dead benefit from the recitation of the "Fātiḥa," which is the "Mother of the Book," then they will, *a fortiori*, benefit from the rest of the Qurʾān's chapters.

Some people say that Qurʾān [recitation] does not reach the dead. God ﷻ inspired me [to understand] that this sentence means two things:

First, it means that the Qurʾān does not reach the dead as chapters and verses. Instead, it ascends into the sky. He ﷻ said, *To Him the good words ascend* (35:10), and the Prophet ﷺ said, "When the Qurʾān is recited, the doors of heaven are opened." This was narrated by the *ḥadīth* master al-Suyūṭī ؓ.[4]

---

misunderstanding of this *ḥadīth*, as many interpreted it to mean that a man cannot acquire good deeds after his death except from these three sources. The author aims to show that this *ḥadīth* only refers to one's works for himself, as it says "*his* works." When a person dies, he cannot perform any more works for his own benefit, but there are three possible ways for someone's own works in his lifetime to continue benefiting him after his death. These works are a charity that keeps giving to others, knowledge that continues to benefit others, and the raising of a good son who will pray for him. This *ḥadīth* is describing one's son as his own work since it was his upbringing of the son that made him a good son who prays for his parent. This is like the *ḥadīth* that was quoted in the commentary on *ḥadīth* 18 of this book: "The person's son is part of what he strived for." Here the author emphasizes that this *ḥadīth* does not discuss the works that others do for a person, and that it does not deny the possibility that the dead can benefit from what others did for them; it only talks about a person's own works for himself.

4. I found the following narration by al-Ṭabarānī in *Kitāb al-duʿāʾ*, vol. 3, p. 1024, *al-Muʿjam al-awsaṭ*, and *al-Ṣaghīr*: "The doors of the heavens are opened for five things: the recitation of the Qurʾān, marching to

Second, it means that it is the reward of the recitation that reaches the dead in the form of great and many good deeds. He ﷺ said, "He who reads the Qur'ān receives for each letter ten good deeds. I do not say *Alif Lām Mīm* is a letter, but *Alif* is a letter, *Lām* is a letter, and *Mīm* is a letter."[5] This means that he who reads *"Alif Lām Mīm"* has thirty good deeds, and they can reach the dead if the reader gifts their reward to him.

The scholars of the earlier generations as well as those who came after them agree that the rewards of charities reach the dead; this is clear and obvious because the charity itself does not reach the dead, but reaches the poor person who benefits from it, and the good deed is rewarded tenfold. For example, if you give a poor man a loaf of bread in charity on behalf of a dead man, then one loaf of bread will reach the poor man, and the dead will receive the reward of that act multiplied by ten or even up to seven hundred times, according to God's multiplication. He ﷻ said, *God multiplies for whom He wills* (2:261).

I heard our shaykh al-Shinqīṭī ﵀ say, "the reward of the recitation of the Qur'ān reaches the dead if the reader gives it to him as a gift by saying before the recitation, 'O God, let the reward of what I will read reach so-and-so.' Before the recitation is better, but it is possible after it."

From this we know that the dead person benefits from the works of the living. As for his own works, they have been cut off because of death. As for the works that he caused during his lifetime, like a continuing charity, or the knowledge that he wrote, or the righteous son who succeeds him and prays for him, they are not cut off from him.

---

face an army, rain, the supplication of the oppressed, and the call to prayer."

5. *Sunan al-Tirmidhī*, vol. 2, p. 733.

Ḥadīth 20

Raising the Servant's Degree

عَنْ أَبِي هُرَيْرَةَ رَضِيَ اللهُ عَنْهُ ، أَنَّ رَسُولَ اللهِ صَلَّى اللهُ عَلَيْهِ
وَسَلَّمَ قَالَ : « إِنَّ اللهَ عَزَّ وَجَلَّ لَيَرْفَعُ لِلْعَبْدِ الدَّرَجَةَ ، فَيَقُولُ : أَيْ
رَبِّ أَنَّى لِي هَذِهِ الدَّرَجَةُ ؟ فَيَقُولُ : بِدُعَاءِ وَلَدِكَ لَكَ »

On the authority of Abū Hurayra ؓ, the Messenger of God ﷺ said,

> God ﷻ will raise the servant's degree [in paradise], so he will say, "O Lord, how did I attain this degree?" He will say, "By your son's supplication for you."

[Narrated by al-Ṭabarānī in *Kitāb al-duʿāʾ*, al-Bazzār in his *Musnad,* and al-Bayhaqī in *al-Sunan al-kubrā*].[1]

The *Muwaṭṭaʾ* (of Mālik) says, "Yaḥyā narrated to me on the authority of Mālik, on the authority of Yaḥyā b. Saʿd, that Saʿīd b. al-Musayyab used to say, 'Men will be raised by the supplication of their sons after them (i.e., after their death).'"[2]

The *ḥadīth* scholar Ibn ʿAbd al-Barr said, "This cannot be known by the mind (and therefore must be based on a prophetic teaching), and has been narrated with a good chain back to the Prophet."

1. Al-Ṭabarānī, *Kitāb al-duʿāʾ*, vol. 3, p. 1386. For al-Bazzār see al-Haythamī's *Kashf al-astār*, vol. 4, pp. 39–40.
2. *Al-Muwaṭṭaʾ*, p. 73. Saʿīd b. al-Musayyab (also pronounced al-Musayyib) is considered to be the greatest scholar of Medina during the generation that followed that of the Prophet's Companions. He died in 94/715.

[Ibn ʿAbd al-Barr] is saying that the statement of the follower [i.e., student of the Prophet's Companions] Saʿīd b. al-Musayyab, which was narrated by Mālik, has also been narrated with a good chain of transmission back to the Prophet ﷺ himself. This was the practice of Ibn ʿAbd al-Barr, to give (other) complete chains for those chains in the *Muwaṭṭaʾ* that had gaps. He narrated through Abū Ṣāliḥ on the authority of Abū Hurayra that the Messenger of God ﷺ said, "The believer will have his degree raised in paradise and say, 'O Lord, how did this happen?' It will be said to him, 'By your son's supplication after you (died).'"[3]

This is specific evidence that the father benefits from the supplication of his son performed in his name. There is also a general evidence for it, which is the saying of God, *Those who came after them say, "Our Lord, forgive us our sins, and the sins of our brothers who believed before us"* (59:10).

In this verse is evidence that the dead benefit from the supplication of the living, whether they are related to them or not.

3. This passage was taken from the version used in the author's other work, which he edited and published in his lifetime, *Fatḥ wa-fayḍ*, p. 238.

Ḥadīth 21

Charity

عَنْ أَبِي هُرَيْرَةَ رَضِيَ اللهُ عَنْهُ ، أَنَّ النَّبِيَّ صَلَّى اللهُ عَلَيْهِ وَسَلَّمَ قَالَ : « مَا مِنْ يَوْمٍ يُصْبِحُ الْعِبَادُ فِيهِ إِلَّا مَلَكَانِ يَنْزِلَانِ فَيَقُولُ أَحَدُهُمَا : اللَّهُمَّ أَعْطِ مُنْفِقًا خَلَفًا ، وَيَقُولُ الآخَرُ : اللَّهُمَّ أَعْطِ مُمْسِكًا تَلَفًا »

On the authority of Abū Hurayra ﵁, the Prophet ﷺ said,

> There is no day which dawns on the servants of God without two angels descending; one of them says, "O God, give the spender a replacement," and the other says, "O God, give the withholder ruin."

It was narrated by al-Bukhārī, Muslim, and al-Nasāʾī. Imam Aḥmad also narrated it on the authority of Abū l-Dardāʾ. It was also narrated by Ibn Ḥibbān in his *Saḥiḥ* and al-Bayhaqī [on the authority of Abū Hurayra], and by al-Ḥākim, who deemed it authentic, [on the authority of Abū Saʿīd al-Khudrī].[1]

Spending is the giving of money in the way of God, and ruin is the loss of money.

The Prophet ﷺ is telling us that every day angels pray for goodness for every charitable giver, and pray against everyone who withholds from spending. So this *ḥadīth* encourages spending and instills an aversion to miserliness.

1. *Ṣaḥīḥ al-Bukhārī*, vol. 1, p. 272. The author composed the names of the narrators of this *ḥadīth* into four lines of poetry.

Al-Qurṭubī ﷺ said, "Spending includes the obligatory and the recommended (types), but he who withholds the recommended (type) does not deserve the supplication of ruin."

Al-Abiyy al-Mālikī, the commentator on the *Ṣaḥīḥ Muslim*, said, quoting al-Qāḍī ʿIyāḍ al-Mālikī ﷺ, "This *ḥadīth* encourages spending, and gives hope for the acceptance of the supplication of the angel. What is meant by spending is spending on the obligatory, because money involves specified rights, and also the recommended, but according to what is customary." Al-Abiyy said, "As for the withholding, it is most likely that he meant the withholding from the obligatory."

Spending is of three types:

1. The obligatory, like the obligatory alms-giving and the cost of pilgrimage. It also includes spending on the wife and children, the parents, on someone in need whom one is legally obligated to spend on, and on saving whoever would die if you did not spend on [them]. It also includes spending to support armed struggle if an enemy enters the country, on learning what is obligatory on the individual to learn if it was only possible by spending, and on the preparation and burial of a dead person in a non-Muslim land by the one who is present. There are also other things that have been made obligatory by the sources of the *sharīʿa*.
2. The recommended, like giving in charity to the poor and needy, in what is other than the obligatory alms-giving.
3. The permissible, like banquets or one's own food and drink, etc.

Since the one who spends on the obligatory is rewarded by the *sharīʿa*, the angel will pray for him, and since by withholding he is blamed by the *sharīʿa*, the angel will pray for ruin against him. Since one is not blamed for leaving the recommended and permissible, the angel does not pray for ruin against him, and since he is rewarded by spending on the recommended, the angel's prayer for replacement applies to him.

It appears to me that everything for which there is a reward is included in the angel's supplication for good, and everything for which there is punishment is included in the angel's supplication for harm. Likewise, everything in which there is no punishment for leaving it, and no reward for doing it, is not included, such as leaving what is recommended, or doing what is permissible.

Beneficial points:

First: God ﷻ, because He loves spending and detests the oppression of the rights of people, made angels descend every day to pray for good for those who spend, and to pray against those who withhold.

Second: God blesses the money of the spender, and gives him an increase of His favor, because the prayer of the angel is answered for goodness for every generous spender and against every miserly withholder.

Third: He who does not spend on what is obligatory for him is not blessed in his earning. Every time such a person thinks he has received an increase, he will in fact be decreased, and every time he thinks he is preserved, he is ruined. This is because the angel's prayer for ruin against him is answered.

Fourth: This *ḥadīth* is in harmony with the saying of God ﷻ, *He will replace whatever you spend, and He is the best of providers* (34:39).

Fifth: This *ḥadīth* shows the great favor of God ﷻ upon His creation, as He refunds the spender in this world, and rewards him on the Day of Rising, each good deed multiplied at least tenfold and up to seven hundred times. The one who spends, therefore, gets two rewards, just like the one who stays up at night in worship—he is rewarded for it in the next life with paradise, and rewarded for it in this life with health in his body, and the removal of affliction.

Sixth: God ﷻ made the hand that spends the upper hand. The Prophet ﷺ said, "The upper hand is better than the lower hand."[2] If one is miserly, his hand becomes even less than the lower hand. The giver's hand is the upper hand, because he is a spender who obeys the command of his Lord, and the receiver's hand is the lower hand, and he is thankful to his Lord for the

---

2. Narrated by al-Bukhārī in his *Ṣaḥīḥ*, vol. 1, p. 270, and also by Muslim and al-Tirmidhī.

blessing, and the miserly one who withholds is neither.

Seventh: The spender has acted according to the manners and characteristics of God ﷻ. The Prophet ﷺ said, "Emulate the qualities of God." The spender has also acted according to the manners and characteristics of the Prophet ﷺ, for he was more generous than the wind that brings rain.

God ﷻ is a generous spender, commanded spending, and loves spending; and the Prophet ﷺ is generous, loves spending and commanded it. So the spender is the beloved of God ﷻ and the beloved of the Messenger of God ﷺ.

Eighth: The withholder has acted according to the manners of Satan because he is miserly and commands to miserliness. God ﷻ said, *He promises you poverty* (2:268), meaning that if you wanted to spend in the way of God he would frighten you with poverty and command you to withhold from spending. The one who withholds from spending is therefore the beloved of Satan, the enemy of the all-Merciful.

You must, O brother in God ﷻ, spend many precious breaths in beholding the Creator, in His remembrance, and in the teaching of wisdom by speaking beneficial words. Know that the more you spend of your knowledge, the more God gives you of it.

Our master ʿAlī (may God be pleased with him and ennoble his countenance) was asked, "Is knowledge better or money?" He said, "Knowledge." They said, "why?" He said, "Because money decreases by spending it, and knowledge increases by it."

Know also that your treasuries are full, for you have ears that hear, eyes that see, hands that grasp, feet that walk, a tongue that speaks, and a mind that thinks.

Spend then of your hearing on the best of speech. He ﷻ said, *Those who listen to what is said and follow the best of it* (39:18). As for your eyes, use them to look at the realms of the skies and the Earth. He ﷻ said, *Did they not look at the sky above them, how We have built it and adorned it, with no rifts in it?* (50:6). And He ﷻ said, *You will not see any flaw in the creation of the All-Merciful. Look again! Do you see any rifts?* (67:3). As for your hands, spend from them in assisting and supporting the weak. As for your your legs, use them to walk to the mosques, especially for the prayers that take place when it is dark. As for your tongue, use it to command what is good and forbid what is evil, and teach the Muslims. And as for your mind, use it to contemplate the creations of God. He ﷻ said, *They reflect on the creation of the heavens and Earth* (3:191).

He who spends goodness from his limbs, God will bring down goodness on him, and the reward of the next life is greater. As for he who spends evil from his limbs, he will find evil in this world, *and the punishment of the next life is greater and more lasting* (20:127).

Know that you will not arrive at what the serious ones achieved until you make all of your limbs sources of pure goodness, and you are constantly aware of God's sight of you, and you teach yourself good manners, and thus you make your soul grow. I do not see anything that will correct you quicker than that.

You must, O brother, listen to what I have said. May God give you success! Soon you will see the wonders of your soul, from you, by you, where there is no veil that veils you, and nothing that preoccupies you. You will witness the Real ﷻ, a witnessing beyond all that could be sensed or imagined—denying and affirming, connected and separated, perishing and abiding.[3] There you will taste the sweetness of faith that the writers and poets described. Among them are those who said,

> I drowned in the ocean of Love . . .

And among them are those who said,

> We drank at the mention of the Beloved . . .

And among them are those who said,

> I witness the reality of Your beauty, and so becomes
> pleasurable to me
> My submission and self-abasement in my love of You!

He who entered the ocean of love and was immersed in it said, "I drowned." His tongue described his state so that he said,

> And let me stand beyond the beyond, without a veil, in the presence of Your name 'the All-Encompassing,' in the station

3. Being in the Sufi states of *fanā'* and *baqā'*.

of audition, so that I am delighted by the pleasure of the divine address.

As for he who drank, he said, "We got drunk"; and he who saw the beauty said, "We found pleasure in witnessing the beauty." They all faced the same direction, but what came to their hearts differed according to the different levels of their preparation.

So prepare your soul by holding on to the Book and the Sunna, so that you are on a firm Muḥammadan footing, present but not present. Al-Ghazālī ﵀ transmitted the saying of our master ʿAlī (may God ennoble his face), "God has men whose bodies are with the people, but their hearts are attached to the inhabitants of the highest spheres."

By doing that I see you, God willing, among those who say,

I have made You in my heart my conversant,
and gave my body to those who want to sit with me.
So my body gives company to him who sits with me,
And my Beloved is in my heart, my only comfort.[4]

And among those who say,

Your beauty is in my eye, your mention in my mouth,
and your love is in my heart—so where could you possibly disappear?

And those who say,

The sun of the day sets at night,
but the sun of the hearts never sets.

And those who say,

Even if I do not set out for the House that is far away[5]
I've set out for the One who never disappears from one's innermost being.
If they return after their pilgrimage then I
shall reside my entire life upon my rituals, never leaving.

---

4. On *uns* see the commentary on *ḥadīth* 6.
5. "Ḥajj" (pilgrimage) literally means "to set out for."

And those who say,

> How amazing it is that I yearn for them,
> and always ask about them, though they are with me!
> My eyes cry over them, though they're in their pupils,
> and my heart longs for them, though they're between my ribs!

You will be always fasting and worshiping at night, in love and enamored, serious and ready, prepared to meet a generous Lord, seizing every opportunity, filling up every space with that which is beneficial, escaping from everything that cuts you off from God, and repeating the lines of al-Bukhārī,

> Avail yourself in leisure of the benefit of a prayer,
> for it may happen that your death will be sudden.
> How many a sound one did I see without ailment,
> whose noble soul departed unexpectedly!

And he who said,

> Prepare for that which is inevitable,
> for death is the appointed time of the servants.
> Do you accept to be the companion of a people,
> who have sustenance for that journey, while you do not?

So die before you die, in order for death to become easier for you, and be alone before you find yourself alone and find that seclusion difficult. Leave your comfort in people out of fear that your separation from them would be too hard for you. Behold your grave before you enter it, lest you dread its desolation. In this much is enough for those who are under the watchful eye of divine care. Someone said in verse,

> If the eyes of care are watching over you,
> then sleep—for you are safe from all that frightens.
> With them catch the Phoenix—for they are your ropes,
> and with them ride the stars—for they are your reigns.

Al-Nawawī ﷺ said, quoting others, "Salvation is (written) from before birth, and divine care (comes) before friendship with God."

I ask God for me and for you, the righteousness of our states, and the reaching of our hopes. Amen.

Ḥadīth 22

The Seeds of Goodness

عَنْ أَنَسِ بْنِ مَالِكٍ رَضِيَ اللهُ عَنْهُ ، قَالَ : قَالَ رَسُولُ اللهِ صَلَّى اللهُ عَلَيْهِ وَسَلَّمَ : « مَا مِنْ مُسْلِمٍ يَغْرِسُ غَرْسًا أَوْ يَزْرَعُ زَرْعًا فَيَأْكُلُ مِنْهُ طَيْرٌ أَوْ إِنْسَانٌ أَوْ بَهِيمَةٌ إِلَّا كَانَ لَهُ بِهِ صَدَقَةٌ »

On the authority of Anas b. Mālik who said, the Messenger of God ﷺ said,

> If any Muslim plants a tree or sows a crop, and then a bird, man, or beast eats from it, he will get for it the reward of a charity.

Narrated by al-Bukhārī.[1]

I say that there is another type of planting and sowing, for the believer plants good offspring that benefit him in this world and the next as in the *ḥadīth*, "Or a righteous son who prays for him."[2]

The believer sows good and righteous works of varying kinds. Their earth is the layers of the hearts, their water is from the sky of the unseen realms, and their sowing is the performance of the obligatory and the abandonment of the forbidden, the acceptance of what is decreed, struggle against the lower self, and thankfulness and patience in times of ease, hardship, and battle. Good tidings,

1. *Ṣaḥīḥ al-Bukhārī*, vol. 1, p. 433. Also narrated by Muslim, Aḥmad, al-Tirmidhī, and others.
2. This is *ḥadīth* 19 in this book.

then, to the land of the hearts upon which the rain of the meanings of the Qurʾān pours down, *so it stirred, and swelled, and produced every kind of joyous growth* (Q 22:5). This results in the self becoming serious about arriving at its glory—it looks at the pleasures of life with suspicion and it escapes from the calamities of the world as it would escape from a monster. It becomes occupied with its Lord after becoming enamored by love of His paradise, and enamored by love of His generosity and honor. The self will bear patiently, along with her body, the decrees of her Lord, until the appointed day comes. On that day she will hear the call, after the greetings and glad tidings, *O soul at peace, return to your Lord well-pleased and well-pleasing* (89:27–28).

Al-Qasṭalānī ﵀ said in his commentary on *Ṣaḥīḥ al-Bukhārī* on the saying of the Prophet ﷺ, "he will get for it the reward of a charity,"

> The use of the word "Muslim" leaves out the disbeliever, which means that the reward in the next life is particular to the Muslim not the disbeliever. This is because the acts that bring one nearer to God are only correct when coming from a Muslim. As for the disbeliever, if he gives a charity or does any kind of goodness, he will not receive a reward for it in the next life.

Yes, the disbeliever will be rewarded in this life for what is eaten from his plants as has been established by evidence. But as for those who say that his punishment in the next life will thus be lessened, this [statement] requires evidence.

Muslim narrated a *ḥadīth* on the authority of ʿĀʾisha ﵂ that says,

> I said, "O Messenger of God, Ibn Jadʿān, in the time before Islam, used to maintain his bonds of kinship and feed the poor. Will that benefit him?" He said, "It will not benefit him, for he never said, 'O my Lord, forgive me my mistakes on the day of accountability.'"[3]

This means that he who does not believe in the resurrection is a disbeliever whose actions will not benefit him. ʿIyāḍ ﵀ transmitted a consensus that the disbelievers will not benefit from their works,

3. *Ṣaḥīḥ Muslim*, vol. 1, p. 111.

nor will they be rewarded for them either with bliss or the lessening of their punishment. Some of them, however, will be punished more than others, depending on their crimes.

As for the *ḥadīth* that Imam Aḥmad narrated from Abū Ayyūb al-Ansārī, "There is no man who plants a tree. . . ." and the *ḥadīth*, "There is no servant. . ." their apparent meaning encompasses both the Muslim and the disbeliever, but general phrases must be understood according to the specific ones (in other sources).

Muslim ﷺ narrated this *ḥadīth* with an addition that I wanted to mention, for the extra benefit. I say with the support of God,

> On the authority of Jābir b. ʿAbdallāh al-Ansārī ﷺ who said, the Messenger of God ﷺ said, "If any Muslim plants a tree then what is eaten from it will be counted as a charity for him, what is stolen from it will be counted as a charity for him, what the beasts eat from it will be counted as a charity for him, what the birds eat from it will be counted as a charity for him, and any loss from it that is caused by anyone will be counted as a charity for him."[4]

Imam al-Nawawī ﷺ said in his commentary on *Ṣaḥīḥ Muslim*,

> These *aḥādīth* show the virtue of planting and the virtue of sowing, and that the reward of the one who does it continues as long as the plants and crops last, and all that comes from them, until the Day of Rising. The scholars have differed on the best of livelihoods. Some said trade, others said a handicraft, and others said planting, and that is the correct one; and its reward in the next life is only for the Muslims.

These *aḥādīth* show many different benefits for the one who plants and sows:

First: If what he owns (of plants and crops) reaches the minimum threshold that makes almsgiving obligatory, he pays its alms-tax, and gets the reward of performing this obligatory duty for it.

Second: He gives from it voluntarily, and is given the reward of the voluntary charity for it. These are two rewards that differ in intention.

---

4. *Ṣaḥīḥ Muslim*, vol. 2, p. 663.

Third: If he gives any dates or seeds to his parents, he is given the reward of having done an obligatory duty and is written as a good son to his parents. If he gives any to relatives, he is written down as someone who maintains the bonds of kinship.

Fourth: If he gives something to his wife and children, he is given the reward of the obligatory for it.

Fifth: If he gives any of it away, he is given the reward of the *hiba* (giving away or transferring to another).

Sixth: If he gives anything as a gift, he is given the reward of the gift, and he would be acting according to the *ḥadīth* of the Prophet ﷺ, "Give gifts to one another and you will love one another."[5]

Seventh: If he loans a person anything, he is given the reward of the loan, eighteen-fold.[6]

On these seven he can make the intention of obtaining the reward.

Eighth: He has the reward of what is eaten by the birds, animals, beasts, and thieves, and what partners in the business or others take from him by force. He is rewarded for these things without the intention.

Ninth, and it is the greatest benefit: The place of his tree will always have a cool shadow, cold water, and dates. The one who planted the tree will then have the reward of every act of sitting in the shade of the tree, eating from its dates, or drinking from its water. It is said that this is from the bliss of this life.

Beneficial point: Shaykh ʿAbd al-Salām said in his commentary on the *Jawharat al-tawḥīd*:

> The difference between the wisdom of an act and its cause, is that the wisdom of it is not the cause of the action. An example of that is the shadow of the tree, for the one who planted the tree did not make the shade a cause for the planting, but it came on its own after the appearance of the tree. As for the cause, it is

---

5. Narrated by Mālik in the *Muwaṭṭaʾ*, p. 357, al-Bukhārī in *al-Adab al-mufrad*, and others.
6. A *ḥadīth* narrated by Ibn Māja and others states that "Charity is multiplied tenfold, while giving a load eighteen-fold." *Sunan Ibn Māja*, p. 352.

the motive behind the action; For example, water is the cause for which a well is dug. He ﷻ said, *I created not the jinn and the humans except to worship Me* (51:56). Meaning, so that they end up worshiping me. This, however, was not the cause for creating them, because the actions of God ﷻ are beyond causes.

You must, O brother in God ﷻ, plant the trees of divine love in the land of your heart, from His saying, *He loves them and they love Him* (5:54). Then water them with the water of striving from His saying, *Strive in (the way of) God as is His due* (22:78), in order for them to bear the fruits of certainty. This certainty is then elevated to the knowledge of certainty, and then even higher to the eye of certainty, and then you will see what those who see cannot see, and hear what those who hear cannot hear, in the presence of, "I am his hearing with which he hears, and his seeing with which he sees, and his tongue with which he speaks."[7]

After that, if any of the fruits and jewels of your speech reach any created being, you will have the reward of charity for it, whether he heard it, read it, or someone else transmitted it to him. That will last for you until the Day of Rising, and your reward will not be cut off while you are in your grave, and by that you enter the field of, "The scholars are the inheritors of the prophets,"[8] for the rewards of the prophets are not cut off after death. You will be dressed in the robe of prophetic inheritance, with which you will be upon the Book and

7. See *ḥadīth* 2 in this book, on the authority of Abū Hurayra, which was narrated by al-Bukhārī. That narration does not have the phrase "his tongue with which he speaks." This phrase is present in the narrations of al-Ṭabarānī in *al-Muʿjam al-kabīr* and al-Bayhaqī in *al-Zuhd al-kabīr* on the authority of the Prophet's Companion Abū Umāma. It is also in the narration of Abū Yaʿlā on the authority of the Prophet's wife Maymūna, and al-Bazzār in his *Musnad*, on the authority of the Prophet's wife ʿĀʾisha. These narrations all have, "I am his heart with which he understands, and his tongue with which he speaks," instead of "his foot with which he walks." A narration by Ibn Abī l-Dunyā in *Kitāb al-awliyāʾ* on the authority of ʿĀʾisha contains all three phrases. For the narration of al-Bazzār see al-Haythamī, *Kashf al-astār*, vol. 4, p. 248.
8. Narrated by Abū Dāwūd, Aḥmad, and al-Tirmidhī in his *Sunan*, vol. 2, p. 683.

the Sunna, completed by a lordly and Muḥammadan completion, separated and connected, engulfed in the beholding of the greatest medium and the greatest curtain (*ḥijāb*)[9] outwardly and inwardly, in waking and in sleep, in all your states and speech. You will be receiving and giving from "the one from whom the secrets burst forth, and the lights sprang forth,"[10] revealing the secrets of the words and phrases, by "the secret that runs through all names and attributes,"[11] where there is no unity or separation, but only love and longing. You will remember him in the presence of the Absolute, as there is no level of divine presence (that you can reach) where the Prophet ﷺ, whose doors never close, is not there. Among [those who enter His presence] are those who were taken by surprise and forgot, but among them are those whose souls were strengthened, so they saw in the presence of God ﷻ, and at the mention of God, the Beloved of God, as they recited His words, *Those who pledge loyalty to you are actually pledging loyalty to God* (48:10). I hope for you to have a great share of this overflowing ocean.

9. Meaning that one cannot reach God except by means of him.
10. From the Ṣalāt al-Mashīshiyya of Ibn Mashīsh.
11. From the Ṣalāt al-Nūr al-Dhātī of Abū l-Ḥasan al-Shādhilī.

Ḥadīth 23

Protection from the Fire

عَنْ عَدِيِّ بْنِ حَاتِمٍ ، أَنَّ النَّبِيَّ صَلَّى اللهُ عَلَيْهِ وَسَلَّمَ قَالَ : « اتَّقُوا النَّارَ وَلَوْ بِشِقِّ تَمْرَةٍ ، فَإِنْ لَمْ تَجِدْ فَبِكَلِمَةٍ طَيِّبَةٍ »

On the authority of ʿAdī b. Ḥātim ﷺ who said, the Prophet ﷺ said,

> Protect yourselves from the fire, even if with half a date, and if you do not find that, then with a good word.

Agreed upon.[1]

This means, make a protective shield between you and the fire on the Day of Rising with charity. The Prophet ﷺ said, "Charity extinguishes the anger of the Lord."[2]

Man should not belittle any charity because God ﷻ accepts it, whether great or small, and rewards it. He ﷻ said, *He who does an atom's weight of good will see it* (99:7).

This *ḥadīth* urges people to give in charity and teaches man not to think little of any charity that he gave for the sake of God ﷻ.

It was revealed in the noble Qurʾān that God ﷻ multiplies a good deed whatever it is. He ﷻ said, *If it is a good deed He multiplies it* (4:40). This means that he makes it grow with Him as a man raises his little foal. The Prophet ﷺ said,

1. *Ṣaḥīḥ al-Bukhārī*, vol. 3, p. 1328. "Agreed upon" means that it is in both *Ṣaḥīḥ al-Bukhārī* and *Ṣaḥīḥ Muslim*.
2. Narrated by al-Tirmidhī, vol. 1, p. 187, and Ibn Ḥibbān on the authority of Anas b. Mālik.

> Whoever gives in charity from honest earnings—and God accepts only the good—God will accept it in His right hand and will then increase it in size for the giver, just as one of you rears his foal, until it is the size of a mountain.[3]

It was related that someone asked the "Mother of the Believers," our lady ʿĀʾisha ﷺ to give him something, so she gave him one grape. He said, "What is this O mother?" She said to him, "Look at how many atoms are in it!" Then she recited to him the saying of God ﷻ, *He who does an atom's weight of good will see it,* and said to him, "this grape that I gave you was from a bunch of grapes that I had saved for the fast-breaking meal of the Prophet ﷺ." He became happy when he knew that and left.[4]

They used to see her ﷺ apply the musk of the Prophet ﷺ to any coin that she wanted to give in charity, before handing it to the poor person. When she was asked about that she replied, "I heard the Prophet ﷺ say, 'Charity falls into the hand of God before it falls into the hand of the asker.'"[5]

"If you do not find..." The wording here switches from addressing a group to addressing each individual. This means, if one truly does not find something to give, or if he finds it is needed for his obligatory expenditure, such as the expenses of his wife, children, and parents, then spending on those is obligatory, and is rewarded as an obligatory act, whereas spending on the poor is recommended, and the obligatory takes precedence over the recommended. Therefore spending on [the wife, children, and parents] is for the person a protection from the fire, and is better than spending on the poor.

"Then with a good word." The good word is the one that is pleasing to God ﷻ and whose speaker is rewarded for it, and that pleases

3. Narrated by al-Bukhārī in his *Ṣaḥīḥ*, vol. 1, p. 266, and by Mālik and others.
4. See Mālik, *Muwaṭṭaʾ*, pp. 387–8, *ḥadīth* 1848 and *ḥadīth* 1849.
5. This prophetic statement was narrated by al-Ṭabarānī in *al-Muʿjam al-kabīr*, and by Ibn ʿAbd al-Barr in *al-Istidhkār*, in his commentary on the *ḥadīth* of al-Bukhārī and Mālik above, "just as one of you rears his foal..."

the one who hears it. God ﷻ has commanded it, for He says, *You shall speak good words to all the people* (2:83). A *ḥadīth* says, "The good word is charity."[6]

God ﷻ gave for us in the noble Qurʾān a similitude for the good word by saying, *Have you not seen how God has coined a similitude: a good word is as a good tree, whose root is firm and whose branches are in the sky, yielding constant fruit by its Lord's leave* (14:24–25).

Here, "tree" refers to the palm tree. God ﷻ has likened the good word to the palm tree, on account of the benefits it contains, and likened the evil word to the colocynth plant for the bitterness of its taste and the foulness of its smell.

The generator of good or bad words is the tongue. The Messenger of God ﷺ took hold of his noble tongue, saying to our master Muʿādh ؓ, "Is there anything that throws people on their faces into the fire other than the harvests of their tongues?"[7]

This *ḥadīth* then teaches us the importance of giving in charity, even if a small amount, that it protects from the fire, and the importance of good speech, that it protects from the fire.

Just as the tongue brings a great number of good deeds, it also brings great sins; as it causes the pleasure of God ﷻ, it causes His displeasure ﷻ. So busy your tongue with what pleases your Creator, and you will be safe, and do not busy it with what angers Him, or you will regret it! One *ḥadīth* states, "May God have mercy on a man who, when he speaks he profits, and stays quiet to remain safe."[8]

Shihāb al-Dīn al-Khafājī ؒ said, "If speech was of silver, then silence is of gold."

The Messenger of God ﷺ said, "Do not speak much without mentioning God, for that hardens the heart, and the furthest person from God is [the one with] a hard heart."[9] Likewise, Mālik narrated the *Muwaṭṭa*ʾ [that Jesus ؑ used to say], "Do not speak much

6. Narrated by al-Bukhārī in his *Ṣaḥīḥ*, vol. 2, p. 579, and Muslim and others.
7. Narrated by Ibn Māja in his *Sunan*, pp. 574–575, al-Tirmidhī and others.
8. Narrated by al-Bayhaqī in *Shuʿab al-īmān*, vol. 7, p. 17.
9. Narrated by al-Tirmidhī in his *Sunan*, vol. 2, p. 616, on the authority of Ibn ʿUmar.

without mentioning God, for your hearts will grow hard, and the hard heart is distant from God."[10]

It is narrated in the commentary of *al-Risāla* of Ibn Abī Zayd ﵀ that the Commander of the Believers, our master ʿUmar b. al-Khaṭṭāb ﵁, entered upon the Commander of the Believers our master Abū Bakr al-Ṣiddīq ﵁ and saw him extending his tongue. ʿUmar said, "What is this O Abū Bakr?" Abū Bakr said, "Leave me for it led me to all sorts of things!"

Abū Zayd al-Mālikī said, "Someone saw al-Ṣiddīq ﵁ in his sleep, after his death. He said to him, 'To what did your tongue lead you?' He said, 'I led it constantly to the repetition of "there is no god but God," so it led me to paradise.'"

One of the righteous said, "God ﷻ made for the tongue two houses, one of bone and one of flesh, but how quickly it emerges if it wants to speak!"

One of the commentators on the *aḥādīth* said that a man passed by a severed head. He looked at it and said, "who killed him?"

God ﷻ made the head speak and it said: "My tongue killed me!"

The man carried the severed head to the king and said to him, "This head speaks!"

The king tried to speak to it, but it did not reply to him! He said to the man, "Do you mock me?" And he commanded that the man be killed. When they took him to his execution, the head spoke to the king and said, "What did the man say to you?" The king ordered that the man be brought back, and said to him, "What did the head say to you?"

He said, "It said to me, 'my tongue killed me.'"

The head immediately replied to the man, "Did you not take heed?"

The king forgave him and released him!

The narrator of this story said after that, in rhyme:

> Guard your tongue, human,
> let it not bite you—it is a snake!
> How many in the cemeteries have died from their tongue,
> though the bravest of men used to fear them!

---

10. Mālik, *al-Muwaṭṭaʾ*, pp. 383–384.

One poet said,

> The wounds of the spearheads heal,
> but what the tongue wounds never heals.

In the safeguarding of the tongue is the safeguarding of the person. Our shaykh, Shaykh Muḥammad Ibrāhīm al-Samālūṭī ﷺ explained the *ḥadīth*, "Safeguard God (i.e., His rights and limits) and He will safeguard you."[11] He said that it means, "safeguard the honor of the people from your tongue, and God will safeguard your honor from their tongues." He continued for an entire hour, teaching and explaining this *ḥadīth* (in this manner).

11. Narrated by al-Tirmidhī in his *Sunan*, vol. 2, p. 641.

Ḥadīth 24

The Traits of the Felicitous

عَنْ جَابِرِ بْنِ عَبْدِ اللهِ رَضِيَ اللهُ عَنْهُ ، قَالَ : قَالَ رَسُولُ اللهِ صَلَّى اللهُ عَلَيْهِ وَسَلَّمَ : « أَلا أُخْبِرُكُمْ بِأَهْلِ الْجَنَّةِ ؟ أَهْلُ الْجَنَّةِ كُلُّ هَيِّنٍ لَيِّنٍ سَهْلٍ قَرِيبٍ »

On the authority of Jābir b. ʿAbdallāh ﵁ who said, the Messenger of God ﷺ said,

> Shall I not tell you who the people of paradise are? The people of paradise are everyone who is soft, gentle, easy, and near.[1]

عَنْ أَبِي عَامِرٍ الأَشْعَرِيِّ أَنَّ النَّبِيَّ صَلَّى اللهُ عَلَيْهِ وَسَلَّمَ قَالَ : « أَهْلُ النَّارِ كُلُّ شَدِيدٍ قَبَعْثَرِيٍّ ، قِيلَ يَا رَسُولَ اللهِ ! مَنِ الْقَبَعْثَرِيُّ ؟ قَالَ : الشَّدِيدُ عَلَى الأَهْلِ ، الشَّدِيدُ عَلَى الْعَشِيرَةِ ، الشَّدِيدُ عَلَى الصَّاحِبِ »

On the authority of Abū ʿĀmir al-Ashʿarī ﵁, the Prophet ﷺ said,

> "The people of the fire are everyone who is stern, big and harsh."

1. Narrated by al-Ṭabarānī in *al-Rawḍ al-dānī ilā l-muʿjam al-saghīr li-l-Ṭabarānī*, vol. 1, p. 72. A different narration by Aḥmad on the authority of Ibn Masʿūd says, the Messenger of God ﷺ said, "Forbidden from entering the fire is everyone who is soft, easy, gentle, and near to the people." Al-Tirmidhī also narrated it on the authority of Ibn Masʿūd thus: "Shall I not tell you who the fire is forbidden from touching? It is forbidden from touching everyone who is near, soft, gentle and easy (*Sunan al-Tirmidhī*, vol. 2, p. 635).

> It was said, "O Messenger of God! Who is the one who is stern, big and harsh?" He said, "He who is harsh on the family, harsh on the clan, harsh on the companion."

Narrated by al-Daylamī, al-Shīrāzī in *al-Alqāb*, and al-Suyūṭī in *Jamʿ al-jawāmiʿ*.[2]

·✻·✻·✻·

The Prophet ﷺ described the people of paradise by saying, "soft, gentle, easy, and near," [when dealing] with the believers, as He ﷻ said, *compassionate among themselves* (48:29). The believer, therefore, is he who is gentle with his believing brother, not tough or hard; easy, not difficult, and his contentment or pleasure is near, not far. One *ḥadīth* states, "The believer is gentle, soft, quickly angered, but near (i.e., quick) to contentment."[3]

The real believer acts according to the saying of God ﷻ, *those who restrain their anger and pardon the people* (3:134), and His saying, *when they are angry, they forgive* (42:37), and His saying, *they repel evil with good* (13:22). Whoever does evil to them, they do something good in return; this characteristic is one of the greatest of noble manners. God has promised the one who acts in this manner that his enemy will become his supporter and will love him greatly, and that is a quick reward in this life for those who have this noble characteristic.

One *ḥadīth* states, "The believer harmonizes with others, and is easy to harmonize with, and there is no good in he who does not harmonize with others, and is not easy to harmonize with."[4]

---

2. al-Suyūṭī, *Jamʿ al-jawāmiʿ*, vol. 3, p. 221.
3. Meaning quickly angered but quickly appeased. I have not found such a tradition. Al-Ghazālī quoted in the *Iḥyāʾ* a tradition that states, "The believer is quick to anger, quick to go back from it," but al-ʿIrāqī said, "I have not found it thus anywhere." Mullā ʿAlī l-Qārī quoted a long *ḥadīth* which states that the perfect believer is the one who is slow to anger and quick to appeasement (al-Qārī, *al-Asrār al-marfūʿa*, p. 364).
4. It was narrated by al-Ṭabarānī in *al-Muʿjam al-awṣat* on the authority of Jābir, and by al-Bazzār in *al-Musnad* on the authority of Abū

He ﷻ said, *He has created harmony between their hearts* (8:63). Harmony between the hearts of the believers is a blessing among the greatest of blessings, and a bounty among the greatest of God's bounties, for with it there is love, cooperation, and support, so that no believer allows harm to befall his brother, severs relations with him, or allows for his surrender to his enemy. Instead, he is a brother to him, generous not miserly, assisting not stubborn, maintaining connections not severing them, bringing into realization the saying of the Real ﷻ, *By His favor you became brothers* (3:103).

The Prophet ﷺ described the people of the fire as harsh on the family, the clan, and the companion. Another *ḥadīth* says of the hypocrite, "When he quarrels he insults."[5] So do not be harsh on your family that they hate you, your clan that they cut you off, or your companions that they leave you.

God ﷻ said, *That is how it will really be: the people of the fire will quarrel with each other* (38:64). God ﷻ described the people of the fire as quarreling while they are in the fire, and described the people

---

Hurayra (see al-Haythamī, *Kashf al-astār*, vol. 4, pp. 227–228). Aḥmad b. Ḥanbal narrated it in his *Musnad* on the authority of Abū Hurayra thus: "The believer is a source of harmony, and there is no good in he who does not harmonize with others, and is not easy to harmonize with" (vol. 15, pp. 106–107). Al-Ḥākim narrated it on the authority of Abū Hurayra thus: "The believer harmonizes with others, and there is no good in he who does not harmonize with others, and is not easy to harmonize with." Al-Ḥākim added, "It is authentic according to the criteria of the two shaykhs [al-Bukhārī and Muslim]" (*al-Mustadrak*, vol. 1, pp. 73–74). The origin of the word used is *ulfa*, which means familiarity, unison, harmony, accord, friendship, and intimacy.

5. Narrated by al-Bukhārī in his *Ṣaḥīḥ*, vol. 1, p. 12, and also by Muslim and al-Tirmidhī. The word used, *fajar*, can be understood to mean "he insults and throws ugly accusations." This is the understanding that was chosen by Mullā ʿAlī l-Qārī when he commented on the *ḥadīth* in *Mirqīt al-mafātīḥ*, and it is the meaning that was intended by the author of this work, judging by the context in which he used the *ḥadīth*. Another meaning of *fajar* is "he deviates from the truth and speaks falsely," which is the meaning understood by al-Nawawī in his commentary on *Ṣaḥīḥ Muslim*. See *Tūḥfat al-aḥwadhī*, al-Mubārakfūrī's commentary on *Sunan al-Tirmidhī*, p. 2013.

of paradise as having sincerity and brotherhood in paradise, as He ﷻ said, *We shall remove any bitterness from their hearts: brothers, sitting on couches, face to face* (15:47). So the people of the fire are people of mutual hate and desertion in this life and the next, and the people of paradise are people of love and affection in this life and the next. He ﷺ said, "The people of kindness in this life are the people of kindness in the next."[6]

6. Narrated by al-Bazzār on the authority of two Companions, Qabīṣa al-Asdī and Ibn ʿUmar. See al-Haythamī, *Kashf al-astār*, vol. 4, p. 102.

Ḥadīth 25

Sacred Matters

عَنْ أَبِي سَعِيدٍ الخُدْرِيِّ رَضِيَ اللهُ تَعَالَى عَنْهُ قَالَ : قَالَ رَسُولُ اللهِ صَلَّى اللهُ عَلَيْهِ وَسَلَّمَ : « إِنَّ لِلّٰهِ عَزَّ وَجَلَّ حُرُمَاتٍ ثَلَاثٍ ، مَنْ حَفِظَهُنَّ حَفِظَ اللهُ لَهُ أَمْرَ دِينِهِ وَدُنْيَاهُ ، وَمَنْ لَمْ يَحْفَظْهُنَّ لَمْ يَحْفَظِ اللهُ لَهُ شَيْئًا : حُرْمَةَ الإِسْلَامِ ، وَحُرْمَتِي ، وَحُرْمَةَ رَحِمِي »

On the authority of Abū Saʿīd al-Khudrī ﵁ who said, the Messenger of God ﷺ said,

> Three things are sacred to God and whoever safeguards them, God will safeguard for him the matters of his religion and worldly life, and whoever does not safeguard them, God will not safeguard anything for him: the sanctity of Islam, my sanctity, and the sanctity of my ties of kinship.[1]

·❁·❁·❁·

What is sacred are the rights due to those three things.

The sanctity of Islam is what is required of a Muslim in order for his Islam to be complete. For example, the Prophet ﷺ said, "The Muslim is the one from whose hand and tongue other Muslims are safe,"[2] and he ﷺ also said, "The Muslim is the brother of the

1. Narrated by Abū Nuʿaym in *Maʿrifat al-ṣaḥāba* and al-Ṭabarānī in *al-Muʿjam al-awṣat* and *al-Muʿjam al-kabīr*. Al-Ṣuyūṭī, *Jamʿ al-jawāmiʿ*, vol. 2, p. 605.
2. *Ṣaḥīḥ al-Bukhārī*, vol. 1, p. 8.

Muslim."[3] The Prophet ﷺ further said, "The fornicator does not commit fornication while he is a believer,"[4] and he ﷺ said, "I have been commanded to fight people until they testify that there is no god but God and Muḥammad is the messenger of God and they establish the prayer and pay the obligatory alms-tax. If they do that, their lives and property are protected from me except for the right of Islam, and their reckoning is up to God."[5] God ﷻ said, *How bad it is to be called a mischief-maker after having accepted faith* (49:11).

In general, he who does what is obligatory in Islam and abstains from what is forbidden has given great importance to the sanctity of Islam, and enters the haven mentioned in the *ḥadīth*, "Safeguard God (i.e., His rights and limits) and He will safeguard you."[6] He who does not act accordingly has not given great importance to the sanctity of Islam, and the recompense of the one who neglects is to be neglected. One *ḥadīth* says, "The ritual prayer supplicates against the one who neglects its prescribed time and says, 'May God neglect you as you neglected me.'"[7]

The sanctity of the Prophet ﷺ is his right that God ﷻ made obligatory on us to fulfill. These rights include obeying him in his speech and actions, respecting him, revering him, and honoring him. One must acknowledge his virtue, his intercession, his rank in the sight of God, and how God elevated his mention and raised his station. One must also know that ever since God ﷻ created the Prophet ﷺ, he has always been increasing in faith, knowledge, lights, stations, blessings, secrets, and goodness.

After joining the highest Companion, the Prophet ﷺ became higher in rank and greater in honor. He also became more expansive in knowledge, unveiling, witnessing, and in his ability to hear and reply to the greetings of the Muslims. It is not permissible for a believer to believe other than that, or that his death is like the

---

3. *Ṣaḥīḥ al-Bukhārī*, vol. 1, p. 459, and in *Ṣaḥīḥ Muslim*.
4. *Ṣaḥīḥ al-Bukhārī*, vol. 3, p. 1373, and in *Ṣaḥīḥ Muslim*.
5. *Ṣaḥīḥ al-Bukhārī*, vol. 1, p. 10.
6. Narrated by al-Tirmidhī in his *Sunan*, vol. 2, p. 641.
7. Narrated by al-Bazzār in his *Musnad*. See al-Haythamī, *Kashf al-astār*, vol. 1, p. 177. Also by al-Ṭabarānī in *al-Muʿjam al-awsaṭ*.

death of other creatures. No! God brought him back to life after his death with a life that surpasses the life of the prophets and messengers—peace and blessings be upon him and them—and the life of the martyrs, the life of the noble angels, and the life of the people living on Earth. You must love him ﷺ more than you love yourself, send peace and blessings upon him, and visit him in his noble Rawḍa[8] so that you obtain for yourself his greeting of peace, and his blessing and the blessing of his gaze upon you, and his supplication for you. I said by the grace of my Lord ﷻ,

> O visitor of that grave and he who is in it
> happiness has come to you, you've gained his nearness.
> Greet him with peace and ask him for the best intercession
> for he is the intercessor, the beloved of his Lord.
> You are the happy one if you arrive at his door.
> Give greetings to that Prophet and his Companions.

The sanctity of the Prophet's ties of kinship is the rights that are due to his kin from us. These include loving them more than our own families, maintaining bonds with them, respecting them, and venerating them. It is to acknowledge their virtue and that God ﷻ chose them as the family and relatives of His Prophet ﷺ.

The grandson of the Messenger of God ﷺ, our master al-Ḥasan, son of our master ʿAlī, said, "God ﷻ did not send a prophet until He chose for him a people, Companions, and a family, and God ﷻ has chosen us as the family of his Prophet ﷺ."

Among them are those who were honored by him ﷺ by way of lineage, and they are his descendants. Others were honored by way of relationship, and they are his wives, the Mothers of the Believers. Others still were honored by way of kinship like his uncles and aunts. Sufficient for you are the sayings of God ﷻ, *Say (to them O Muḥammad): I ask of no reward from you for this but the love of the relatives* (42:23); *God's wish is but to remove impurity from you, O members of the household, and to purify you thoroughly*

8. A part of the mosque of Medina that is considered a piece of paradise on Earth.

(33:33); and, *The mercy of God and His blessings be upon you, O members of the household* (11:73).

There are many *aḥādīth* about the virtues of the members of the household of prophecy . Among the greatest ways to maintain bonds with them is to visit them after their death, give them greetings of peace, and ask God to be pleased with them.

Ḥadīth 26

Visiting the Righteous

عَنْ أَنَسٍ قَالَ : قَالَ أَبُو بَكْرٍ رَضِيَ اللَّهُ عَنْهُ بَعْدَ وَفَاةِ رَسُولِ اللَّهِ صَلَّى اللَّهُ عَلَيْهِ وَسَلَّمَ لِعُمَرَ : انْطَلِقْ بِنَا إِلَى أُمِّ أَيْمَنَ ، نَزُورُهَا كَمَا كَانَ رَسُولُ اللَّهِ صَلَّى اللَّهُ عَلَيْهِ وَسَلَّمَ يَزُورُهَا ، فَلَمَّا انْتَهَيْنَا إِلَيْهَا بَكَتْ ، فَقَالَا لَهَا : مَا يُبْكِيكِ ؟ مَا عِنْدَ اللَّهِ خَيْرٌ لِرَسُولِهِ صَلَّى اللَّهُ عَلَيْهِ وَسَلَّمَ ، فَقَالَتْ : مَا أَبْكِي أَنْ لَا أَكُونَ أَعْلَمُ أَنَّ مَا عِنْدَ اللَّهِ خَيْرٌ لِرَسُولِهِ صَلَّى اللَّهُ عَلَيْهِ وَسَلَّمَ ، وَلَكِنْ أَبْكِي أَنَّ الْوَحْيَ قَدِ انْقَطَعَ مِنَ السَّمَاءِ ، فَهَيَّجَتْهُمَا عَلَى الْبُكَاءِ فَجَعَلَا يَبْكِيَانِ مَعَهَا

On the authority of Anas ﵁, who said,

> Abū Bakr ﵁ said to ʿUmar after the death of the Messenger of God ﷺ, "Let us go to Umm Ayman to visit her as the Messenger of God ﷺ used to visit her."
>
> [They said,] "When we reached her she cried."
>
> They said to her, "What makes you cry? What God has for His Messenger ﷺ is better for him."
>
> She said, "I do not cry because I do not know that what God has is better for His Messenger ﷺ, rather I cry because revelation has been cut off from the heavens."
>
> This moved them to tears and they began to cry with her.

Narrated by Muslim.[1]

1. *Ṣaḥīḥ Muslim*, vol. 2, p. 1049.

Al-Nawawī 🕮 said,

> This *ḥadīth* shows the virtue of visiting the righteous; and
> the visiting of the more virtuous to the less virtuous; and the
> following of the example of the Messenger of God 🕮; and the
> man's visiting of the righteous woman and listening to her talk;
> and the taking of a scholar or the like as a companion in visits,
> worship, and similar things; and crying with grief at the parting
> of the righteous and the loved ones, even if they have moved
> on to something better than their previous state; and crying
> without a sound.

Ḥadīth 27

Reverence, Mercy, Recognition

عَنْ عُبَادَةَ بْنِ الصَّامِتِ أَنّ رَسُولَ اللهِ صَلَّى اللهُ عَلَيْهِ وَسَلَّمَ قَالَ :
« لَيْسَ مِنْ أُمَّتِي مَنْ لَمْ يُجِلَّ كَبِيرَنَا ، وَيَرْحَمْ صَغِيرَنَا ، وَيَعْرِفْ لِعَالِمِنَا حَقَّهُ »

On the authority of ʿUbāda b. al-Ṣāmit ﵁, the Prophet ﷺ said,

> He who does not revere our elders, have mercy on our youth, and know the rights of our scholars is not from my community.

Narrated by Aḥmad b. Ḥanbal, al-Ḥākim, and my master Aḥmad b. Idrīs in *Rūḥ al-sunna*.[1]

·✿·✿·✿·

To revere the elders is to show them respect and to honor them because of their old age, and this has been the custom of the nobles and the Arabs until this day.

---

1. This is the wording of Aḥmad in his *Musnad*, vol. 37, p. 416, and al-Ṭabarānī in *Makārim al-akhlāq*. The author, following his shaykh in *Rūḥ al-sunna* (p. 158), has *yubajjil* instead of *yujill*, and recognized that this is not the standard wording by stating, "this is how it was narrated by my master Aḥmad b. Idrīs in *Rūḥ al-sunna*." Their narration also has "he is not one of us" instead of "he is not from my community," which is the wording in the narration of al-Bayhaqī in *al-Sunan al-kubrā*, al-Ṭabarī in *Tahdhīb al-āthār*, and al-Ḥākim in *al-Mustadrak*, vol. 1, p. 211.

To show mercy to the young is to show compassion and sympathy for them because of their weakness and because of their youth and intellect.

To know the rights of the scholars is to know the rights carried by the Muḥammadan inheritance. He ﷺ said, "The scholars are the inheritors of the prophets."[2] It is also to know the right of their virtue over others. He ﷺ said, "The virtue of the scholar over the worshiper is like my virtue over the least of you."[3] Therefore, it is obligatory on every Muslim to know the rights of the scholars. Scholars must be respected for their role as successors of the Prophet. He ﷺ said, "May God have mercy on my successors." Someone said, "Who are your successors O Messenger of God?" He said, "They are those who will come after I am gone, who will narrate my *aḥādīth* and my Sunna, and teach them to the people."[4]

The community is well as long as the scholars are in it, and the community is well as long as the scholars are venerated, and their sayings are listened to and acted upon. Al-Būṣīrī ﷺ said,

> We fear not misguidance after you, while among us
> are the scholars, the inheritors of the light of your guidance.

2. Narrated by Abū Dāwūd, Aḥmad, and al-Tirmidhī in his *Sunan*, vol. 2, p. 683.
3. Narrated by al-Tirmidhī in his *Sunan*, vol. 2, p. 684.
4. Al-Suyūṭī, *al-Jāmiʿ al-ṣaghīr* (see al-Nabahānī, *al-Fatḥ al-kabīr*, vol. 1, p. 233).

Ḥadīth 28

Seeking God through Service

عَنْ أَبِي هُرَيْرَةَ ، قَالَ : قَالَ رَسُولُ اللهِ صَلَّى اللهُ عَلَيْهِ وَسَلَّمَ : « إِنَّ اللهَ عَزَّ وَجَلَّ يَقُولُ يَوْمَ الْقِيَامَةِ : يَا ابْنَ آدَمَ ، مَرِضْتُ فَلَمْ تَعُدْنِي ، قَالَ يَا رَبِّ : كَيْفَ أَعُودُكَ وَأَنْتَ رَبُّ الْعَالَمِينَ ؟ قَالَ : أَمَا عَلِمْتَ أَنَّ عَبْدِي فُلَانًا مَرِضَ فَلَمْ تَعُدْهُ ؟ أَمَا عَلِمْتَ أَنَّكَ لَوْ عُدْتَهُ لَوَجَدْتَنِي عِنْدَهُ ؟ يَا ابْنَ آدَمَ ، اسْتَطْعَمْتُكَ فَلَمْ تُطْعِمْنِي ، قَالَ يَا رَبِّ : وَكَيْفَ أُطْعِمُكَ وَأَنْتَ رَبُّ الْعَالَمِينَ ؟ قَالَ : أَمَا عَلِمْتَ أَنَّهُ اسْتَطْعَمَكَ عَبْدِي فُلَانٌ ؟ فَلَمْ تُطْعِمْهُ ، أَمَا عَلِمْتَ أَنَّكَ لَوْ أَطْعَمْتَهُ لَوَجَدْتَ ذَلِكَ عِنْدِي ؟ يَا ابْنَ آدَمَ ، اسْتَسْقَيْتُكَ فَلَمْ تَسْقِنِي ، قَالَ يَا رَبِّ : كَيْفَ أَسْقِيكَ وَأَنْتَ رَبُّ الْعَالَمِينَ ؟ قَالَ : اسْتَسْقَاكَ عَبْدِي فُلَانٌ ، فَلَمْ تَسْقِهِ ، أَمَا إِنَّكَ لَوْ سَقَيْتَهُ وَجَدْتَ ذَلِكَ عِنْدِي ؟ »

On the authority of Abū Hurayra ﵁, who said, the Messenger of God ﷺ said,

> God ﷻ will say on the Day of Rising, "O son of Adam, I fell ill and you visited Me not." He will say, "O Lord, and how do I visit You when You are the Lord of the worlds?" He will say, "Did you not know that My servant so-and-so had fallen ill and you visited him not? Did you not know that had you visited him you would have found Me with him?"

> "O son of Adam, I asked you for food and you fed Me not." He will say, "O Lord, and how do I feed You when You are the Lord of the worlds?" He will say, "Did you not know that My servant so-and-so asked you for food and you fed him not? Did you not know that had you fed him, you would have found that with Me?"
>
> "O son of Adam, I asked you to give Me drink and you gave Me not to drink." He will say, ""O Lord, how should I give You to drink when You are the Lord of the worlds?" He will say, "My servant so-and-so asked you to give him to drink and you gave him not to drink. Had you given him to drink you would have surely found that with Me."

Narrated by Muslim.[1]

·❁·❁·❁·

The noble Ibn Idrīs said, "He who is for the creation a shield, a mercy, and a shade under which they could rest, God will be so for him; he who honors a servant out of regard for his Master, has honored the Master. . . ."

He ﷺ also said, "He ﷻ explained the reference to Himself in His saying: 'I was hungry,' 'I was ill,' and 'I asked for something to drink,' by His saying, 'My servant so-and-so was hungry.' So dealing with the servant while regarding the Master is dealing with the Master without doubt."

I say: if you know that your Lord is present with others, did you reach the certainty that He is with you? Did you respect and take heed of this fact that He is with you, in your treatment of yourself? If [your self] was hungry out of ignorance, did you feed it knowledge? If it was ill with sins and heedlessness, did you treat it with repentance and seek His forgiveness? If it was thirsty out of love of the world, did you quench its thirst by making it renounce that love?

---

1. *Ṣaḥīḥ Muslim*, vol. 2, p. 1094. It was also narrated by al-Bukhārī in *al-Adab al-mufrad*, and Ibn Ḥibbān in his *Ṣaḥīḥ*.

If you know that the All-Knowing One is with you, and that He loves the scholars and despises the ignorant, then hurry to the gatherings of knowledge to obtain that knowledge that takes you to God's love. In one *ḥadīth* God says, "O Abraham, I am most knowledgeable, and I love everyone who is knowledgeable."[2] I have said by the grace of my Lord,

> Rush to the people of the sciences, for they are
> the people of nourishment, by them the selves are lit.
> If others gave what is precious, they have given
> the most precious thing of all: the healing honey.

Rush also to the sincere repentance that will take you to God's love for you. He ﷻ said, *God loves the repentant* (2:222). How great is the repentance that takes to love! He who has repented (*tāba*) has turned back (*anāba*); and he who has turned back has returned (*āba*); and he who has returned has knocked on the door (*bāb*); and he who has knocked on the door, the door will soon be opened for him; and he for whom the door has opened, has seen the people of the realities (*albāb*),[3] those from whom the veil (*ḥijāb*) has been lifted. I said by the grace of my Lord,

> Repent if you want the love of the Forgiving One
> for God forgives all sins.
> He is not disappointed by he who comes to him, repentant,
> he is saved by his repentance from what is other than Him.
> The heart is not straight in its actions
> until it repents to the One, the Subduer.

The love of the world is an unsettling state of thirst and worry, so remove the thirst of your soul by making it renounce the perishing world and desire the everlasting one. If it desires, it renounces; and

---

2. Mentioned by Ibn ʿAbd al-Barr (original footnote), and al-Subkī in *Ṭabaqāt al-Shāfiʿiyya al-kubrā*, vol. 6, p. 288.
3. "The people with hearts/intellects," an expression used regularly in the Qurʾān. It also means "the people of the kernel," and many Sufis understand "the kernel" to mean the spiritual substance and the secret of things.

if it renounces, it finds; and if it finds, it becomes serious; and if it becomes serious, it rushes forth; and if it rushes forth, it arrives; and if it arrives, it connects.

Ḥadīth 29

On Account of an Animal

عَنْ ابْنِ عُمَرَ رَضِيَ اللهُ عَنْهُمَا ، عَنِ النَّبِيّ صَلَّى اللهُ عَلَيْهِ وَسَلَّمَ ، قَالَ :
« دَخَلَتِ امْرَأَةٌ النَّارَ فِي هِرَّةٍ رَبَطَتْهَا فَلَمْ تُطْعِمْهَا وَلَمْ تَدَعْهَا تَأْكُلُ مِنْ خَشَاشِ الأَرْضِ »

On the authority of ʿAbdallāh b. ʿUmar ﷺ that the Prophet ﷺ said,

> A woman entered the fire on account of a cat which she tied up and neither fed it nor did she allow it to eat the earth's insects and rodents.

Narrated by al-Bukhārī, Muslim, Imam Aḥmad, and Ibn Māja, all from Abū Hurayra, and narrated by al-Bukhārī also from Ibn ʿUmar.[1]

·❁·❁·❁·

"A woman entered . . ." Ibn Ḥajar al-ʿAsqalānī said,[2]

> I have not seen her name anywhere. There is a narration that she is from the tribe of Ḥimyar, and another narration that she is Jewish, and there is no contradiction between them because a group of Ḥimyar entered Judaism, so she was sometimes referred to by her religion and sometimes by her tribe.
>
> His saying, "which she tied up," means with a rope or the like. In the narration found in the section on the excellence

1. *Ṣaḥīh al-Bukhārī*, vol. 2, p. 646.
2. In *Fatḥ al-Bārī*, the most famous commentary on *Ṣaḥīh al-Bukhārī*.

of giving water in al-Bukhārī, it says, "She locked it up until it died of hunger. . . ."

Al-Qasṭalānī said,[3]

> This is one of the things that our lady ʿĀʾisha corrected for Abū Hurayra 🙏. She said to him, "Do you know what the woman was? The woman, beside what she did, was a disbeliever. The believer is too honored by God to be tormented for a cat. So when you narrate from the Messenger of God 🕌, look carefully at how you narrate.

This contains many topics of discussion:

> First: This contradicts the narration in the *Fatḥ*[4] that she was Jewish, and the Jews of the old days are not called disbelievers. The answer to that, however, is that it is possible that she was a woman of Ḥimyar who remained with her disbelief and polytheism, or that she entered Judaism only outwardly, but did not abandon her disbelief. By that her disbelief is combined with her being Jewish.
> Second: The scholars have agreed about the one who perpetrates a great sin and dies without having repented from it: his affair is left with his Lord.

Al-Laqqānī 🙏 said,

> If someone dies without repenting from his sin then his affair is left with his Lord.

If he repented, however, then the scholars have agreed that God accepts his repentance and forgives him what he did before, even if he was a disbeliever.[5]

3.   In his own commentary on *Ṣaḥīḥ al-Bukhārī*.
4.   Ibn Ḥajar's *Fatḥ al-Bārī* is the most famous commentary on *Ṣaḥīḥ al-Bukhārī*.
5.   This is based on the opinion that the disbelievers are punished also for their individual sins, not just for rejecting the faith. See also the commentary on *ḥadīth* 22 for a discussion on whether or not disbelievers are rewarded for their good works in the next world or only in this world.

Ḥadīth 30

A Garden of Paradise

عَنْ أَبِي هُرَيْرَةَ رَضِيَ اللهُ عَنْهُ ، أَنَّ رَسُولَ اللهِ صَلَّى اللهُ عَلَيْهِ وَسَلَّمَ ، قَالَ : « مَا بَيْنَ بَيْتِي وَمِنْبَرِي رَوْضَةٌ مِنْ رِيَاضِ الجَنَّةِ ، وَمِنْبَرِي عَلَى حَوْضِي »

On the authority of Abū Hurayra ﷺ the Messenger of God ﷺ said,

> What is between my house and my pulpit is a garden from the gardens of paradise, and my pulpit is on my basin.

Narrated by al-Bukhārī.[1]

Shaykh Ibn Abī Jamra said, "God only made this spot a garden from the gardens of paradise because it was the walkway of the Prophet ﷺ."

God has honored His Prophet ﷺ and whatever is attributed to him. He made prayer in the mosque that he ﷺ built equal to a thousand prayers and that is because of the mosque's attribution to him, not because of the space that he built. No matter how much the mosque expands, it will still contain that reward until the Day of Rising, as long as it is considered his mosque. He ﷺ said, "If this mosque was expanded to Sanaa it would still be my mosque," as narrated by al-Daylamī on the authority of Abū Hurayra.[2] The

1. *Ṣaḥīh al-Bukhārī*, vol. 1, p. 223.
2. Also narrated by Ibn Abī Shayba in *Akhbār al-madīna* (see al-Sakhāwī,

ḥadīth means that prayer in it is equal to one thousand normal prayers as long as [the mosque] is attributed to him ﷺ, even if it was expanded to Sanaa, Yemen.

God made the town that he ﷺ chose for his residence a sacred sanctuary. He ﷺ said about Medina, "O God I make sacred what is between its two black mountains as Abraham made Mecca sacred."[3] The sanctity of what is between the two black mountains means that its trees are not cut down, its game is not disturbed, and its fresh herbage is not cut. All of that is to honor him, and out of respect for him ﷺ; while the game of Mecca is inviolable and there is a penalty for hunting it, the game of Medina is inviolable but there is no penalty for hunting it.

We pray in the prayer niche that he ﷺ used to pray in,[4] just as he ﷺ prayed in the place that our master Moses ؑ sat,[5] and at the Station of Abraham ؑ.[6] More than all the prophets and messengers ؑ, our

---

al-Maqāṣid al-ḥasana, p. 424).

3. *Ṣaḥīḥ al-Bukhārī*, vol. 2, p. 560. Also narrated by Muslim with different wording.
4. On praying in the exact spot where the Prophet Muḥammad prayed, see the *ḥadīth* of Ibn ʿUmar narrated by Mālik in the *Muwaṭṭaʾ*, quoted in al-Jaʿfarī, *Fatḥ wa fayḍ*, p. 248.
5. The *ḥadīth* about the Prophet Muḥammad praying in the spot where Moses sat was narrated by al-Ṭabarānī in *al-Muʿjam al-kabīr*, al-Bazzār in his *Musnad*, and al-Bayhaqī in *Dalāʾil al-nubuwwa*. They narrated the Prophet's description of his Night Journey to Jerusalem on the authority of Shaddād b. Aws. In this *ḥadīth* the Prophet Muḥammad described how he was ordered during the journey by the angel Gabriel to dismount from his heavenly mount Burāq and to pray under the tree under which the Prophet Moses sat in Madyan, and then again in the spot where the Prophet Jesus was born in Bethlehem. For the narrations of al-Ṭabarānī and al-Bazzār see al-Haythamī, *Kashf al-astār*, vol. 1, pp. 35–37. Al-Bayhaqī narrated it in *Dalāʾil al-nubuwwa*, vol. 2, pp. 355–357, and said, "This chain of narrators is correct." See also al-Jaʿfarī, *al-Sirāj al-wahhāj*, pp. 47–49, where it is also attributed to al-Tirmidhī. Al-Nasāʾī narrated a similar *ḥadīth* with small differences on the authority of Anas b. Mālik in his *Sunan*, vol. 1, pp. 71–72.
6. Praying at the Station of Abraham, where the Prophet Abraham stood while building the Kaʿba, is mentioned in Q 2:125.

Prophet ﷺ is deserving of respect for his relics and traces, as well as prayer near them, and supplication at their location.

Ḥadīth 31

Blessings upon the Prophet

عَنْ أَبِي هُرَيْرَةَ رَضِيَ اللهُ عَنْهُ ، قَالَ : قَالَ رَسُولُ اللهِ صَلَّى اللهُ عَلَيْهِ وَسَلَّمَ : « رَغِمَ أَنفُ رَجُلٍ ذُكِرْتُ عِنْدَهُ فَلَمْ يُصَلِّ عَلَيَّ »

On the authority of Abū Hurayra ﵁, who said that the Messenger of God ﷺ said,

> May the nose of the man who does not invoke blessings upon me if I am mentioned in his presence be covered in dirt.

Narrated by al-Tirmidhī and al-Ḥākim.[1]

« وَرَجُلٍ ذُكِرْتَ عِنْدَهُ فَلَمْ يُصَلِّ عَلَيْكَ ، فَأَبْعَدَهُ اللهُ ، قُلْ : آمِين ، فَقُلْتُ : آمِين »

> [Gabriel said] "May God distance anyone who does not invoke blessings upon you when you are mentioned. Say Amen." I said, "Amen."

Narrated by al-Mundhirī.[2]

·✿·✿·✿·

1. *Sunan al-Tirmidhī*, vol. 2, p. 908. It is also narrated by Aḥmad b. Ḥanbal and others. "May his nose be covered in dirt" is an ancient Arab expression.
2. Also narrated on the authority of several Companions of the Prophet by al-Bukhārī in *al-Adab al-mufrad*, Ibn Ḥibbān in his *Ṣaḥīḥ*, al-Bazzār in his *Musnad*, al-Ḥākim in *al-Mustadrak*, and others. Al-Ḥākim

Among God's favors upon His Prophet ﷺ is that he made the invocation of blessings upon him obligatory whenever his name is mentioned, regardless of whether the Prophet is still living or after he died. God ﷻ did not give this favor to any other created being but him ﷺ. Also among those favors is that he who invokes one blessing upon him ﷺ will be sent ten blessings by God; and that the invocation of blessings upon him ﷺ emancipates one from the fire. This is the case regardless of whether those blessings were sent during the Prophet's life or after his death. He ﷺ said,

> He who invokes one blessing on me, God will send ten blessings on him for it. He who invokes blessings on me ten times, God will send a hundred blessings on him for it. He who invokes blessings on me a hundred times, God will send a thousand blessings on him for it. He who invokes blessings on me a thousand times, God will make his skin and hair forbidden for the fire.[3]

---

narrated it on the authority of Kaʿb b. ʿUjra and said, "This *ḥadīth* has a correct chain of narrators" (*al-Mustadrak*, vol. 4, p. 170).

3. Muslim narrated in his *Ṣaḥīḥ* on the authority of Abū Hurayra that the Prophet said, "Whoever invokes one blessing on me, God will send ten blessings on him" (vol. 1, p. 172). It was also narrated by al-Bukhārī in *al-Adab al-mufrad*, Aḥmad in his *Musnad*, Abū Dāwūd in his *Sunan*, al-Tirmidhī in his *Sunan*, al-Nasāʾī in his *Sunan*, and others. Al-Ṭabarānī narrated in *al-Muʿjam al-ṣaghīr* on the authority of Anas b. Mālik that the Prophet said, "He who invokes one blessing on me, God will send ten blessings on him for it. He who invokes blessings on me ten times, God will send a hundred blessings on him for it. He who invokes blessings on me a hundred times, God will write between his eyes, 'Free from hypocrisy and free from the fire,' and He will give him residence on the Day of Rising with the martyrs." Muḥammad b. Sulaymān al-Jazūlī wrote in *Dalāʾil al-khayrāt* that it has been narrated that the Prophet said, "He who invokes one blessing on me, God will send ten blessings on him. He who invokes blessings on me ten times, God will send a hundred blessings on him. He who invokes blessings on me a hundred times, God will send a thousand blessings on him. He who invokes blessings on me a thousand times, God will make his body forbidden for the fire. . ." (pp. 22–23).

Ḥadīth 32

The Sleep of the Prophets

عَنْ عَطَاءٍ عَنِ النَّبِيِّ صَلَّى اللهُ عَلَيْهِ وَسَلَّمَ ، قَالَ : « إِنَّا مَعْشَرَ الأَنْبِيَاءِ تَنَامُ أَعْيُنُنَا ، وَلا تَنَامُ قُلُوبُنَا »

On the authority of ʿAṭāʾ, the Prophet ﷺ said,

We prophets, our eyes sleep, but our hearts do not sleep.

[Narrated by Ibn Saʿd in *al-Ṭabaqāt al-kubrā*].[1]

Know that the prophets, peace and blessings be upon them, were different than the rest of creation in the smaller death.[2]

1. Ibn Saʿd, *al-Ṭabaqāt al-kubrā*, vol. 1, p. 145. It is classified as *mursal ṣaḥīḥ*, meaning that it is considered authentic despite the fact that the Companion who narrated it has been omitted from the chain. That is because it goes back to someone whose *aḥādīth* are all considered authentic, even when he omits the Companion between himself and the Prophet. The author attributed this *ḥadīth* to *Ṣaḥīḥ al-Bukhārī*. This specific *ḥadīth* is not in the *Ṣaḥīḥ*, though there are many similar to it in al-Bukhārī's collection, and they will be quoted after the commentary.
2. The smaller death is sleep, as compared to the normal death. The Qurʾān says, *God takes the souls when they die, and the souls of the living when they sleep. He keeps hold of those whose death He ordained and sends the others back until their appointed time* (39:42).

They also differed from them in the greater death. He ﷺ said, "The prophets are alive in their graves, praying." Narrated by al-Bayhaqī.[3]

O you who desires to make the prophets like the rest in death, have you not seen these *aḥādīth*? Did you not hear what God ﷻ said about the martyrs: *They are alive with their Lord, receiving sustenance* (3:169)? The prophets ﷺ are better than the martyrs.

Shaykh Taqī l-Dīn al-Subkī l-Shāfiʿī, author of *Jamʿ al-jawāmiʿ*, and the *ḥadīth* master al-Suyūṭī, and other scholars said: The life of the Prophet ﷺ after death is taken from the verse of the martyrs by way of priority.

I say: It is in the Muḥammadan Sunna as well.

Translator's Note

The *aḥādīth* in *Ṣaḥīḥ al-Bukhārī*, "Section: The Prophet ﷺ, his eyes slept, but his heart did not sleep."

> The Prophet Muḥammad said to his wife ʿĀʾisha, "My eyes sleep, but my heart does not sleep."[4]
>
> The Prophet's Companion Anas b. Mālik said regarding the night of the Prophet's Night Journey to Jerusalem,
>
> Three persons [angels in the form of men] came to him [i.e., the Prophet] while he was asleep in the Sacred Mosque, and this was before he received his first revelation. The first of them said, "Which of them is he?" The middle one said, "He is the best of them." The last of them said, "Then take the best of them." That was all that happened that night and he did not see them again until they came another night [i.e., the night of the Night Journey]. That was all that was seen by his heart, as the eyes of the Prophet ﷺ were asleep but his heart never slept. Likewise are all the prophets, their eyes sleep but their hearts do not sleep. Gabriel then took charge of him and ascended with him to the heavens.[5]

---

3. This is *ḥadīth* 12 in this book.
4. Narrated by al-Bukhārī and Muslim, see *Ṣaḥīḥ al-Bukhārī*, vol. 2, pp. 701–702.
5. *Ṣaḥīḥ al-Bukhārī*, vol. 2, p. 702.

Ḥadīth 33

Visions of the Prophet

عَنْ أَبِي هُرَيْرَةَ قَالَ : سَمِعْتُ النَّبِيَّ صَلَّى اللهُ عَلَيْهِ وَسَلَّمَ يَقُولُ : « مَنْ رَآنِي فِي المَنَامِ فَسَيَرَانِي فِي اليَقَظَةِ »

On the authority of Abū Hurayra ﷺ who said, I heard the Prophet ﷺ say,

> He who saw me in his sleep will see me in a waking state.

Narrated by al-Bukhārī, Muslim, and Abū Dāwūd.[1]

The commentators on *Ṣaḥīḥ al-Bukhārī* differed on the meaning of this *ḥadīth*. A group said that he will see him in this life, and another group said that he will see him in the next. The first group replied to the second: the believer's sighting of the Prophet ﷺ on the Day of Rising is not dependent on one seeing him in his sleep in this life.

A group objected that seeing him in this life in a waking state necessitates his moving from his noble grave and his multiplication. The scholars answered that what is established is that he ﷺ is in the Rawḍa like the sun in the sky, which is seen by every human and in every country, without it moving or multiplying. This is what al-Suyūṭi accepted, and he composed a treatise on it called *Tanwīr al-ḥalak fī jawāz ruʾyat al-nabī wa-l-malak* [Illuminating the darkness on the possibility of seeing the Prophet and the angels], which he opened by citing this *ḥadīth*.

1. *Ṣaḥīḥ al-Bukhārī*, vol. 3, p. 1415.

Among those who proved this and confirmed it is our shaykh and teacher, the noble shaykh Aḥmad b. Idrīs ﷺ. He said that he received all of his litanies from the Prophet ﷺ while awake. His student, the great scholar of the Muslim West, the noble Muḥammad b. ʿAlī l-Sanūsī ﷺ agreed with him on that and mentioned it in his books.

Ḥadīth 34

The People of Remembrance

عَنْ أَبِي هُرَيْرَةَ ، قَالَ : قَالَ رَسُولُ اللهِ صَلَّى اللهُ عَلَيْهِ وَسَلَّمَ : « إِنَّ لِلهِ مَلَائِكَةً يَطُوفُونَ فِي الطُّرُقِ يَلْتَمِسُونَ أَهْلَ الذِّكْرِ ، فَإِذَا وَجَدُوا قَوْمًا يَذْكُرُونَ اللهَ تَنَادَوْا : هَلُمُّوا إِلَى حَاجَتِكُمْ ، قَالَ : فَيَحُفُّونَهُمْ بِأَجْنِحَتِهِمْ إِلَى السَّمَاءِ الدُّنْيَا ، قَالَ : فَيَسْأَلُهُمْ رَبُّهُمْ وَهُوَ أَعْلَمُ مِنْهُمْ مَا يَقُولُ عِبَادِي ؟ قَالُوا : يَقُولُونَ يُسَبِّحُونَكَ ، وَيُكَبِّرُونَكَ ، وَيَحْمَدُونَكَ ، وَيُمَجِّدُونَكَ ، قَالَ : فَيَقُولُ : هَلْ رَأَوْنِي ؟ قَالَ : فَيَقُولُونَ : لَا وَاللهِ مَا رَأَوْكَ ، قَالَ : فَيَقُولُ : وَكَيْفَ لَوْ رَأَوْنِي ؟ قَالَ : يَقُولُونَ : لَوْ رَأَوْكَ كَانُوا أَشَدَّ لَكَ عِبَادَةً ، وَأَشَدَّ لَكَ تَمْجِيدًا ، وَتَحْمِيدًا ، وَأَكْثَرَ لَكَ تَسْبِيحًا ، قَالَ : يَقُولُ : فَمَا يَسْأَلُونِي ؟ قَالَ : يَسْأَلُونَكَ الْجَنَّةَ ، قَالَ : يَقُولُ : وَهَلْ رَأَوْهَا ؟ قَالَ : يَقُولُونَ : لَا ، وَاللهِ يَا رَبِّ مَا رَأَوْهَا ، قَالَ : يَقُولُ : فَكَيْفَ لَوْ أَنَّهُمْ رَأَوْهَا ؟ قَالَ : يَقُولُونَ : لَوْ أَنَّهُمْ رَأَوْهَا كَانُوا أَشَدَّ عَلَيْهَا حِرْصًا ، وَأَشَدَّ لَهَا طَلَبًا ، وَأَعْظَمَ فِيهَا رَغْبَةً ، قَالَ : فَمِمَّ يَتَعَوَّذُونَ ؟ قَالَ : يَقُولُونَ : مِنَ النَّارِ ، قَالَ : يَقُولُ : وَهَلْ رَأَوْهَا ؟ قَالَ : يَقُولُونَ : لَا ، وَاللهِ يَا رَبِّ مَا رَأَوْهَا ، قَالَ : يَقُولُ : فَكَيْفَ لَوْ رَأَوْهَا ؟ قَالَ : يَقُولُونَ : لَوْ رَأَوْهَا كَانُوا أَشَدَّ مِنْهَا فِرَارًا ، وَأَشَدَّ لَهَا مَخَافَةً ، قَالَ : فَيَقُولُ : فَأُشْهِدُكُمْ أَنِّي

قَدْ غَفَرْتُ لهمْ ، قَالَ : يَقُولُ : مَلَكٌ مِنَ الملائِكَةِ : فِيهِمْ فُلَانٌ لَيْسَ مِنْهُمْ

إِنَّمَا جَاءَ لِحَاجَةٍ ، قَالَ : هُمُ الجُلَسَاءُ لَا يَشْقَى بِهِمْ جَلِيسُهُمْ »

On the authority of Abū Hurayra ☙, who said, the Messenger of God ☙ said,

> God has angels who travel the highways and byways seeking out the people of remembrance. When they find people remembering God ☙ they call out to one another, "Come to what you hunger for!" and they enfold them with their wings in layers stretching up to the lowest heaven. Their Lord—who knows best—asks them, "What are My servants saying?"
>
> They say, "They are glorifying You, proclaiming Your greatness, praising You, and magnifying You."
>
> He says, "Have they seen Me?"
>
> They say, "No, by God, they have not seen You."
>
> He says, "How would it be if they were to see Me?"
>
> They say, "If they were to see You, they would worship You even more intensely and magnify You even more intensely and glorify You even more intensely."
>
> He says, "What are they asking for?"
>
> They say, "They are asking You for the Garden."
>
> He says, "Have they seen it?"
>
> They say, "No, by God, Our Lord, they have not seen it."
>
> He says, "How would it be if they were to see it?"
>
> They say, "If they were to see it, they would yearn for it even more strongly and seek it even more tirelessly and would have an even greater desire for it."
>
> He says, "What are they seeking refuge from?"
>
> They say, "From the Fire."
>
> He says, "Have they seen it?"
>
> They say, "No, by God, Our Lord, they have not seen it."
>
> He says, "How would it be if they were to see it?"
>
> They say, "If they were to see it, they would flee from it even more determinedly and have an even greater fear of it."
>
> He says, "I make you all My witnesses in that I have forgiven them."

One of the angels said, "Among them is so-and-so who is not one of them. He came to get something he needed."

He says, "They are the people that, whoever sits with them, shall never suffer (because of having sat with them)."[1]

· ❁ · ❁ · ❁ ·

This *ḥadīth* which was narrated by al-Bukhārī ﵀ in his *Ṣaḥīḥ*, and was copied by our shaykh ﵀ in *Rūḥ al-sunna*, is the greatest evidence for the circles of remembrance and of people engaging in congregational remembrance. It shows the virtue of remembrance, and the virtue of sitting with those engaging in remembrance.

It also provides evidence that he who visits the grave of a prophet, the grave of someone from the people of the household of prophecy, the grave of a Companion of the Prophet ﷺ, or a friend of God ﵁ and sits near him, even if very briefly, is referred to by this *ḥadīth*, "They are the people that, whoever sits with them, shall never suffer (because of having sat with them)."

1. *Ṣaḥīḥ al-Bukhārī*, vol. 3, p. 1301. "*Lā yashqā*" (literally, 'shall not suffer') means, 'will not be of the people of the fire.' Its opposite is *yasʿad* (literally, 'to be happy') and means, 'to be of the people of paradise.' Here the emphasis is on the fact that it is due to them that others are saved from suffering, out of God's honoring of them, so He honors their guests.

Ḥadīth 35
Circles of Remembrance

عَنْ أَنَسِ بْنِ مَالِكٍ رَضِيَ اللهُ عَنْهُ أَنَّ رَسُولَ اللهِ صَلَّى اللهُ عَلَيهِ وَسَلَّمَ قَالَ : « إِذَا مَرَرْتُمْ بِرِيَاضِ الجَنَّةِ فَارْتَعُوا " ، قَالُوا : وَمَا رِيَاضُ الجَنَّةِ ؟ قَالَ : " حِلَقُ الذِّكْرِ »

On the authority of Anas b. Mālik ﵁, the Prophet ﷺ said,

> "If you pass by the gardens of paradise, then eat from them!" They said, "And what are the gardens of paradise?" He said, "The circles of remembrance."

Narrated by Aḥmad b. Ḥanbal, al-Tirmidhī, and al-Bayhaqī in *Shuʿab al-īmān*.[1]

The first time I heard this *ḥadīth* was from my shaykh, the gnostic of God ﷻ the noble Muḥammad al-Sharīf, the son of the gnostic of God ﷻ the noble ʿAbd al-ʿĀlī, the son of the gnostic of God ﷻ, my master the noble Aḥmad b. Idrīs ﵁.

Shaykh Muḥammad al-Sharīf ﵀ said, "It is understood from this *ḥadīth* that it is desirable to come together in circles of remembrance, and that the gnostics find pleasure in the remembrance of God ﷻ, as the people of paradise find pleasure in its bliss."

He is saying that coming together in the circles of remembrance is a sunna and not an innovation in the religion as some claim,

1. *Sunan al-Tirmidhī*, vol. 2, pp. 900–901.

because of the mention of circles of remembrance in the *ḥadīth*. The [Prophet's] Companions 🕌 did that, and the Prophet 🕌 approved, as illustrated by the *ḥadīth* in *Ṣaḥīḥ Muslim*.[2]

As for their finding pleasure in the remembrance, this occurs for different reasons. The first is the disappearance of all that is other than God—even one's self—from the spiritual eye of the heart. That is why the shaykh used to always say while he was in remembrance, "Make yourself disappear O you who is engaging in remembrance!" and I did a lot of remembrance with him, and praise is due to God. The disappearance of what is other than God results in lights, and it is like the tasting of the tongue but for the heart.

The second reason is the witnessing of God the transcendent, a witnessing that is free from any modalities and beyond anything imaginable, until the effect of the witnessing appears to the soul. It is like the bliss of paradise, and nothing surpasses it except the vision of God in paradise. As the author of *Bad' al-amālī* 🕌 said in describing the people of paradise when they witness the Real 🕌,

> They will forget the bliss when they see Him,
> so what great loss awaits the Mu'tazilī.[3]

It means that they will forget the bliss of paradise because of the bliss of the vision of the divine. Likewise the gnostics in this world forget the bliss of the world when they encounter in their hearts and souls the pleasure of the witnessing of the Real, High, and Transcendent is He. My master ʿAbdallāh al-Maḥjūb al-Mīrghanī 🕌 said,

> Witness the remembrance with the one being remembered,
> and pass away from the gardens and palaces of paradise

The words of Shaykh Muḥammad al-Sharīf 🕌 indicate to us that the pleasure found in remembrance is truly great.

Hear, our brother, then listen with your heart to what we say. The knower of God, when he engages in the remembrance of God 🕌,

---

2. The *ḥadīth* referred to here will be quoted after the commentary.
3. The Mu'tazilī denied the possibility of the vision of God. *Bad' al-amālī* is a poem on theology by ʿAlī b. ʿUthmān al-Ūshī (d. 569), of the Māturīdī theological school.

his soul, body, and the hair on his body find pleasure, and he feels it. In this state he cannot be burned by fire, because he is in a place of connection to the divine, which turns all harmful things into beneficial ones.

Translator's Note

The above-mentioned *ḥadīth* is in *Ṣaḥīḥ Muslim:*

> Abū Saʿīd al-Khudrī said that Muʿāwiya said, "The Messenger of God came to a circle of his Companions and said, 'What has made you sit together?"
>
> They said, "We sat to remember God and to praise Him for guiding us to Islam and for the favors that He bestowed upon us."
>
> He said, "By God nothing else made you sit together?"
>
> They said, "By God nothing else made us sit together!"
>
> He said, "Know that I did not make you swear on this because I doubted you, but because Gabriel came to me and informed me that God ﷻ is showing you off to the angels!"[4]

4. *Ṣaḥīḥ Muslim*, vol. 2, p. 1140. Also narrated by al-Tirmidhī and al-Nasāʾī.

Ḥadīth 36

Polishing the Heart

عَنْ عَبْدِ اللهِ بْنِ عُمَرَ عَنِ النَّبِيِّ صَلَّى اللهُ عَلَيْهِ وَسَلَّمَ أَنَّهُ كَانَ يَقُولُ :
« إِنَّ لِكُلِّ شيءٍ صِقَالَةً ، وَإِنَّ صِقَالَةَ الْقُلُوبِ ذِكْرُ اللهِ عَزَّ وَجَلَّ ، وَمَا
مِنْ شيءٍ أَنْجَى مِنْ عَذَابِ اللهِ مِنْ ذِكْرِ اللهِ » قَالُوا: وَلَا الْجِهَادُ فِي سَبِيلِ
اللهِ ؟ قَالَ : « ولو أَنْ يَضْرِبَ بِسَيْفِهِ حَتَّى يَنْقَطِعَ »

On the authority of ʿAbdallāh b. ʿUmar who said that the Prophet ﷺ used to say,

> "For everything there is a burnisher, and the burnisher of the hearts is the remembrance of God. There is nothing that saves one from the punishment of God more than the remembrance of God."
>
> They said, "Not even armed struggle in the cause of God?"
>
> He said, "Not even if one were to strike with his sword until it broke."

Narrated by my master Aḥmad b. Idrīs in *Rūḥ al-sunna*.[1]

---

1. *Rūḥ al-sunna*, p. 126. Also by al-Bayhaqī in *Shuʿab al-īmān*, vol. 2, p. 62. It has been narrated with the word for burnisher starting with the letter *sīn* as well as *ṣād* (see al-Suyūṭī, *Jamʿ al-jawāmiʿ*, vol. 2, p. 596, n. 6). I have found it printed with the letter *ṣād* (*ṣiqāla*) in the works of Ibn Idrīs and al-Jaʿfarī, and in al-Bayhaqī's *Kitāb al-daʿawāt al-kabīr*; and I have found it printed with a *sīn* (*siqāla*) in al-Bayhaqī's *Shuʿab al-īman* and al-Suyūṭī's *Jamʿ al-jawāmiʿ*.

This *ḥadīth* shows that

1. Remembrance polishes the hearts, and in neglecting it they rust like metal. Another *ḥadīth* narrated by Ibn ʿUdayy states, "Hearts rust as metal rusts, and their polish is the remembrance of God."[2]
2. The remembrance of God brings safety and security from the punishment of God.
3. It has a great virtue in the sight of God. If the servant engages in the remembrance of his Lord and struggles in His way, then he has combined the two virtues, the virtue of remembrance and the virtue of struggle; likewise for he who engages in the remembrance of his Lord and struggles against his desires and his ego.

2. The full *ḥadīth* is: On the authority of Ibn ʿUmar, the Prophet ﷺ said, "Hearts rust as metal rusts when it is exposed to water." They said, "What is their polish, O Messenger of God?" He said, "Much remembrance of God" (ʿAbdallāh Ibn ʿUdayy, *al-Kāmil fī ḍuʿafāʾ al-rijāl*, vol. 1, p. 420).

Ḥadīth 37

Satan's Whispers

عَنْ أَنَسِ بْنِ مَالِكٍ: قَالَ رَسُولُ اللهِ صَلَّى اللهُ عَلَيْهِ وَسَلَّمَ : « إِنَّ الشَّيْطَانَ وَاضِعٌ خَطْمَهُ عَلَى قَلْبِ ابْنِ آدَمَ ، فَإِنْ ذَكَرَ اللهَ خَنَسَ ، وَإِنْ نَسِيَ الْتَقَمَ قَلْبَهُ »

On the authority of Anas 🌸, the Prophet 🌼 said,

> Satan has placed his snout on the heart of the son of Adam. If he remembers God, he retreats, and if he forgets, he puts his heart into his mouth.

Narrated by ʿAbd al-Razzāq, Ibn Abī l-Dunyā, Abū Yaʿlā in his *Musnad*, and al-Bayhaqī in *Shuʿab al-īmān*.[1]

---

1.   Al-Bayhaqī, *Shuʿab al-īmān*, vol. 2, p. 74. Ibn Abī l-Dunyā's narration is from *Makāʾid al-shayṭān*. Ibn Idrīs also narrated it in *Rūḥ al-sunna*, p. 129. Al-Ṭabarī narrated in his Qurʾān commentary that the Prophet's cousin Ibn ʿAbbās said, "Satan is sitting on the heart of the son of Adam. If he forgets or becomes absentminded, he whispers into it, and if he remembers God he retreats." He also narrated that Ibn ʿAbbās said, "Everyone is born with the whisperer on his heart. If he remembers God, he retreats, and if he is absentminded, he whispers. That is why God says, *The one who whispers and retreats* (114:4)." It was also narrated thus by al-Bayhaqī and al-Ḥākim, who declared it an authentic narration (al-Suyūṭī, *al-Durr al-manthūr*, vol. 6, pp. 721–722).

In this *ḥadīth* the Prophet ﷺ tells us how Satan whispers into the heart of man, that he comes from the left side and extends his snout—i.e., his trunk—to the heart. If he finds it busy in the remembrance of God, he retreats, meaning that he turns back and escapes. If he finds him not thinking of God, he puts the person's heart in his mouth, meaning that he takes over his heart and whispers into it that which angers God ﷻ. Some narrations say that, "he begins to put false hopes into him." This means that he whispers into him distant hopes of the vanities of the world and its adornments to keep him distracted from the remembrance of God ﷻ, and he instills in him doubts and false imaginings. He ﷻ says, *He promises them and gives them false hopes, but Satan's promises are nothing but delusion* (4:120). May God give us and you refuge from the whisperings of the accursed Satan.

One of the righteous men asked his Lord ﷻ to show him in his sleep how Satan whispers into the heart of the believer. He was shown a cup full of water, and a frog approaching it. When the frog came near it, the cup shook, and the frog turned back and escaped. It was said to him, "This cup is like the heart: its shaking is like the remembrance of God ﷻ, and the frog is like Satan."

Know, our brother in God ﷻ that when a thought occurs in your heart telling you to do or say something, you must present it to the Book and the Sunna. If they accept it, then know that it is from the angels, so hurry in doing it, and if they do not accept it, then escape from it as you would escape from a wild beast, and know that it is from Satan.

Sometimes, Satan might whisper things to a man that, if he uttered them in turn, he would be a disbeliever. When a person reaches that state, then let him know that he has reached the completion of faith. He should not argue with Satan for arguing only increases his hold, as has been related by my master Aḥmad Zarrūq ؓ. I heard my shaykh, the *ḥadīth* scholar Ḥabībullāh al-Shinqīṭī ؓ quote the following rhymed composition of that rule,

> That which Satan whispers
> and the heart rejects—that is (an indication of) faith.

So do not argue then with the accursed one
for that will only increase his hold on you.
A rule that was established by Zarrūq
whose words never stop delighting.

Translator's Note

Shaykh Aḥmad b. Idrīs said in *al-ʿIqd al-nafīs*,

> The [Prophet's] Companions ﷺ complained to the Prophet ﷺ and said, "O Messenger of God, Satan whispers things to us that we find too horrible to mention." The Prophet said, "That is pure faith!"[2]
>
> That is because Satan is like the thief, and the thief only tries to enter inhabited houses. As for houses in ruin, there is nothing there for the thief to take. *When they are touched by an instigation from Satan, those who fear God remember (God) and at once they have insight* (7:201).[3]

2. Narrated by Muslim, al-Nasāʾī, Aḥmad, al-Bayhaqī and others. See the narration of Muslim on the authority of Abū Hurayra, vol. 1, p. 68.
3. *al-ʿIqd al-nafīs*, p. 30.

Ḥadīth 38

Formulas of Remembrance

عَنْ أَبِي بَكْرٍ عَنِ النَّبِيِّ صَلَّى اللّٰهُ عَلَيْهِ وَسَلَّمَ قَالَ : « عَلَيْكُمْ بِلا إِلَهَ إِلا اللّٰهُ وَالاسْتِغْفَارِ فَأَكْثِرُوا مِنْهُمَا فَإِنَّ إِبْلِيسَ قَالَ : أَهْلَكْتُ النَّاسَ بِالذُّنُوبِ وَأَهْلَكُونِي بِلا إِلَهَ إِلا اللّٰهُ وَالاسْتِغْفَارِ ، فَلَمَّا رَأَيْتُ ذَلِكَ أَهْلَكْتُهُمْ بِالأَهْوَاءِ وَهُمْ يَحْسَبُونَ أَنَّهُمْ مُهْتَدُونَ »

On the authority of Abū Bakr ﵁, the Prophet ﷺ said,

> Hold tight to "there is no god but God" and the asking of God's forgiveness, and repeat them often. Iblīs[1] has said, "I caused the people's ruin with sins, and they caused my ruin with 'there is no god but God' and the asking of God's forgiveness. When I saw that, I caused their ruin by making them follow their desires while thinking that they are guided."

Narrated by Abū Yaʿlā in his *Musnad* and by my master Aḥmad b. Idrīs in *Rūḥ al-sunna*.[2]

---

1. The name of Satan.
2. Abū Yaʿlā l-Mawṣilī, *Musnad Abī Yaʿlā l-Mawṣilī*, vol. 1, p. 123. This *ḥadīth* seems to be a commentary on the Qurʾānic verses: *If anyone shuts his eyes to the remembrance of the all-Merciful, We assign him an evil one as a companion. They debar them from the path, while they think that they are guided* (43:36–37). The author also attributed it to ʿAbd al-Razzāq in his work *Fatḥ wa fayḍ*, p. 120.

In this *ḥadīth* there is a command from the Prophet ﷺ to repeat often, "there is no god but God" and ask God's forgiveness. Remembrance with "there is no god but God" calls the self to repentance and regret, and repentance calls the self to seek God's forgiveness, and with the seeking of His forgiveness, sins are forgiven.

As for the desires, He ﷺ reminded us of, *he whose evil work was adorned for him so that he saw it as good and beautiful* (35:8). It is a work of disobedience in the image of obedience, so that when one is done with it, he does not feel regret or repent for it, and is thus deprived of being forgiven for it. It could also be that one speaks to God ﷻ after committing the disobedient act with speech that is not befitting, such as by using the excuse of divine decree and apportionment.

Ibn ʿAbbād al-Shāfiʿī spoke eloquently on this matter in his commentary on the *Aphorisms* of Ibn ʿAṭāʾillāh al-Sakandarī l-Mālikī. He then mentioned the following *ḥadīth*. He ﷺ said, "If the servant commits a sin and says, 'O Lord, I have wronged and sinned,' God ﷻ says, 'I have acted with mercy and forgiveness.' But if he says, 'You willed and decreed,' God ﷻ says, 'Neither will I act with mercy nor will I forgive.'"

My master Abū l-Ḥasan al-Shādhilī ؓ said about the repentance of Adam ؑ, "It is so that he would be an example to his children in repentance and good works." This means that our master Adam ؑ, when he ate from the tree, ascribed the error to himself and said, *Our Lord, we have wronged our souls: if You do not forgive us and have mercy, we shall certainly be of the losers* (7:23). Likewise the believers, if one of them does something wrong he speaks to God ﷻ with the speech of his father Adam and says, "My Lord I have wronged my soul" and does not use the excuse of predestination. Among the supplications of the Prophet is to say, "At your service, O Lord, at your service! All goodness is in Your hands, and evil is not attributed to you!"[3]

3. Narrated by Muslim in his *Ṣaḥīḥ*, vol. 1, pp. 307–308, and others. *Labbayk* means, "Here I am, at Your service," but literally means, "My whole being is Yours," as it comes from "My *lubb* (essence/heart) is Yours."

Ḥadīth 39

Dealing with God, the Self, and Others

عَنْ أَبِي ذَرٍّ قَالَ: قَالَ لِي رَسُولُ اللهِ صَلَّى اللهُ عَلَيْهِ وَسَلَّمَ : « اتَّقِ اللهَ حَيْثُمَا كُنْتَ ، وَأَتْبِعِ السَّيِّئَةَ الحَسَنَةَ تَمْحُهَا ، وَخَالِقِ النَّاسَ بِخُلُقٍ حَسَنٍ »

On the authority of Abū Dharr [al-Ghifārī] ﵁ who said, the Messenger of God ﷺ said to me,

> Fear God wherever you are, follow a bad act with a good one and it will wipe out the first, and treat people with beautiful manners.

Narrated by al-Tirmidhī.[1]

·❁·❁·❁·

He ﷺ is commanding us to fear God (have *taqwā*) in our three types of dealings: our dealings with God ﷻ, our dealings with the self, and our dealings with people. Whoever does well in all these dealings lives safe and will be resurrected safe and secure on the Day of Rising; God will let him enter paradise with the people of *taqwā*, who will be safe.

When it comes to dealing with Him ﷻ, it is to have *taqwā* in private and in public. This is the directive of God ﷻ to us and to those who came before us: *We have directed those who were given the Book before you, and you, to fear God* (4:131).

Taqwā was defined by our master ʿAlī (may God ennoble his face) as, "Fear of the Majestic One, acting according to the revelation,

---

1. *Sunan al-Tirmidhī*, vol. 2, p. 516. Also narrated by Aḥmad and others.

contentment with what is little, and preparing for the day of departure." This is because fear of God ﷻ makes the self desire to do good and righteous works, energizes it for that, and stops it from committing offenses and lowly acts. He who knows God fears Him, and he who fears Him has *taqwā*, and he who has *taqwā* obeys His commands and avoids His prohibitions. *With this God puts fear in His servants. O servants of Mine! Be, then fearful of Me!* (39:16).

Acting according to the revelation is acting according to the Book of God ﷻ in what He commanded and forbade, because it is the straight path: whoever travels it reaches the pleasure of God, and whoever turns away from it will be of those who perish. *A blessed Book that We sent down to you so that they reflect on its verses and so that the men of understanding may be mindful* (38:29).

Contentment with little is to submit to God's decree and apportionment and to thank Him for all states, because He knows and we do not know, and He is the knower of the unseen. How many times did wealth make its owners wretched, and how many times did simplicity bring happiness! *It may be that you dislike something which is good for you, and it may be that you like something which is bad for you, and God knows and you do not know* (2:216).

Preparing for the day of departure is being ready for death, which comes without a known appointed time, arriving suddenly by the command of God. How many a healthy man was among the living in the morning and among the dead in the evening. He was with his children and loved ones, and became the captive of his grave and its sand. The intelligent one is he who prepares himself to meet the One whose command is "be!" and it is.

Dealing with the self is to strive for its righteousness, success, purification, and the acquisition of good manners. It is to return to God often and to do good deeds after bad ones so that God forgives the self what it did before and writes it among the repentant. *Surely good deeds remove evil deeds. This is a reminder to the mindful* (11:114). He who neglects himself has brought it loss, and that is a great injustice. Success is for the one who rectifies himself with the *sharīʿa*, and great disappointment awaits him who neglects it. *Prosperous is he who purified it, and failed has he who corrupted it* (91:9–10).

Treating people with beautiful manners is to reconnect with those who cut you off, give to those who deprived you, forgive those who were unjust to you, and to have forbearance with those who act with rage. Forbearance is water and anger is fire, and the one who has water will overcome the one who has fire. Beware of anger, for it is a terrible companion! It is because of anger that a person injures his neighbors, divorces his wife, curses the religion and the *sharīʿa*; and it is because of anger that blood is shed, and fathers and mothers are cursed. The origin of every great calamity is anger. It is the knife of separation, the signpost of evil, the cry of destruction, the great misfortune of humanity, and the evil of society. It severs brotherhood, intoxicates minds, suspends wisdom, and corrupts intelligence. Anger is the fire of enmity and the darkness of ignorance. He who wants to live happily, then, should beware of anger, choose forbearance as his companion, and behave according to the manners of the most forbearing of all the worlds ﷺ.

Ḥadīth 40

The Three Mosques

عَنْ أَبِي هُرَيْرَةَ رَضِيَ اللهُ عَنْهُ، عَنِ النَّبِيِّ صَلَّى اللهُ عَلَيْهِ وَسَلَّمَ قَالَ: « لا تُشَدُّ الرِّحَالُ إِلَّا إِلَى ثَلَاثَةِ مَسَاجِد : مَسْجِدِي هَذَا ، وَمَسْجِدِ الحَرَامِ ، وَمَسْجِدِ الأَقْصَى »

On the authority of Abū Hurayra ﵁, the Prophet ﷺ said,

> There is no journey except to three mosques: this mosque of mine [in Medina], the Sacred Mosque [in Mecca], and al-Aqṣā Mosque [in Jerusalem].

Narrated by al-Bukhārī and Muslim.[1]

·❁·❁·❁·

The Prophet ﷺ wanted to show the virtue of these three mosques over others, and to show that the rest of the mosques are equal to one another in virtue. It is not permissible to move from one mosque to another with the belief that praying in the other mosque is better than the first. This is because prayer in all mosques is rewarded equally, except in the Sacred Mosque, where a single prayer equals a hundred thousand prayers, in the Mosque of the Prophet ﷺ, where one prayer equals a thousand prayers, and in al-Aqṣā Mosque, where one prayer equals five hundred prayers.

Therefore, the meaning of the *ḥadīth* is that no one is to move from one mosque to another mosque believing that prayer in the

1. This is the wording in *Ṣaḥīḥ Muslim*, vol. 1, pp. 566–567.

second is better than in the first; except for these three mosques, because of their virtue.

These three mosques, then, are exceptions to mosques in general. The Prophet ﷺ wanted to show in this *ḥadīth* that worship in all mosques is equal in reward, so no one should prefer one mosque over another, and therefore move to it, except for the three mosques. The virtue of worship in these three permits us to move to them from other mosques. This virtue is something that we learn from the Prophet ﷺ, not something we can infer with our minds.

The jurists understood from this *ḥadīth* that if a man vowed to pray two units of prayer to God in al-Azhar Mosque, for example, then it is permissible for him to fulfill his vow by praying them in any mosque whatsoever. However, if he vowed to pray two units in one of the three mosques, then he must travel to that mosque.

There are many people who, if you say to them, "I want to visit the Prophet ﷺ," they would say, "He ﷺ said, 'There is no journey except. . . .'" If you say to them, "I want to visit one of the Friends of God ﷺ," they would say to you, "There is no journey except. . . ." These people have misunderstood this *ḥadīth* because the *ḥadīth* is talking about mosques, not about visiting graves.

The phrase used by the Prophet ﷺ, "There is no journey" is meant to include any type of movement from one location to another, whether it is a long journey or a short one. The expression is one that is used for long journeys only because they are more common. This is what my Lord ﷻ inspired in me, and after studying the writings of the *ḥadīth* commentators I found the correct opinion to be the one that I have mentioned to you here. The Commander of the Faithful [in the science of *ḥadīth*], Ibn Ḥajar al-ʿAsqalānī ﷺ said on this *ḥadīth*,

> Precedence must be given to the most fitting interpretation, which is that there is no journeying to a mosque in order to pray in it, except to the three. This nullifies the claim of those who forbid journeying to visit the noble grave [of the Prophet] and the graves of the righteous.

Ibn Ḥajar ﷺ said, "That is one of the ugliest matters reported from Ibn Taymiyya." By this he meant Ibn Taymiyya's prohibition of journeying for the sake of visiting the grave of the Prophet ﷺ.

Beneficial point: That which leads to the obligatory is obligatory. For example, paying the amount that the pilgrimage company requires—if the pilgrimage depends on it—becomes obligatory. Likewise, if the minor pilgrimage depends on spending a certain amount, then going by the opinion that performing the minor pilgrimage is a *sunna*, paying that amount is also *sunna*. This means that one receives the reward of performing the *sunna* for the money paid for the minor pilgrimage. The fact that visiting the graves of the Muslims is recommended has been established by the verbal and actual *sunna* of the Prophet ﷺ. The verbal is his saying, "Do visit them,"[2] and the actual is his visiting the graves in the al-Baqīʿ cemetery.

If it is established that visiting graves is a *sunna*, then that which leads to it is also a *sunna*. So, if you walk to the cemetery as the Prophet ﷺ walked to al-Baqīʿ, then your walking is a *sunna*, meaning that you will get the reward of doing a *sunna* for it. Similarly if you rented a horse and paid for it so that you can visit the cemetery, your paying for its rental is a *sunna*, meaning that you get rewarded for it accordingly. Likewise, if a man's parents called him to come to them in Upper Egypt, his going to Upper Egypt becomes obligatory on him because obedience to one's parents is obligatory. So if he pays for the train ride and goes to his parents in Upper Egypt, he is given the reward of an obligatory action for the money he paid. Therefore, he who says that journeying to visit graves is forbidden and uses the *ḥadīth* of, "There is no journey except . . ." is wrong because he ﷺ said, "Do visit them." This is a general command that covers journeys by foot or riding. Therefore, the prohibition of such a journey and objection to visitors is without evidence.

2. This is *ḥadīth* 15 of this book, narrated by Muslim, ʿAbd al-Razzāq, and others. See *ḥadīth* 15 and *ḥadīth* 16.

Ibn ʿUmar said that the Messenger of God ﷺ used to journey to the mosque of Qubāʾ riding and on foot.[3] Ibn Ḥajar al-ʿAsqalānī said, "In this *ḥadīth* there is evidence that the 'no' in 'There is no journey except . . .' is not intended as a prohibition."[4]

3. Muslim narrated, "The Messenger of God ﷺ used to go to the Mosque of Qubāʾ, riding and on foot, and pray two units of prayer" (*Ṣaḥīḥ Muslim*). Al-Bukhārī narrated that this took place every Saturday, and that Ibn ʿUmar used to always do the same (*Ṣaḥīḥ al-Bukhārī*, vol. 1, p. 223).
4. Meaning that it is intended solely to indicate the virtue of the three mosques over other mosques. Muslim narrated, "The Messenger of God ﷺ used to go to the mosque of Qubāʾ, riding and on foot, and pray two units of prayer." In *Ṣaḥīh al-Bukhārī* a *ḥadīth* states that this took place every Saturday. In the *Sunan* of Ibn Māja and other works is the statement of the Prophet, "He who purifies himself in his house then goes to the mosque of Qubāʾ and prays in it will have the reward of a minor pilgrimage." Another states, "One prayer in the mosque of Qubāʾ is like doing the minor pilgrimage." (See both in *Sunan Ibn Māja*, p. 207).

Appendix

The *Ḥadīth* of the Muḥammadan Sunna with a commentary by Shaykh Aḥmad b. Idrīs

Edited and published by Shaykh Ṣāliḥ al-Jaʿfarī as *Shahd mushāhadat al-arwāḥ al-taqiyya min baḥr ʿulūm jadd al-sāda al-idrīsiyya* [The honey that pious souls drink from the ocean of the sciences of Shaykh Aḥmad b. Idrīs]

Introduction

All praise is due to God, and the most excellent salutations upon His Prophet Muḥammad. The Prophet ﷺ said, "The scholars are the inheritors of the prophets." From ancient times, the prophets sent to the Children of Israel and other nations represent a measure of the incalculable blessings that God bestowed upon humanity. Sometimes sent to reaffirm, and other times to renew the divine writ, their timely interventions through the ages also reveal something about those who inherited the Trust, for confirmation and renewal was necessary only when corruption and degeneration came to pass. That is until, at last, there came Muḥammad ﷺ, the Seal of the Prophets. The nation of God's final messenger is truly blessed because it has and will have scholars who are guided to convey the divine writ until the end of days. God's final Messenger affirmed this in his saying, "From my nation there are persons who are guided, and ʿUmar is among them." There are no more messengers then, but inheritors—message-bearers upon right guidance.

Among the scholars who have served Islam and conveyed the message of our master Muḥammad ﷺ is Aḥmad b. Idrīs, the great imam who spent a lifetime as a wayfarer—from Morocco, to Mecca, Medina, and then southern Arabia, he finally came to rest in Ṣabyā in the Yemen. With each step and every footfall, Imam Aḥmad discharged the trust inherited from the Prophet ﷺ.

Imam Aḥmad b. Idrīs ranked among those guided, and now, even long after he has passed away, he remains a blessing for the Muslim community, for great scholars are careful to bequeath the trust to those who come after them. Imam Aḥmad had a profound influence on the scholarly, intellectual, and social life of the Muslim nation. Though his was a life of constant migration, the Idrīsiyya school blossomed and God knows best, because of the Shaykh's encyclopedic knowledge, his strict adherence to the rules of the *sharīʿa*, his complete dedication to the guidance of the Prophet ﷺ, and his ongoing concern for the comprehensive spiritual upbringing of his students. This was demonstrated most clearly with the spread of his school in the East and the West at the hands of great scholars whose qualifications, spiritual leadership, and adherence to the prophetic guidance were fully attested to. Imam Aḥmad never sought to spread his path and increase the number of his students—his only aim was to spread the teachings of the religion and to guide those who sought knowledge.

While the noble Imam Aḥmad inherited from the Prophet ﷺ in another sense, as a descendant of the Prophet, perhaps the truest measure of his blessing was his ceaseless striving and absolute selflessness in serving God's religion—and these characteristics he passed on to his students. Among his many students were Imam Jaʿfar al-Nātī in Eritrea and Imam Ṣāliḥ al-Jaʿfarī in Egypt.

One of the blessings of Imam Aḥmad was the spread of his path in Eritrea at the hands of the great imam and peerless scholar, Shaykh Jaʿfar al-Nātī, who received his education at the hands of Shaykh Muḥammad al-Dandarāwī in Medina al-Munawwara, the city of the Messenger ﷺ. Shaykh Jaʿfar al-Nātī returned to Eritrea at the command of Shaykh al-Dandarāwī, who directed him to spread the path in his native land. On his return, he was received by Shaykh al-Amīn, the shaykh of the Qādiriyya path. He settled in a small village near the port city of Massawa, which grew into the town of Amatere (from the Arabic *amā tarā*, "do you not see?"). Within a very short period he established a unique school, where he dedicated his life to teaching the memorization and meanings of the Qurʾān, the sciences of the *sharīʿa*, and Sufism. Amatere became a base of scholarship, a center to which students of knowledge from all parts of Eritrea traveled. At the school of Shaykh Jaʿfar the Qurʾān was recited continuously, even throughout the nights, when bonfires allowed his students to recite without interruption until the morning. The Shaykh traveled throughout Eritrea in order to spread knowledge and offer guidance, and his path flourished along the length of the Eritrean seaboard.

Sincerity to the divine writ and steadfastness in the prophetic tradition is at the heart of this work, the first English biography of Imam Ṣāliḥ al-Jaʿfarī, a translation of forty *aḥādīth* collected by the imam, and a short treatise by his mentor, Imam Aḥmad b. Idrīs. As befits a student of knowledge, sincerity underscores the efforts of our beloved Sayyid Samer Dajani—may God enable us and ennoble him.

(Shaykh) Faid Mohammed Said
Alubudiya.co.uk

محمد رسول الله

The *Ḥadīth* of the Muḥammadan Sunna

حَدِيثُ السُّنَّةِ المُحَمَّدِيَّةِ

رُوِيَ عَنْ سَيِّدِنا عَلِيٍّ كَرَّمَ اللهُ تَعالَى وَجهَهُ أَنَّهُ قالَ : سَأَلْتُ رَسُولَ اللهِ صَلَّى اللهُ عليهِ وَسَلَّمَ عَنْ سُنَّتِهِ ، فَقَالَ صَلَّى اللهُ عَلَيْهِ وآلِهِ وَسَلَّمَ :

« المَعْرِفَةُ رَأْسُ مَالِي ، وَالْعَقْلُ أَصْلُ دِينِي ، وَالحُبُّ أَسَاسِي ، وَالشَّوْقُ مَرْكَبِي ، وَذِكْرُ اللهِ أَنِيسِي ، وَالثِّقَةُ كَنْزِي ، وَالحُزْنُ رَفِيقِي ، وَالْعِلْمُ سِلَاحِي ، وَالصَّبرُ زادِي ، وَالرِّضا غَنِيمَتِي ، وَالْعَجْزُ فَخْرِي ، وَالزُّهْدُ حِرْفَتِي ، وَالْيَقِينُ قُوَّتِي ، وَالصِّدْقُ شَفِيعِي ، وَالطَّاعَةُ حَسْبِي ، وَالْجِهَادُ خُلُقِي ، وَقُرَّةُ عَيني فِي الصَّلاةِ ، وَهَمِّي لِأَجْلِ أُمَّتِي ، وَشَوقِي إِلَى رَبِّي »

It has been narrated that our master ʿAlī (may God ennoble his face) said, I asked the Messenger of God ﷺ about his *sunna*. He ﷺ said,

Knowledge of God is my capital; intellect is the basis of my religion; love is my foundation; longing is my vessel; remembrance of God is my comfort; trust is my treasure; sorrow is my companion; knowledge is my weapon; patience is my provision; contentment is my trophy; powerlessness is my pride; detachment is my trade; certainty is my strength; truthfulness is my intercessor; obedience is my honor; struggle is my character; my pleasure is in prayer; my concern is for my community; and my longing is for my Lord.[1]

1. Quoted by al-Qāḍī ʿIyāḍ in *al-Shifā bi-taʿrīf ḥuqūq al-Muṣṭafā*, pp. 146–

The meaning of his saying ﷺ, "Knowledge of God is my capital."

It is to know God ﷻ: He is the First, for there is nothing before Him, and the Last, for there is nothing after Him, and the Outer, for there is nothing above Him, and the Inner, for there is nothing beneath Him. This is the definition with which God ﷻ defined Himself as it came to us from His Prophet ﷺ. He ﷺ used to say in his supplication, "You are the First, for there is nothing before You, and You are the Last, for there is nothing after You, and You are the Outer, for there is nothing above You, and You are the Inner, for there is nothing beneath You."[2]

So knowledge of God is to erase the entire universe from one's sight, and to turn one's face only toward God ﷻ. *Wherever you turn, there is the face of God* (Q. 2:115). That is the capital, and with it come divine self-disclosures.[3]

The meaning of his saying ﷺ, "Intellect is the basis of my religion."

The intellect is the starting point of every goodness and God did not bless a servant with a blessing greater than the intellect. With it he is able to differentiate between truth and falsehood, faith and disbelief, and with it he is able to distinguish what is permissible from that which is forbidden. With it he can understand which things please God ﷻ and which things anger Him; it, therefore, is the starting point of every blessing. Knowledge of God, which is the foundation of faith, is only acquired through it.

When God created the intellect He said to it, "Come!" and so it came. Then he said to it, "Go!" and so it went.[4] When it understood

---

147. A slightly different version was quoted by Abū Ḥāmid al-Ghazālī in *Iḥyāʾ ʿulūm al-dīn* (Beirut: Dār al-Kitāb al-ʿArabī, 2005), p. 1822.

2. Narrated by Muslim in his *Ṣaḥīḥ*, vol. 2, p. 1144, and several others. It is based on the verse, *He is the First and the Last; the Outer and the Inner; He has knowledge of all things* (57:3).

3. *Tajalliyāt* (sing. *tajalli*): Literally, "a coming forth into the light," "an effulgence," "a revealing." "A term in mysticism meaning an epiphany, a manifestation of the numinous, an emanation of inward light, an unveiling of divine secrets, and enlightening of the heart of the devotee." Cyril Glassé, *The New Encyclopedia of Islam*, p. 445.

4. See the *aḥādīth* in al-Bayhaqī, *Shuʿab al-īmān*, vol. 6, pp. 348–350.

(*ʿaqila*) how to follow orders, and understood the commands and prohibitions, it was called an *ʿaql*. This word is taken from the fetters (*ʿiqāl*) of riding beasts, because it keeps people tied to what God loves and is pleased with.

The meaning of his saying ﷺ, "Love is my foundation."

Love is the foundation of knowledge of God. There is a *ḥadīth* that says, "There is no faith for he who has no love," meaning love of God.

The best kind of love is when God and His Messenger are more beloved to the person than anything other than them. *Say (to them O Muḥammad), "If you love God then follow me, and God will love you"* (3:31). So when one follows him and does the things that are beloved to God ﷻ, God will love him. What is required is that he follow the Messenger of God ﷺ in what he commands and forbids, and then, when God loves him, the servant will most surely become devoted to God. One of the supplications of David ﷺ was, "O God, I ask You for the love of You, and for the love of those who love You, and I ask You for those works that will make me attain Your love. O God, make Your love more beloved to me than myself, my family, and cold water [in immense heat]."[5] The reason he enumerated these particular things is because they take hold of the heart and distract it from God ﷻ. If one does not occupy himself with God ﷻ and instead occupies himself with these things, then it is feared that he will become ungrateful for God's blessings, and we seek refuge in God ﷻ from that.

The meaning of his saying ﷺ, "Longing is my vessel."[6]

The human body is a vessel for the soul, and longing is the wind that drives this vessel. As long as there is attachment to God ﷻ, the vessel moves.

5. *Sunan al-Tirmidhī*, vol. 2, p. 896.
6. Similarly, in a long *ḥadīth* describing the different qualities of the believer, the Prophet says to Muʿādh b. Jabal, "Longing is his riding beast, prayer is his cave [of refuge] . . . and truthfulness is his leader." Narrated by Abū Nuʿaym in the *Ḥilya*, vol. 10, p. 31.

Longing is higher than love because love is to be inclined toward God ﷻ, and longing is to hurry toward Him without pause; it is possible to have an inclination without longing, but when there is longing then inclination is definitely present.

The meaning of his saying ﷺ, "Remembrance of God is my comfort."[7]

In one *ḥadīth* is the supplication, "O God, You are the companion in travel."[8] The traveler does not find *uns*[9] on his journey except in his companion, and as one *ḥadīth* states, "There is no breath that a human breathes, except that he has taken a step forward with it toward the afterlife." Therefore, the breaths constitute the journey. If the remembrance of God is the *anīs* on that journey, then that is the best companion! He who remembers God on his journey has found *uns* in the greatest of things.

The meaning of his saying ﷺ, "Trust is my treasure."

It is mentioned in one *ḥadīth*, "He who wants to be the richest of people, then let him trust in what is in the hands of God more than he trusts in what is in his own hands."[10] Another *ḥadīth* states, "The believer's treasure is his Lord."[11] Another *ḥadīth* contains the

---

7. *Anīs:* that which brings *uns*, which is comfort, contentment, and intimacy in the presence of another, and dispels the feeling of desolation.
8. *Ṣaḥīḥ Muslim*, vol. 1, p. 550.
9. See footnote 7 above.
10. Narrated by Abū Nuʿaym in the *Ḥilya* and Ibn Abī l-Dunyā in *Makārim al-akhlāq*, pp. 8–9. The author wrote it as, "None of you believes until he trusts in what is in the hands of God more than he trusts in what is in his own hands" both in this work and in *Rūḥ al-sunna* (p. 73). Ibn Māja and al-Tirmidhī narrated it thus on the authority of Abū Dharr al-Ghifārī: The Messenger of God ﷺ said, "Detachment from this world does not mean considering what is permissible as forbidden, or doing away with one's wealth. Rather, detachment from this world means not trusting in what is in one's own hands more than in what is in the hand of God. . . ."
11. Narrated by al-Daylamī in *al-Firdaws* (see Ibn Idrīs, *Kīmyāʾ al-yaqīn*,

supplication, "O God, none can prevent what You give, and none can give what You withhold."[12] Therefore, nothing remains with the servant except his trust in God ﷻ. If God did not give us what is in our own hands or what is in the hands of others, then we would not be able to take anything.

The meaning of his saying ﷺ, "Sorrow is my companion."

It is mentioned in one *ḥadīth*, "He who feels sorrow over missing out on something from his worldly life draws nearer to the fire by the distance of a journey of a thousand years. He who feels sorrow over missing out on something from his next life draws nearer to paradise by the distance of a journey of a thousand years."[13]

Sorrow increases according to the greatness of what one feels sorrow about, and one feels sorrow and sadness over what one has missed. If one's sadness is over what he has missed of divine self-disclosures, then that is the best of sorrows.

The meaning of his saying ﷺ, "Knowledge is my weapon."

Knowledge is the foundation of knowledge of God and the foundation of all goodness. With knowledge and sound contemplation, one arrives at sensing the greatness of God in his heart. He ﷻ said, *A lesson to ponder, O people of insight!* (59:2), and that is not possible without knowledge.

The meaning of his saying ﷺ, "Patience is my provision."

The servant is traveling in his breaths and moments, and his provision for his journey is his adherence to [God's] commands and prohibitions. He cannot do that without patience, for if he did not have patience, his lower self would lead him to that which angers God ﷻ.

---

p. 13, n.1).

12. *Ṣaḥīḥ al-Bukhārī*, vol. 1, p. 161, and *Ṣaḥīḥ Muslim* and others.
13. Narrated by Abū ʿAbdallāh Muḥammad al-Rāzī (Ibn al-Ḥaṭṭāb) in his *Mashyakha*, p. 273. Quoted by al-Muttaqī l-Hindī in *Kanz al-ʿummāl*, vol. 3, p. 197, and Ibn Idrīs in *Rūḥ al-sunna*, p. 142.

The meaning of his saying ﷺ, "Contentment is my trophy."

The greatest trophy is being content with the apportionment of God ﷻ. It has been related that God ﷻ said to Moses ﷺ, "O Moses, if you are content with Me, then I am content with you. But if you are displeased and are not content with My decree, then you deserve My displeasure."

The meaning of his saying ﷺ, "Powerlessness is my pride."

Powerlessness is to admit that there is no might or power except in God ﷻ.

He ﷺ said, "Impoverishment is my pride, and in it I pride myself."[14] Impoverishment is the loss of all things from the heart, and having their place filled with the love of God ﷻ. This is the impoverishment that the Messenger of God ﷺ was proud of. Impoverishment, then, when it is the heart being in need of God ﷻ, is a praiseworthy impoverishment and a source of pride. As for the impoverishment from which one seeks refuge, and which he ﷺ linked to disbelief in his saying, "O God I seek refuge in You from rejection of faith and impoverishment,"[15] and in his saying, "Impoverishment is almost rejection of faith,"[16] it is the absence of the Real from the heart, and the attachment of the heart to things that keep one away from God ﷻ. When all these things are gone from the heart and the heart is filled with attachment to God ﷻ, then that is the impoverishment which the Messenger of God ﷺ was proud of.

The meaning of his saying ﷺ, "Detachment is my trade."

Detachment is a high and noble rank; one's heart is not attached to a single thing, and one turns away from things altogether. It is to have no desire for them, and to only take from them that which brings one nearer to one's Lord and Master. It is to have trust in God ﷻ

---

14. See al-Sakhāwī, *al-Maqāṣid al-ḥasana*, p. 480.
15. Narrated by al-Nasāʾī in his *Sunan*, vol. 1, p. 221, al-Ḥākim in his *Mustadrak*, and Aḥmad and others.
16. Narrated by al-Bayhaqī in his *Shuʿab al-īmān*, vol. 9, p. 12, and Abū Nuʿaym in his *Ḥilya*.

and [to ensure] that nothing enters one's heart except one's Lord, for one *ḥadīth* states, "The believer's treasure is his Lord";[17] and this is the paradise that is granted in this world. He who is such, then his food is the best of food and his clothes are the best of clothes; as for he who is occupied with things other than his Lord, he is always in torment.

He who turns to God ﷻ with his whole being, and detaches himself from this world, God ﷻ will make it his servant, as one *ḥadīth* states, "God ﷻ says to the world, 'O world, serve him who serves Me, and tire him who serves you.'"[18]

One of the friends of God was asked, "Why is it that you do not care for this world?"

He said, "Because it does not care for me!"[19]

A king once said to one of the friends of God: How abstemious you are, O so-and-so!

He said: You are more abstemious than I!

He said: How is that?

He said: You are content with little of the palaces and women of paradise, and all that is eternal. As for me, I am content with little of these worldly things that will perish.[20]

So look at this admonition that this Sufi gave to that king!

The meaning of his saying ﷺ, "Certainty is my strength."

---

17. Narrated by al-Daylamī in *al-Firdaws* (see Ibn Idrīs, *Kīmyāʾ al-yaqīn*, p. 13, n. 1).
18. Narrated by al-Shihāb in his *Musnad* on the authority of Ibn Masʿūd as a saying of the Prophet, and by Abū Nuʿaym in his *Ḥilya* as a saying of Jaʿfar al-Ṣādiq (*Ḥilyat al-awliyāʾ*, vol. 3, p. 194).
19. Here the same word for detachment (*zuhd*) is used, but I translated it according to its meaning of "not wanting something, or not caring about it," instead of detachment, because of the context in which it was employed.
20. As with the story above, the word used here is the same, *zuhd*, but I chose to translate it as "being abstemious" and as "being content with little" according to the context, as the Arabic word captures all these meanings, but it is difficult to use the same translation in English in different contexts.

Certainty is the spiritual witnessing of the Real ﷻ. He ﷻ said, *Those who are upright in their testimonies* (bi-shahādātihim) (70:33), but according to some other readings the verse says *their witnessing* (bi-shahādatihim). The witnessing (*shuhūd*) of the Real is the source of their strength, and they are always upright by their witnessing, one witnessing after another.

Translator's Note

The Qurʾān came in different canonical readings that give different shades of meanings to certain verses, all of which are accepted as true. Here the author is looking at a different reading of this verse that says "witnessing" (i.e., to bear witness in court) instead of "testimonies." Then he is giving a deeper, more spiritual level of interpretation of the meaning carried by this verse. Here the witnessing is not the bearing of witness in court, but the spiritual witnessing of God ﷻ, and the *bi-* that comes before that word is now understood in its meaning of "by" instead of "in," so that it means, "by their witnessing." Thus the meaning is, *Those who are kept upright by their witnessing (of God).*

The word *qāʾimūn* literally means 'standing upright,' and also means 'alive.' That is because when something is standing, then it is alive. God's name al-Qayyūm means that He is the One upon whom all existence depends. He is the sustainer of life. Without Him, everything falls down, lifeless.

The author, therefore, is saying that this verse means, "Those who are sustained by their spiritual witnessing of God." He means that they are constantly nourished and strengthened by their spiritual witnessing of God.

The meaning of his saying ﷺ, "Truthfulness is my intercessor."

Ṣidq (being truthful and sincere) is the best intercessor with God ﷻ. *Who is more truthful than God in speech?* (Q. 4:87), so if God has given someone truthfulness, then He has given him His description and His characteristic. If one is truthful in turning to his Lord and Master, then there is no intercessor for him greater than that. The basis of the path to God ﷻ is truthfulness and the knowledge that one's Lord only created him to worship Him. The servant remains truthful in his worship, directing himself toward his Lord—*It would be better for them to be true to God* (Q. 47:21)—and so becomes truthful and sincere in seeking knowledge. He knows why his Lord created him, and turns to Him with his entirety, his heart and body. Truthfulness is a sword that does not miss, and a horse that does not stumble.

Know that the Qurʾān's miraculous inimitability is due to its truthfulness. One of the friends of God—my master Muḥyī l-Dīn b. ʿArabī—said, "I was asked, 'Do you know what made the Qurʾān miraculously inimitable?' I said, 'No.' I was told, 'Because it is pure truth.'"

So be truthful and your speech will be miraculous.

You must be truthful in your companionship with the Real ﷻ and His creation, so do not be with the Real except with truthfulness, and do not accompany His creation except with truthfulness. The reality of truthfulness is to turn to God ﷻ with your entirety.

He ﷺ said, "A man will keep speaking the truth, and looking carefully into only speaking the truth, until he is written down with God as a man of truth (*ṣiddīq*). . . . A man will keep lying, and looking carefully into lying, until he is written down with God as a liar."[21]

To look into something in this context means to examine the act that one is about to do, so that, if it is truthful, he would do it, and if not, he would leave it. One of the kinds of looking carefully into lying is the selling of a product by false oaths, because he who

21. Narrated by Muslim in his *Ṣaḥīḥ*, vol. 2, p. 1106, and by Abū Dawūd and others. Al-Bukhārī narrated it without the phrase "looking carefully into . . ." *Ṣiddīqiyya* (being a *ṣiddīq*) is a spiritual rank that comes below the prophets and above the martyrs, as mentioned in the Qurʾān: *Whoever obeys God and the Messenger will be among those He has blessed: the messengers, the* ṣiddīqīn, *the martyrs, and the righteous* (4:69). Commentators on the Qurʾān said, "They are those of great truthfulness and sincerity, and so reach the level of certainty and come to see things as they really are. They are the friends of God, the knowers of God." (See the commentary of Ibn ʿAjība which quotes al-Bayḍāwī).

is swearing thinks that it will bring God's provision closer to him. However, by lying, one is actually distancing the provision from himself. One *ḥadīth* states, "There are three types of people that God will not speak to or look at or purify on the Day of Rising, and they will have a painful punishment: he who lets his garment drag on the floor behind him (out of pride); he who only gives to others in order to remind them of his favor on them and seek their gratitude; and he who sells his products by false oaths."[22] This angers God ﷻ and will be a cause of losing one's provision.

So you must be truthful in dealing with the Real and with His creation, and God willing, much good will come to you.

The meaning of his saying ﷺ, "Obedience is my honor."

[The Arabic word] *ḥasbī* means [two things in Arabic]: "my honor," and "my sufficiency." If one obeys God, then God will satisfy him and protect him from every harm and every worry.

One *ḥadīth* states, "A woman is sought in marriage for four things: her wealth, her beauty, her noble lineage (i.e., her honor), and her religion. Take the one with the religion, and may your hands have dust in them!"[23] This means, may your hands grab the sand of paradise so that it sticks to them, and this phrase is a good supplication from the Prophet ﷺ.

Another *ḥadīth* states, "He who marries a woman for her wealth, God will only increase him in poverty, and he who marries a woman for her prestige, God will only increase him in lowliness, and he who marries a woman for her beauty, God will only increase him in worthlessness, and he who marries a woman for her religion, God will increase her blessings upon him and his blessings upon her."[24]

The meaning of his saying ﷺ, "Struggle is my character."

---

22. Narrated by Muslim in three traditions with slightly different wording, see his *Ṣaḥīḥ*, vol. 1, p. 58, *ḥadīth* 306–309.
23. *Ṣaḥīḥ al-Bukhārī*, vol. 3, p. 1067, *Ṣaḥīḥ Muslim*, and others.
24. Narrated by al-Ṭabarānī in *al-Muʿjam al-awsaṭ* and Abū Nuʿaym in *al-Ḥilya*, vol. 5, p. 245, but instead of "for her religion" they have, "so he can lower his gaze, protect his private parts, or reconnect ties of kinship."

Struggle is of two kinds: the struggle against the disbelievers, which is the call (i.e., invitation) to God ﷻ; and the struggle against the self's lower desires, and that is to call it to sincere devotion to God ﷻ.

He ﷺ said, "Every prophet has a trade, and my trade is impoverishment and struggle."[25] Impoverishment is the emptiness of the heart of all things and its being filled with God ﷻ. He ﷺ chose impoverishment because its winds are powerful, and only perfect men can remain firm in it.

A man came to one of the friends of God who was seated, and put some money in his lap. The friend of God said to him, "You wanted by this charity of yours for me to be written among the rich and be left waiting for five hundred years, standing in sweat, while the impoverished are in paradise?! I have no need of it!"[26] He stood up and the coins fell from his lap. The man said, "I never saw anyone more powerful and honorable than him when he left the money and stood up, nor anyone more lowly and abased than my own self when I went after the coins as they rolled on the floor."

The people of God are more afraid of the loss of their poverty than the rich are afraid of the loss of their wealth. He ﷻ said, *Man exceeds all bounds when he thinks he is self-sufficient* (96:6–7), and He ﷻ said, *O people, you are the poor in need of God* (35:15). The Prophet ﷺ, therefore, held on to the impoverishment with which God described him until he met his Lord ﷻ, for what is meant by "people" is him, because he ﷺ is their origin, as everything is part of the handful of light which is his light. He ﷺ did not want to share with his Lord in the characteristic of being rich.

---

25. The narration I found says, "I have two trades—whoever loves them, loves me, and whoever hates them, hates me. They are impoverishment and struggle." (Narrated by Ibn al-Najjār in *Dhayl Tārīkh Baghdād*). See also the commentary on "Powerlessness is my pride."

26. In reference to the *ḥadīth* that the poor will enter paradise 500 years before the rest of people. Narrated by Ibn Māja, Aḥmad, al-Tirmidhī, al-Nasāʾī, Ibn Ḥibbān and others (see *Sunan al-Tirmidhī*, vol. 2, p. 603). There is also reference to the *aḥādīth* that it will be so hot on the Day of Rising that people will be standing in pools of their own sweat (*Ṣaḥīḥ al-Bukhārī*, vol. 3, p. 1324).

The meaning of his saying ﷺ, "My pleasure is in prayer."

He did not just say "prayer . . ." but rather said, "in prayer . . ." and that is because he is absent from the actions that he performs [in the prayer] due to his immersion in his greatest pleasure. What is meant by his greatest pleasure is the spiritual witnessing of his Beloved ﷻ in the prayer. He ﷺ used to say to Bilal, "Bring us comfort by it, O Bilal!" meaning by the prayer, because in it is the witnessing of the Real ﷻ.[27]

The meaning of his saying ﷺ, "My concern is for my community."

Concern for the affairs of the Muslims is an essential right of Islam, as the *ḥadīth* states, "He who is not concerned with the affairs of the Muslims is not one of them."[28] God ﷻ said, *Let not your soul perish with grief over them* (35:8), referring to the Prophet's constant worry; he ﷺ said, "I take hold of the knots on your waist belts to keep you back from the fire while you are rushing into it like moths rush into a torch."[29] Yet they overpower him, meaning that they go against his guidance and they throw themselves into the fire.

What is meant by the community is both the community of invitation [i.e., those who have not yet accepted the message] and the community of acceptance [i.e., the Muslims]. That is because he ﷺ is a mercy to all the worlds. God ﷻ said, *We sent you not but as a mercy to the worlds* (21:107).

The meaning of his saying ﷺ, "And my longing is for my Lord."

He ﷻ said, *We are closer to him than his jugular vein* (50:16). If that is so, then how could there be longing? But this is like the saying of the one who said,

27. Meaning, recite the call to prayer so that we may pray and find our greatest pleasure in that prayer. The *ḥadīth* is narrated by Abū Dāwūd in his *Sunan*, vol. 2, p. 834 and Aḥmad.

28. Narrated by al-Ḥākim in the *Mustadrak*, vol. 4, p. 352, and Ibn Bishrān in *al-Amālī*.

29. Narrated by al-Bukhārī and others with different wording (see *Ṣaḥīḥ al-Bukhārī*, vol. 3, p. 1315).

> How amazing it is that I yearn for them,
> and always ask about them, though they are with me!
> My eyes cry over them, though they are in their pupils,
> and my heart longs for them, though they are between my ribs!

Everyone is given of this longing according to his ability, and if it becomes firmly fixed in a person, then it turns into fervent love and ardor. When it turns into fervent love and ardor in a person then he will become lost in the object of his desire like Majnūn. He said to Layla, "Leave me, for my love of you distracts me from you!" That is what being lost in his love did to him: his feeling of oneness with her made him not need [to actually be with] her! This is the station of extinction.[30] The reality of extinction is unity:

---

30. Ibn ʿArabī, in *Kitāb al-ḥujub,* discusses this spiritual state and calls it "extinction in love." He explains that the person who reaches this station is in perpetual contact with the object of his love, which is his being in love with the original beloved. Because of this the lover is in perpetual bliss and pleasure. He quotes another poet who, when he saw his love of his beloved growing larger and larger, and his life drawing near its end, and there was no hope of fulfilling his desires, did not give up, but he made that love that he always had the new object of his love. He became in love with his love of the beloved for the rest of his life. That way, whether he got his beloved or not, he always had the pleasure of having the love of the beloved. "In such a station," he explains, "being abandoned by his beloved is inconceivable, because the immaterial spiritual image which resides in the very self of the lover, out of his witnessing of the object of his love, is firmly implanted therein, and has no existence except in him. . . . As for the union with a separate entity, it is followed by separation and pain, because it does not last, for states change in such a station. And this will make the one who is like [Qays] fear that parting: he feared the pain that would come after bliss, and therefore came to be repelled by the outward image, because it is foreign to him, whereas the one who fell in love with the image that is nearer to him (and in fact resides in his soul) has found satisfaction; as you know, the nearer neighbor has more right over the farther one. And it is rare to find someone who has tasted this, especially on the path of God most high." (*Kitāb al-ḥujub*, p. 104).

"When I love him I become his hearing with which he hears . . ."[31] as is befitting of Him ﷻ. What is meant here is not what those without insight might imagine, for God ﷻ is free from that and far above it, and [what they imagine] is disbelief and error. The unity that is mentioned by the people of God, may God ﷻ be pleased with them, is a matter that is experienced, and not something that could be expressed in words. It is of the sciences of the experiential, not of the sciences of the books.

> You do not love me if you do not become extinct in me,
> and you are not extinct in me if my image does not appear in you!

God is the guide and the cause of success. May God shower the Prophet and his family with peace and blessings with every glance and every breath, as many times as all that is contained in the knowledge of God.

[The copyist wrote]

This is the end of the blessed treatise, and copying it was completed on Friday the second of Muḥarram in the year 1320 of the noble migration (*hijra*). Peace and blessings be upon the one who migrated and his family and companions.

Written by the lowly servant
who is in need of the generosity of God,
Muḥammad b. ʿAlī l-Yamanī l-Idrīsī.

31. *Ṣaḥīḥ al-Bukhārī*, vol. 3, p. 1319.

Bibliography

Abū Dāwūd, Sulaymān. *Sunan Abū Dāwūd*. 2 vols. Vaduz: Thesaurus Islamicus Foundation, 2000.

Abū Nuʿaym, Aḥmad. *Ḥilyat al-awliyāʾ wa ṭabaqāt al-aṣfiyāʾ*. 10 vols. Cairo: al-Saʿāda, 1974.

Addas, Claude. "Abu Madyan and Ibn ʿArabi," in *Muhyiddin Ibn ʿArabi: A Commemorative Volume*, edited by S. Hirtenstein and M. Tiernan. Shaftesbury, Dorset, UK: Element Books, 1993.

ʿAqīla, Muḥammad b. Aḥmad. *al-Fawāʾid al-jalīla fī musalsalāt Ibn ʿAqīla*. Beirut: Dār al-Bashāʾir al-Islāmiyya, 2000.

Bang, Anne K. *The Idrīsī State in ʿAsīr 1906–1934: Politics, Religion and Personal Prestige as Statebuilding Factors in Early Twentieth-Century Arabia*. London: Hurst and Company, 1996.

al-Bayhaqī, Aḥmad. *Dalāʾil al-nubuwwa wa maʿrifat aḥwāl ṣāḥib al-sharīʿa*. 7 vols. Beirut: Dār al-Kutub al-ʿIlmiyya, 1984.

———. *Shuʿab al-īmān*. 14 vols. Riyadh: Maktabat al-Rushd, 1989.

Bernstein, Marver H. "The Appeal of Communism in Arab Countries." *World Politics* 9, no. 4 (July 1957), pp. 623–629.

al-Bukhārī, Muḥammad b. Ismāʿīl. *Ṣaḥīḥ al-Bukhārī*. 3 vols. Vaduz: Thesaurus Islamicus Foundation, 2000.

Dajānī, Aḥmad Ṣidqī. *al-Ḥaraka al-sanūsiyya nashʾatuhā wa numuwwuhā fī l-qarn al-tāsiʿ ʿashar*. Beirut: 1967, 1988.

Dajani, Zahia Ragheb. *Egypt and the Crisis of Islam*. New York: Lang, 1990.

al-Ghazālī, Abū Ḥāmid Muḥammad. *Iḥyāʾ ʿulūm al-dīn*. Beirut: Dār al-Kitāb al-ʿArabī, 2005.

Glassé, Cyril. *The New Encyclopedia of Islam*. Walnut Creek, CA: AltaMira Press, 2002.

al-Hajrasī, Muḥammad Khalīl. *al-Jawhar al-nafīs fī ṣalawāt Ibn Idrīs*. Cairo: al-Maṭbaʿa al-Azhariyya li-l-Turāth, 1988.

al-Ḥākim, Muḥammad b. ʿAbdallāh. *al-Mustadrak ʿalā l-ṣaḥīḥayn*. 5 vols. Beirut: Dār al-Kutub al-ʿIlmiyya, 2002.

al-Haythamī, Nūr al-Dīn ʿAlī. *Kashf al-astār ʿan zawāʾid al-Bazzār*. 4 vols. Beirut: Muʾassasat al-Risāla, 1979.

——. *Majmaʿ al-zawāʾid wa manbaʿ al-fawāʾid*. 12 vols. Beirut: Dār al-Kitāb al-ʿArabī, 1982.

Hirtenstein, S. and M. Tiernan (eds.). *Muhyiddin Ibn ʿArabi: A Commemorative Volume*. Shaftesbury, Dorset, UK: Element Books, 1993.

Ibn Abī l-Dunyā, ʿAbdallāh. *Makārim al-akhlāq*. Beirut: Dār al-Kutub al-ʿIlmiyya, 1989.

——. *Man ʿāsha baʿd al-mawt*. Cairo: Maktabat al-Sunna, 1993.

——. *al-Manāmāt*. Cairo: Maktabat al-Qurʾān, 1988.

Ibn al-ʿArabī, Muḥyī l-Dīn. *Kitāb al-ḥujub*, in Ibn al-ʿArabī, *ʿAnqāʾ maghrib fī khatm al-awliyāʾ wa shams al-maghrib*. Beirut: Dār al-Kutub al-ʿIlmiyya, 2009.

Ibn Ḥajar al-ʿAsqalānī, Aḥmad. *Fatḥ al-bārī sharḥ ṣaḥīḥ al-Bukhārī*. 13 vols. Beirut: Dār al-Maʿrifa, 1959.

Ibn Ḥanbal, Aḥmad. *Musnad al-imām Aḥmad b. Ḥanbal*. 50 vols. Beirut: Muʾassasat al-Risāla, 2001.

Ibn al-Ḥaṭṭāb, al-Rāzī. *Mashyakhat al-shaykh al-ajall Abī ʿAbdallāh Muḥammad al-Rāzī*. Riyadh: Dār al-Hijra, 1994.

Ibn Idrīs, Aḥmad. *Awrād sayyidī Aḥmad b. Idrīs*. Cairo: Dār Jawāmiʿ al-Kalim, 2008.

——. *al-Fuyūdāt al-rabbāniyya bi-tafsīr baʿḍ al-āyāt al-qurʾāniyya.*Cairo: Dār Jawāmiʿ al-Kalim, n.d.

——. *al-ʿIqd al-nafīs fī naẓm jawāhir al-tadrīs*. Cairo: Dār Jawāmiʿ al-Kalim, 2006.

——. *Kīmyāʾ al-yaqīn*. Cairo: Dār Jawāmiʿ al-Kalim, 2004.

——. *The Letters of Aḥmad Ibn Idrīs*. Edited and translated by Albrecht Hofheinz and Einar Thomassen. London: Hurst and Company, 1993.

——. *Majmūʿat aḥzāb wa awrād wa rasāʾil*. Cairo: Muṣṭafā l-Bābī l-Ḥalabī, 1940.

——. *Rūḥ al-sunna*. Cairo: Dār Jawāmiʿ al-Kalim, 2007.

——. *Shahd mushāhadat al-arwāḥ al-taqiyya*. Cairo: Dār Jawāmiʿ al-Kalim, 2004.

——. *Sharḥ al-ṣudūr*. Cairo: Dār Jawāmiʿ al-Kalim, 2004.

Ibn Māja, Muḥammad. *Sunan Ibn Mājah*. Vaduz: Thesaurus Islamicus Foundation, 2000.

Ibn Saʿd, Muḥammad. *Kitāb al-ṭabaqāt al-kabīr*. 11 vols. Cairo: Maktabat al-Khānjī, 2001.

Ibn ʿUdayy, Abū Aḥmad. *al-Kāmil fī duʿafāʾ al-rijāl.* 9 vols. Beirut: Dār al-Kutub al-ʿIlmiyya 1997.

Ibrāhīm, Yaḥyā Muḥammad. *Madrasat Aḥmad b. Idrīs al-Maghribī wa atharuhā fī l-Sūdān.* Beirut: Dār al-Jīl, 1993.

al-Jaʿfarī, ʿAbd al-Ghanī. *al-Kanz al-tharī fī manāqib al-Jaʿfarī.* Cairo: Dār Jawāmiʿ al-Kalim, 1990.

———. *Quṭūf min sīrat sayyidī l-shaykh Ṣāliḥ al-Jaʿfarī.* Cairo: Dār Jawāmiʿ al-Kalim, n.d.

———. *al-Ṭarīqa al-Jaʿfariyya: shaykhan wa-minhājan.* Cairo: Dār Jawāmiʿ al-Kalim, 1993.

al-Jaʿfarī, Ṣāliḥ. *al-ʿAjab al-ʿujāb fī mā warada min aḥwāl al-mawtā baʿda dafnihim bi l-turāb.* Cairo: Dār Jawāmiʿ al-Kalim, 2001.

———. *Aʿṭār azhār aghṣān ḥaẓīrat al-taqdīs fī karāmāt al-ʿālim . . . al-sayyid Aḥmad b. Idrīs.* Cairo: N.p., 1974.

———. *Awrād al-ṭarīqa al-Jaʿfariyya.* Cairo: Dār Jawāmiʿ al-Kalim, 2000.

———. *Dars al-jumuʿa bi-l-Azhar.* 10 vols. Cairo: Dār Jawāmiʿ al-Kalim, n.d.

———. *Dīwān al-Jaʿfarī.* 12 vols. Cairo: Dār Jawāmiʿ al-Kalim, n.d.

———. *Fatḥ wa fayḍ wa faḍl min Allāh.* Cairo: Dār Jawāmiʿ al-Kalim, 1991.

———. *al-Fawāʾid al-Jaʿfariyya min anwār al-aḥādīth al-nabawiyya.* Cairo: Dār Jawāmiʿ al-Kalim, 1992.

———. *al-Fuyūḍāt al-Jaʿfariyya bi-sharḥ al-awrād al-Idrīsiyya.* Cairo: Dār Jawāmiʿ al-Kalim, 1993.

———. *al-Ilhām al-nāfiʿ li-kulli qāṣid.* Cairo: Dār Jawāmiʿ al-Kalim, 1996.

———. *al-Maʿānī l-raqīqa ʿalā l-durar al-daqīqa.* Cairo: Dār Jawāmiʿ al-Kalim, 1997.

———. *Miftāḥ mafātiḥ kunūz al-samāwāt wa-l-arḍ.* Cairo: Dār Jawāmiʿ al-Kalim, 2008.

———. *Minbar al-Azhar.* Cairo: Dār Jawāmiʿ al-Kalim, 1993.

———. *al-Muntaqā l-nafīs fī manāqib quṭb dāʾirat al-taqdīs mawlāna al-sayyid Aḥmad b. Idrīs.* Cairo: Dār Jawāmiʿ al-Kalim, 1998.

———. *al-Sīra al-nabawiyya al-Muḥammadiyya.* Cairo: Dār Jawāmiʿ al-Kalim, 1993.

———. *al-Sirāj al-wahhāj fī qiṣṣat al-isrāʾ wa-l-miʿrāj.* Cairo: Dār Jawāmiʿ al-Kalim, n.d.

———. *al-Ṣalawāt al-Jaʿfariyya.* Cairo: Dār Jawāmiʿ al-Kalim, 2008.

al-Jazūlī, Muḥammad b. Sulaymān. *Dalāʾil al-khayrāt*. Beirut: Dār al-Kutub al-ʿIlmiyya, 2008.

al-Kattānī, Muḥammad b. Jafʿar. *Al-Arbaʿīn: Collection of Forty Ḥadīths on the Duty of Loving the Noble Family of the Prophet Muḥammad*. London: Turath Publishing, 2010.

al-Lamaṭī, Aḥmad b. al-Mubārak. *Pure Gold from the Words of Sayyidī ʿAbd al-ʿAzīz al-Dabbāgh*. Translated by John O'Kane and Bernd Radtke. Leiden: Brill, 2007.

Mālik b. Anas. *al-Muwaṭṭaʾ*. Vaduz: Thesaurus Islamicus Foundation, 2000.

al-Mawṣilī, Abū Yaʿlā Aḥmad. *Musnad Abī Yaʿlā l-Mawṣilī*. 13 vols. Beirut: Dār al-Maʾmūn li-l-Turāth, 1989.

al-Mirghanī, Muḥammad ʿUthmān. *Tāj al-tafāsīr li-kalām al-malik al-kabīr*. vol. 1. Cairo: Supreme Council for Islamic Affairs, 2005.

al-Mubārakfūrī, Muḥammad. *Tuḥfat al-aḥwadhī bi-sharḥ Jāmiʿ al-Tirmidhī*. Beirut: Dār al-Fikr, 1979.

Muslim b. al-Ḥajjāj al-Qushayrī. *Ṣaḥīḥ Muslim*. 2 vols. Vaduz: Thesaurus Islamicus Foundation, 2000.

al-Muttaqī l-Hindī, ʿAlī. *Kanz al-ʿummāl fī sunan al-aqwāl wa-l-afʿāl*. 18 vols. Beirut: Muʾassasat al-Risāla, 1989.

al-Nasāʾī, Aḥmad. *Sunan al-Nasāʾī*. 2 vols. Vaduz: Thesaurus Islamicus Foundation, 2000.

O'Fahey, R. S. *Enigmatic Saint: Aḥmad b. Idrīs and the Idrīsī Tradition*. London: C. Hurst and Co., 1990.

——— and Ali Ṣāliḥ Karrar. "Enigmatic Imam: The Influence of Aḥmad b. Idrīs." *International Journal of Middle East Studies* 19, no. 2 (May 1987), pp. 205–219.

al-Qāḍī ʿIyāḍ. *al-Shifā bi-taʿrīf ḥuqūq al-Muṣṭafā*. Beirut: Dār al-Fikr, 1988.

al-Qārī, Mulla ʿAlī. *al-Asrār al-marfūʿa fī l-akhbār al-mawḍūʿa*. Beirut: Dār al-Amāna, 1971.

al-Qasṭalānī, Aḥmad. *al-Mawāhib al-ladunniyya bi-l-minaḥ al-muḥammadiyya*. 4 vols. Beirut: al-Maktab al-Islāmī, 2004.

Radtke, Bernd, R. S. O'Fahey, and John O'Kane. "Two Sufi Treatises of Aḥmad b. Idrīs." *Oriens* 35 (1995), pp. 143–178.

Radtke, Bernd, et al. *The Exoteric Aḥmad b. Idrīs: A Sufi's Critique of the Madhāhib and the Wahhābīs*. Leiden: Brill, 2000.

Ṣabbāgh, Maḥmūd ʿAbd al-Ghanī. "al-Ṣūfiyya wa-majālisuhā wa-muʾaththirātuhā fi l-Ḥijāz," in *al-Taṣawwuf fī l-khalīj*. Dubai: Al-Mesbar Studies & Research Centre, 2001.

al-Sakhāwī, Muḥammad b. ʿAbd al-Raḥmān. *al-Maqāṣid al-ḥasana fī kathīrin min al-aḥādīth al-mushtahira ʿalā l-alsina*. Beirut: Dār al-Kitāb al-ʿArabī, 1985.

al-Ṣanʿānī, ʿAbd al-Razzāq. *al-Muṣannaf*. Johannesburg: al-Majlis al-ʿIlmī, 1983.

al-Shawkānī, Muḥammad b. ʿAlī. *Nayl al-awṭār*. Cairo: Dār al-Ḥadīth, 1993.

al-Subkī, Tāj al-Dīn ʿAbd al-Wahhāb. *Ṭabaqāt al-shāfiʿiyya al-kubrā*. 10 vols. Cairo: Hajr, 1992.

al-Suyūṭī, Jalāl al-Dīn. *al-Durr al-manthūr fī l-tafsīr al-maʾthūr*. 7 vols. Beirut: Dār al-Kutub al-ʿIlmiyya, 2000.

——. *Jamʿ al-jawāmiʿ*. Cairo: al-Azhar al-Sharīf, 2005.

——. *al-Jāmiʿ al-ṣaghīr fī aḥādīth al-bashīr al-nadhīr*. Beirut: Dār al-Kutub al-ʿIlmiyya, 2002.

——. *Tanwīr al-ḥalak fī ruʾyat al-nabī wa l-malak*. Cairo: Maṭbaʿat al-Saʿāda, 1910.

al-Samīn, Muṣṭafā (ed.). *Naẓm al-Ājurrūmiyya*. Cairo: Dār Jawāmiʿ al-Kalim, n.d.

al-Sanūsī, Muḥammad b. ʿAlī. *al-Majmūʿa al-mukhtāra*. Edited by Muḥammad ʿAbduh b. Ghalbūn. Manchester, UK: N.p., 1990.

Sedgwick, Mark. *Saints and Sons: The Making and Remaking of the Rashīdi Aḥmadi Sufi Order, 1799–2000*. Leiden: Brill, 2005.

al-Ṭabarānī, Abū l-Qāsim Sulaymān. *Kitāb al-duʿāʾ*. 3 vols. Beirut: Dār al-Bashāʾir, 1987.

——. *al-Rawḍ al-dānī ilā l-muʿjam al-saghīr li-l-Ṭabarānī*. 2 vols. Amman: Dār ʿAmmār, 1985.

al-Ṭabarī, Muḥammad b. Jarīr. *Tārīkh al-umam wa-l-mulūk*. Amman: International Ideas Home, n.d.

Thābit, Muḥammad Khālid. *Min aqṭāb al-umma fī l-qarn al-ʿishrīn*. Cairo: al-Muqaṭṭam, 2009.

Thomassen, Einar and Bernd Radtke (eds.). *The Letters of Aḥmad b. Idrīs*. London: Hurst & Company, 1993.

al-Tirmidhī, Abū ʿĪsā Muḥammad. *Sunan al-Tirmidhī*. 2 vols. Vaduz: Thesaurus Islamicus Foundation, 2000.

al-Tirmidhī, al-Ḥakīm. *Nawādir al-usūl fī aḥādīth al-rasūl*. 4 vols. Beirut: Dār al-Jīl, 1992.

al-Ṭuʿmī, Muḥyī l-Dīn. *al-Nūr al-abhar fī ṭabaqāt shuyūkh al-Azhar*. Beirut: Dār al-Jīl, 1992.

Trimingham, J. Spencer. *The Sufi Orders in Islam*. New York: Oxford University Press, 1998.

Vikør, Knut S. *Sufi and Scholar on the Desert Edge: Muḥammad b. ʿAlī al-Sanūsī and his Brotherhood*. London: Hurst and Company, 1995.

Voll, John. "Two Biographies of Aḥmad b. Idrīs al-Fāsī (1760–1837)." *International Journal of African Historical Studies* 6, no. 4 (1973), pp. 633–645.

About the Author

Samer Dajani earned a bachelor's degree in Arab and Islamic Civilizations from the American University in Cairo and a master's degree in Islamic studies from the School of Oriental and African Studies at the University of London, where he is currently working on a PhD. He studied with Muslim scholars in Egypt, Morocco, and the United Kingdom. Samer Dajani has a written *ijāza* (authorization) from Shaykh ʿAbd al-Ghanī Ṣāliḥ al-Jaʿfarī, Shaykh Ṣāliḥ al-Jaʿfarī's son and head of the Jaʿfariyya *ṭarīqa*, to teach *al-Fawāʾid al-Jaʿfariyya*, the work he has translated here.

Shaykh Ṣāliḥ al-Jaʿfarī was born in 1910 in the Sudan; he arrived in Cairo at the age of twenty to study at al-Azhar, where he obtained the highest degree at the time—the ʿĀlimiyya. He then taught in al-Azhar Mosque and in 1953 earned a PhD from the Faculty of Sharīʿa. He became the imam of al-Azhar Mosque and was known for his Friday lessons, which were popular and well-attended. He was the founder of the Sufi order, al-Jaʿfariyya al-Aḥmadiyya al-Muḥammadiyya, which is active in education and social work and has followers around the world. Shaykh al-Jaʿfarī wrote approximately fifteen works on various Islamic sciences, edited many others, and composed twelve volumes of poetry. He died in Cairo in 1979.

Colophon

Reassurance for the Seeker is set in Minion Pro 11/14, an Adobe typeface designed by Robert Slimbach and released in 2000. Minion Pro is inspired by classical, old style typefaces of the late Renaissance, a period of elegant and highly readable type designs. It combines the aesthetic and functional qualities that make text type highly readable for computerized typesetting needs. Additional glyphs were created to meet the needs of the Arabic transliteration for the text.

The Arabic text is set in Amiri 13/27, a digital interpretation by Dr. Khaled Hosny of the metal typeface of the Amīriyya Press at Bulaq. It strikes a balance between the beauty of *naskh* calligraphy on one hand and the constraints and requirements of elegant metal handset typography on the other. The Amiri typeface was chosen because it best reflects the era during which the text was composed, as Shaykh al-Jaʿfarī lived during a formative period for Arabic movable type printing. The Amiri typeface represents the apogee of the period before printing moved on to make use other developing technologies. Additional glyphs were used from AGA Arabesque and KFGQPC Arabic Symbols.